A VICTORIAN SON

STUART CLOETE IN 1918

STUART CLOETE

A VICTORIAN SON

AN AUTOBIOGRAPHY
1897-1922

COLLINS
ST JAMES'S PLACE, LONDON
1972

William Collins Sons & Co Ltd
London · Glasgow · Sydney · Auckland
Toronto · Johannesburg

First published 1972
© Stuart Cloete 1972

ISBN 0 00 211041 5

Set in Monotype Garamond
Made and Printed in Great Britain by
William Collins Sons & Co Ltd Glasgow

TO THE WOMEN IN MY LIFE,
THE MOST IMPORTANT OF WHOM WERE
MY MOTHER AND THE TWO GIRLS WHO
MARRIED ME, EILEEN AND TINY

CONTENTS

Part One
THE CHILD

Part Two
THE BOY

Part Three
THE MAN

FOREWORD

Never before had the clock of progress moved so fast as during this period (1897-1922). Empires dissolved in the acid of new liberties. Millions died in the greatest war the world had ever suffered. More millions were liquidated or displaced in the name of freedom as the seeds of anarchy, which we reap today, were sown.

This is the life story of a survivor of those times, when even survival was an achievement. It is a story of thoughts, moods and action: of vanished beauties, of pretty girls who are now grandmothers, and young men who are mostly dead; of fine horses, of dogs, of books, of country days and war. A kaleidoscope of changing memories, hopes and regrets which together comprise the life of a man – any man – and his times.

Part One

THE CHILD

THE INFANT

I WAS born in 1897, the year of Queen Victoria's Diamond Jubilee, which celebrated the sixtieth year of her reign.

From pole to pole the Union Jack whipped in arctic gales or sagged in the tropic heat of this Empire upon which the sun never set. Since then, in the years of which I shall write, the bunting which once dominated the skies has shrunk in the laundry of time to the size of a woman's handkerchief.

But then, in the year in which I was born, Britannia ruled the waves. The Pax Britannica was a reality. London was the centre of the world: in children's school atlases country after country, whole continents, were painted red with unquestioned British dominion.

The Procession was the greatest in terms of variety yet to be seen, and the last. The golden coach of the old Queen Empress drawn by eight postillioned Flemish creams was accompanied by her Household Cavalry – the Life Guards and the Blues. Behind her came detachments of turbaned Indian Lancers, of Canadian North-West Mounted Police, of British Cavalry, of Foot Guards, of Highland Regiments with their skirling pipes and swinging kilts, of soldiers from the West Indies, from West Africa, from Fiji. Men of every colour from every colony, dominion and protectorate marched in a brotherhood of arms. There were carriages in which rode emperors, kings, princes and rajahs.

The crowds cheered from the scarlet barrier of the Foot Guards who lined the route. The streets echoed to the hammer of marching heels, the clatter of iron-shod hooves and the clink of cavalry accoutrements. They rang with British glory. Eyes were dazzled with panoply, with flags, with standards. The ears reverberated to the martial music.

At sea the great grey battleships which guarded Great Britain and her possessions fired their salvoes of salutes.

This was the world into which I was born. The very zenith of

British glory. I have lived to see its nadir. I fought for an empire and find myself in a Coloured Commonwealth with an England that has broken every promise she ever made. I have gone from a world that thought with Tennyson and Kipling to one in which the predominant influence is the London School of Economics. I have lived in the reigns of six monarchs – Queen Victoria, King Edward VII, King George V, King Edward VIII, King George VI and Queen Elizabeth. Born in the reign of one queen, it is probable that I shall die in the reign of another. In my lifetime most kings have toppled from their thrones: The Czar of all the Russians, the Kaiser, the Kings of Spain, Portugal, Italy, Serbia, Montenegro, Bulgaria, Jugoslavia, Romania and Greece. The Austro-Hungarian Empire no longer exists. The United States of America has taken over the leadership of the world, and Communism – the new political religion – threatens all that remains of the ancient order. There have been two world wars and a third is more than a possibility.

I have moved from the horse and buggy days of my childhood into the era of the atomic bomb, jet propulsion and space travel which has landed a man on the moon. As a child I saw Blériot set off from Hardelot Plage to Cap Gris Nez where he started his flight over the English Channel. I have seen the last great mass of cavalry standing by ready for the breakthrough which never came, and fought with the first tanks. I remember men being allowed to smoke only in rooms set apart for the purpose, wearing smoking jackets and even caps which were changed before they rejoined the ladies. I remember being told in whispers of a woman who had been divorced. Such women were completely unacceptable socially even if they were the innocent party. Apart from divorced women there were other more borderline cases: women who were said to have had a past, that is, men in their lives to whom they had not been married. Young girls were never allowed out without a maidservant or chaperone. If they were found to have been alone with a man for more than five minutes they were considered compromised and their virginity held in question.

Gold was king in this world of five per cent security. An English sovereign was exchangeable at par everywhere and no

passport was required to travel anywhere except in Russia or the
Ottoman Empire.

And all this little more than half a century ago! Four such
periods would go back to the American Revolution, twenty to
the Battle of Hastings, forty to the Crucifixion.

Having passed the age allotted to man by the Bible – eight
hundred and forty months – (a man who lives a thousand months,
to the age of eighty-three years and four months, is a rarity) –
there is a certain interest in thinking of the past and in dividing it
into manageable periods; into blocks each of which has its own
characteristics. The first twenty years of anyone's life are more or
less spent in growing up, not that a human being is developed or
even fully matured by then, but it is an approximation. The next
twenty years in the life of a man or a woman are the period which
is dominated by the sexual urge. Biologically speaking, at forty,
both men and women can be and often are grandparents. Sex
may continue to manifest itself till an advanced age but the fury
has gone out of it. The spear is blunted. This is the period of
maturity. Success has either been achieved or not achieved by
forty. The ladder must, by this time, be at least partially climbed.
After sixty comes the last period of life – the evening, where
thought and memory replace action. Where a man not only puts
his material affairs in order but tries to sort out his life, to evaluate
his failures and successes. Where, with sufficient perspective, he
can at last begin to see the wood without being confused by the
trees.

Looking back, he finds with surprise that many of the things he
thought so good when they happened turned out badly, and
many of the things he complained about at the time have turned
out well. Like a patchwork quilt, the events of the past begin to
form a pattern. A sequence is seen, the interaction of cause and
effect. By a strange paradox now that there is less time, there is
more time. Urgency is the enemy of leisure and urgency has gone.
There is time to think about such questions as love and death.
Time to fish in the ragbag of memory, hauling out each fragment
and trying to reconstruct the cloth from which it was cut. It is
into this bag that the psychoanalyst dips his hand when he says:
What do you remember about this or that? Refusing to remember,
living on hope without memory, may be a primary cause of

neurosis. A plant might as well try to live without roots. It can for a few days, in water. In man the water is excitement, booze, women . . . An autobiography is the antidote to this danger. Its essential ingredient is truth, but truth about oneself is not easy to take, much less to write.

A man leads many lives. And a writer more than most. To write an autobiography is an act of autosurgery in which the life of the patient is not taken into account. There is only one essential – not to give a damn.

There is the outward chronological physical life – childhood, school, marriage, work, travel and the rest. Things owned, money made or lost, people known, places visited. These are the bones of a man's life, but the other, the shadows cast by the flesh in the still pool of his spirit, are what really matter. There must be thought before there can be action and each thought is the effect of a previous cause. At any given time a man is the sum of his experiences. Such experiences are vital. A perfume, a sight, a sound, a voice, can evoke a memory and set off a chain reaction – often of women, for they are an intrinsic part of most men's lives.

Women have always been of the greatest importance to me. I have been in love with one girl or another since I was six years old. It would appear to me that woman in the abstract – the principle of woman, as it were, her essence – represents all that is most beautiful in the world. Every desire, every perfume, every colour of the spectrum, every texture of softness, all that is delicate, ephemeral and lovely is epitomized in the woman of a man's dream and his desire. She is God, she is the world itself, the very stars of the heavens all rolled into one, into the point where biology, art and religion meet in an emotion which science has been unable to explain. Biology is not enough. Religion fails because of the biological factor.

So there it is. A story. That of a man's life as near as he can tell it, a sort of analysis of motive, of cause and effect, but with a lot left in the air unanswered because there are no answers. Roughly chronological, except where chronology must be sacrificed to trace the effects of causes, to follow the skein of events forward into the future or back into the past.

Why did I want to be a soldier? Why did I have a passion for the Indian Cavalry in general and for the Bengal Lancers in particular? This goes back to two coloured prints of Indian officers in uniform that hung in the hall of our flat in Paris. One infantry and one cavalry. It was the long-skirted coats with chain mail epaulettes of the cavalry that attracted me. Even Lord Roberts has acknowledged that it was the uniforms of the Royal Bengal Artillery with their tiger skin and scarlet helmets that made him join them. The splendour of the Napoleonic uniforms, the flags, eagles and martial music had a psychological purpose: their aim was to attract men into Napoleon's service and hold them with panoply and thoughts of glory.

I cannot have been more than three years old when I was much excited by the Boer War which was then in progress. There were no photographs in the papers in those days but I remember a picture, a drawing in black and white, that appeared in the *Daily Telegraph*, I imagine, since that was my father's paper, of a boy trumpeter with a bandaged head, galloping madly through bursting shells for reinforcements. My father coloured the picture for me. The horse brown, the boy in khaki with a red blob of blood on the white bandage round his head. The picture was hung in my nursery.

There was another picture, a French picture, of a boar hunt in colour. The boar stood at bay, surrounded by hounds which I assisted by stabbing the boar with a pen. I still have the picture. I found it only the other day.

Another picture was Lady Butler's 'Charge of the Light Brigade'. A wonderful picture of British Hussars and Lancers sabring the Russians as they served the guns. And there was the famous 'Thin Red Line' picture – a coloured print of the Battle of the Alma. These all hung in my nursery. Everything was glory to me. My people for generations had been soldiers. A child has not seen war. I did not know how many of the noble six hundred died or that those fine English chargers had starved in the snows of the Crimean winter. I knew nothing of Florence Nightingale. Only glory. *La gloire* of the French. The *Marseillaise*. The reviews. The cuirassiers in their bright cuirasses and helmets with black horse-tails hanging down over their shoulders. Their bay and brown horses. The trumpeters had white horsetails dyed red on their helmets and rode grey chargers. I saw them dismounted, dragging their long sabres on the pavements as they courted servant girls and nurses. I heard the clink of their spurs and the clash of steel, of bits and accoutrements. Only glory. I was taught to recite 'The Charge of the Light Brigade' with gestures as I stood on a footstool. I used to play with my father's sword and he would tell me stories of campaigns. Of the Kaffir Wars and rebellions, and the Colonies, and other older wars when we had fought the French; of how my great-grandfather had been captured by Napoleon and forced to serve in his Guard, of my great-grand-uncle, General Sir Josias Cloete, who had fought as a cornet of horse in the Battle of Waterloo when he was fifteen. Only glory.

Perhaps that is the way to make a soldier or a priest, an assassin or an actor. By example, by exposition, by environment. Pictures, tales, things. Objects like swords, uniforms, books, plans, maps, ornaments, toys. I had boxes of lead soldiers and guns and forts. Without knowing it, I was being formed, compressed as it were into a semi-hereditary mould. It resembled in a way the old apprenticeship to a trade which was often carried on from father to son. Perhaps being a soldier and a gentleman was in those days a kind of trade. I learnt as a blacksmith's son or the joiner's boy learn the use of their fathers' tools. The way the painters used to learn their art and the surgeon's apprentice acquired his skill.

After boyhood I never loved my father. But I never saw him drunk. I never saw him behave in an undignified manner except when he flew into a passion. I was always, till I grew up, afraid of him, and called him 'sir'. He beat me, very rightly I think, and it did me no harm. Had I been raised today I should have been a delinquent. I do not think severity matters at all if it is accompanied by respect and justice. I cannot at any time imagine myself being punished by a man I did not respect. And my father was no nagger. When it was over it was done and the subject never mentioned again. There was never any conflict between us about my mother. You cannot be jealous of God. He was God.

Only one was greater – my mother's father, old John Park, who had a great white beard and lived upstairs in the big London house in Wetherby Gardens. Whenever he saw me he gave me a stick of golden twisted barley sugar. It was transparent. If you didn't crunch it up it lasted a long time. I saw him very seldom. I was taken to London every year by my mother but had no idea he was drinking himself to death in those fine apartments above the dining- and drawing-rooms. His favourite son, and my mother's favourite brother, Jim, had been drowned in an accident in Sweden where the family had big timber interests. The other son, Ted, ran off with his own aunt. This was the first scandal I ever heard and I don't think I knew it was a scandal until much later. Ted's uncle had married a very beautiful woman much younger than himself and on one occasion when she wanted to go to Paris to buy clothes young Ted, a couple of years her junior, was sent with her as her courier and protector. He protected her so well that they never came back. At least not till much later. When her husband died they married and went to live near Bourne End where they had a fine herd of Jersey cattle. My grandmother drove in her carriage each week to Paddington Station to pick up the ten pounds of sinful yellow butter that Ted sent her from his farm. I remember it still as being very good. I wonder if that is one reason why I like Jersey cattle and have had two herds of my own?

Anyway that's the first scandal, the first skeleton in the cupboard. But where is the family with no scandal? If someone suggests that my mother ever looked at any man but my father I am supposed to knock him down, and once I should have. Now I am old enough to know my mother was a woman, and like any other beautiful woman, was no doubt tempted in her day. I know nothing much about her except what she hinted to me before she died. But she was very old then, over eighty, and liked to talk of her adventures. She may have been exaggerating and anyway it is of no importance.

I speak of principles. Any decent young man will defend his mother's honour whether she had any or not. His grandmother he will defend less vigorously, and if it is suggested that his great-grandmother was a bit fast – that she was, for instance, the friend of a peer or a millionaire – there is a tendency to laugh it off. After all, a peer . . . But again, in principle, it does not matter whose bed it is, anything out of wedlock is adultery. A terrible word in those days. We have two parents, four grandparents, eight great-grandparents, sixteen great-great-grandparents, so it goes into hundreds, into thousands. So we can be certain that there were criminals, murderers and whores among them. To lighten the insult there must also be dukes, kings, queens, bishops, curates, respectable serving-maids, game-keepers, sailors and soldiers, knights and troubadours, even men of colour.

Where was I? How old? Three? That is still far too forward. I must go back to my birthday and perhaps even to the day I was conceived. I was born at 3 a.m. on July 23rd, 1897, in an apartment in Paris – 150 Rue Longchamps – but we soon moved to the fifth floor of a new building – 51 Rue Pergolese. It is reasonable to suppose I was conceived in October 1896. Perhaps the Chinese are right in calculating age from the date of conception. My father was forty-seven at the time of my birth and my mother about ten years younger. As there was a gap of twelve years between me and my nearest brother I can only assume that I was a mistake, an accident after a party, or that my mother, having borne five sons, thought she would like a daughter and was convinced that the run of boys could not continue. But it did and there I was. My conception may have been unexpected but once I was on the way my mother was delighted, convinced I would be a girl. I had to be, on the law of averages. It was not then realized that any couple who have had three children of the same sex are likely to continue the series. The fact that I turned out to be a boy did not deter my mother. I was a beautiful child, a sort of Shirley Temple prototype. A little horror that no woman could resist. Looking back, I cannot imagine why I did not turn out a homosexual. My dear mother followed the prescription for producing one with academic exactitude. I should have been a classic case but it didn't work that way. Quite the opposite. I have, I think, taken a more than usual interest in women; they have been the flowers of my life. Anyone who tells a boy that women are not the key to happiness and pleasure is in error. In marriage or out of it, as friends, as lovers, as objects of art and beauty, there is nothing like a dame. But with girls, as with a lot of other things, you get back what you give in thought and consideration. When I started jumping horses my father said: 'Throw your heart over first.' I have, I think, applied this maxim to everything I have tried to do.

When I went to Africa I met Josie Dale Lace at the Turffontein Races in Johannesburg. She had been a great friend of my mother's and was a character and still a very handsome woman, though in her seventies. She wore a monocle. One of her sons had married Claudine Cloete, one of my very pretty cousins. In the great days of the Golden City, Josie had driven a team of zebras through the streets. My mother said she was a wonderful whip.

She said: 'So you're Edie's baby?' She looked at me closely and then went on: 'You've got a spot in your eye. You'll be lucky.' She was right. I had been lucky, and have been lucky ever since.

But how extraordinary it is to look back at my childhood in Paris and to think that so many of those little rich, and near rich, kids playing in the Avenue du Bois, rolling their hoops and whipping their tops, were doomed: the boys to be wounded or killed, the girls to lose their fathers, brothers, husbands and lovers. How very odd the trick that fate was to play on us because our fathers had made love to our mothers between certain dates. Between, say, 1877 and 1897. Odd that all those years of love-making and child-raising, of hope and anxiety, of education, were suddenly to go up the spout. And that was not the lot. More than a thousand years of breeding had gone to make a British stock that was second to none and the cream of it was lost. The French, too, when they had scarcely recovered from Napoleon's sacrifice to Mars. Only ninety-nine years had passed since Water-loo and here we were in 1914 at it again, fighting on some of the same battlefields with the French as allies and the Germans as enemies. What would the Iron Duke or Marshal Blücher have thought of that?

But all unknowing we played happily amid scenes of un-believable beauty and perhaps of decadence, if decadence can be evaluated – which I doubt. In many ways the present seems much more decadent to me. To the modern liberal the turn of the century was decadent because the old class structure was still more or less intact. This was enough to damn it ideologically and socially. The socialist, thinking in near-totalitarian terms, sees anything that is out of the ordinary as decadent. Democracy must be commonplace.

In this old world of ours there were strings that led back into the medieval past. Everywhere one saw the peasant costumes of the country people. The tonsured monks and nuns dressed as they had been in the twelfth century. There were horses, carts and carriages; sailing ships and rowing boats. There was continuity. Today was not yet entirely divorced from yesterday.

Our apartment had a hall, a big drawing-room, my mother's bedroom, my father's bedroom, my brother Lovel's room and my nursery where I slept with my nurse and later my governess. There was a balcony in front of the apartment over the street which was reached by french windows from the drawing-room. We had flower-boxes on it and my father had chicken wire stretched along the iron balustrade to prevent my falling over. He also had a long coil of rope to use in case of fire. It reached to a roof two floors below. The sixth-floor garrets were used by the servants from all the apartments, each of which also had a cellar in the basement – a fascinating place where we kept trunks and oddments and visited by guttering candlelight. Each cellar door was fastened with a big galvanized padlock. To reach the flat there was a wide staircase with a red and green carpet and a lift that one worked by pulling a rope. The apartment was heated by hot air – the calorifer which came up from a furnace in the basement and entered the various rooms through a slot in the wainscoting which was regulated by adjusting a small brass slide. In my nursery additional heat was supplied by a large oil-lamp with a red glass wire-covered chimney that led into a hollow blue enamel table which diffused the warmth and was used for keeping food warm and drying clothes on the rail that ran round it. I have never forgotten the cheerful red glow of the big lamp chimney.

There was also a Chinese screen covered in beige material on which sparrow-like birds and fronds of bamboo were embroidered in silver. This screen had a damaged corner and I found it was filled with Chinese newspapers. I used to fish out small pieces and was much intrigued with the printed Chinese letters.

A Fräulein used to come once a week to talk German to me, teach me to read Gothic script and write the now obsolete pointed German handwriting. I liked neither and soon forgot the little I had learned. I did however like *Strüwelpeter* and still remember the cover of the book and his picture with long fingernails and straight-up hair.

My brother, Lance, who had been in Peking during the Boxer Rebellion, brought back some brass vases and jars and half a dozen beautiful pictures painted on silk: butterflies, flowers, dragonflies, Chinese ladies in a garden and a picture of a writhing mass of silkworms eating mulberry leaves. No one liked this subject and when I asked for it it was given to me. I had it framed on my own and chose a moulding that looked like carved ivory. I was then about seven. Lance also brought back a lot of small pictures painted on rice paper and some silver boxes beautifully decorated with blue and green enamel.

The apartment was quite near the Bois de Boulogne. To reach it, all we had to do was walk up the Rue Laurent Pischa and cross the road. In those days the Bois was worth seeing. Paris, the world itself, was filled with beauty, with variety. Nothing was uniform, nothing regimented. There was terrible poverty, terrible oppression, but there was hope. There were not millions in concentration camps doing forced labour. The most civilized nation of the world, the nation of scientists and composers, of Kaiser Wilhelm and his White Hussars, had not yet devised ovens for cooking men to make soap and fertilizer out of their remains. I was brought up to think that only missionaries were cooked by cannibals. As I was not reared in a religious manner, though I went to Sunday School and said my prayers, it did not seem particularly reprehensible. Especially as even then I realized that a cooked missionary was a necessary part of progress. There almost had to be a barbecued missionary before a punitive expedition could be sent to avenge him and establish a fort to prevent any recurrence of the tragedy. The next stage was to build a trading station under the guns of the fort, declare a protectorate, and finally assimilate the area as a colony. In my culture the baked missionary went with the pretty uniforms of the Indian Lancers, with the panoply of war. Life as I saw it was blood-coloured, uniformed, mounted on a snorting charger.

This was the Paris of Manet, of Monet, of Renoir. Loubet was President. Sarah Bernhardt used to drive to the races in a victoria drawn by two thoroughbred bay mules. What a sight it was! Hundreds of vehicles – broughams, victorias, dogcarts, open cabs, private hansoms, coaches. What horses, what harness – silver-mounted, or brass polished like gold. What clothes! What hats plumed with ostrich feathers, what lace-edged parasols! What colour!

Every day my nurse Elsa took me walking in the Avenue du

Bois, now the Avenue Foch. That was a picture too. Some hundreds of well-dressed children – little boys in sailor suits, in kilts, in Little Lord Fauntleroy outfits, little girls in skirts so short that they showed their lace-edged drawers. In winter they wore black or white kid gaiters with buttons right up to their naked thighs. If the girls of today in their mini skirts and boots were reduced in height to two foot six they would look very like these little girls of three or four in my time. Every child was accompanied by a nurse – a *nou-nou* – in uniform, with long wide coloured ribbon streamers from her cap, or in national peasant costume. Norman girls. *Bretonnes. Arlésiennes.* Girls wearing starched caps from every *département* of France. Many of them wore long gold heirloom ear-rings. There were also English nurses. This was a real sign of status. They wore brown, grey or dark blue bonnets and long cloaks. Very starched and hygienic.

Being Paris, no fresh milk was drinkable and so a wet-nurse had been obtained for me from Alsace. Elsa was a fine big deep-chested blonde girl, who took me to her splendid bosom. She stayed with us till I was seven or eight and I loved her dearly.

Elsa was the only Alsatian in the Bois. She wore her national costume, an immense black moiré silk bow on her head and a scarlet flannel dress over which came a black velvet corset laced in front to show the dress beneath. A black moiré silk apron and white stockings. Black shoes with silver buckles completed the outfit. This was a costume world of nurses and children, of prams, hoops, tops, dolls and dogs in which everyone behaved as if he was alone in a garden at home, except of course that we were all dressed up. The English nannies looked shocked at the bulging peasant breasts that were presented so openly to the babies of the rich under the phallic flowering of the horse chestnuts. They were shocked at the openness with which little boys had their tiny flies undone. At the way little girls had their lace-edged drawers pulled down and were held out with raised legs. It was a bit too natural for England. But in the end what did it matter? Looking back now, what did anything matter? How few of us are alive today.

It was at once all very intimate and sophisticated. One saw a nurse disinfect with a lighted match a needle taken from her blouse to pierce a little girl's ears. She held a cork on the side of the ear near the head and pushed a threaded needle through it. She then cut the thread and did the other ear. For some days the child ran about with a dangling piece of cotton through each ear to keep the wound open. There was no hygienic nonsense about any of this and when the nurse decided the ear was ready for it she put a fine gold hoop through the hole. Most little girls were wearing them by the time they were five.

This is what the children saw as they played with their hoops and spun the tops they whipped with little fishskin whips.

Sometimes if my father was riding in the Bois he would meet us and take me up in front of his saddle for a canter. That is when the association with horses, which has meant so much to me, began. He took me to business conferences where I sat as still as a mouse for hours. He bought me a picture of two racehorses at the Hôtel Drouout, the big Paris auctioneers. My first picture, it hung over my bed for years. While I was a child he was a good father to me. At that time I loved him. I admired him. I was afraid of him. We were not pals, we were father and son.

CHAPTER 2

LULLABY

PEOPLE sang lullabies to children when I was a baby, but everyone sang then. The servants sang when they cleaned the windows or did the laundry; house-painters sang on their ladders. They were young, of course: young girls and men in their prime. Housemaids, dairymaids, gardeners, grooms. They were full of life. They had eaten no de-natured foods. They had no DDT in their livers, no strontium 90 in their bones.

If anyone wanted music in those days he had to make it for himself. There was no radio, no TV. The gramophone had only just been invented. All middle-class girls learned to play the piano and to sing. It did not matter if they had no ear. There was drawing-room music, the family singing round the piano while mother played. There were more advanced musical groups which played a variety of instruments. There were street bands and occasional soloists. Sometimes we heard something beautiful – a wonderful woman's voice, or a violin played by a man who had been driven into the streets by bad luck, drink or illness.

I have the feeling that though there was so much misery – the French word *misère* seems to express it better – so much poverty, there was also more contentment. Everyone knew what he was, who he was and where he was. Servants – imagine even using the word today – were loyal to the families they worked for, and the families reciprocated with pensions and care in their old age. Paternalism. Family businesses were run by fathers, sons, sons-in-law and nephews. Nepotism, another dirty word.

The poor were by no means content. But God was not yet dead – it took a couple of world wars to kill him – and the impoverished workers could look at their masters with a certain amount of patronage. They might have to work ten hours a day and live in poverty for fifty or sixty years, but the rich when they died would frizzle in hell for ever. A very comforting thought that was encouraged by the Establishment who were more interested in a good time now than celestial comfort in a problematical hereafter.

Slavery in America had only been ended by the Civil War, just over thirty years ago. It was only fifty-odd years since, in England, legislation had been passed to stop the use of half naked, often pregnant, women and young girls doing the work of pit ponies in the coal mines.

I think the chimney sweeps I saw walking, soot covered, carrying the brushes of their trade in their hands, still drove the small boys who followed them up the chimneys of the great hotels of the rich in Paris. A large private house was then called an hotel. (There were not many real hotels, not many restaurants – only *bistros* where the working class could eat cheaply and drink their wages away.)

Often only seven or eight years old, they sometimes got stuck or were suffocated by the soot which they had to scrape and brush down on to themselves before it could fall into the hearth below. The use of boys as chimney sweeps had been declared illegal in England, but still seemed to persist in France.

These reforms were resisted violently. As was the Criminal Amendment Act in 1885 which raised the age of consent from thirteen to sixteen, and ended brothel-keeping in England and the export of English girls to the Continent. Brothels – *maisons tolérées* – were legal in France till recent times. But prostitutes are still registered with the police and carry cards permitting them to solicit.

Girls and women were then sweated in the garment trades. Seamen were abused. Darwin's theory of the survival of the fittest had been manipulated to fit a policy of *laissez-faire* in which the devil took the hindmost. This was a period of unbelievable hypocrisy which I knew nothing about as a middle-class baby, or even later as a boy. The class whose births, marriages and deaths were announced in the correct columns of the right newspapers: *The Times, Morning Post* and *Telegraph*. Those on the next rung up the social ladder had their names in the Court Circular. Still, there was something to be said for hypocrisy: it implied a standard to which at least lip service must be given.

When I was teething and could not sleep my father carried me up and down, singing: 'O Susannah', 'I dreamt that I dwelt in marble halls', 'Old MacDonald had a Farm', 'Camptown Races'. My mother sang me to sleep with English lullabies and in French with '*Au Clair de la Lune*' and '*Alouette, gentille Alouette*'. Elsa sang me soft German songs but she did not have to do much singing. If I was restless she pushed her warm young milky breast into my mouth.

As a result of all this I am still touched by women's voices in English, French and German. They strike a chord of sentiment which moves me. I have never regretted being moved by such things. Sensitivity has always seemed to me a good thing, something to be cultivated rather than repressed. I have always been touched by beauty: a horse, a woman, a flower. Seldom scenery. Never a magnificent view. Rather a dell of moss-covered rocks in a wood in Ireland, a fairy kind of place, or the moors of Cumberland or Scotland. Wild marshlands. The vastness of Serengeti. This, I suppose, is a kind of religion. It is here that I feel close to all living things, part of them, part of a scheme. Close to something inexplicable that may be another word for God. On the plains of East Africa one is looking back through a peep-hole pricked in time. The animals one sees – zebra, giraffe, lion – are animals that were here ten thousand years ago. The same in the sense that water running in a river is the same. There is a kind of terrible innocence in East Africa. A Garden of Eden whose existence is drawing to a close for the pressure of population must end it.

In the early nineteen-hundreds this was a wonderful world. Empty. Beautiful. Free. But this comes later. I was a suckling then. A little pig sucking and banging away at Elsa's breasts.

My father, Laurence Woodbine Graham, was a South African and my mother Scottish – Edith Margaret Park. I was named Edward Fairley Stuart. Edward Fairley after an uncle of my mother's who was my godfather whom I never met, in the hope he would be flattered into leaving me his fortune. This did not come about. Stuart because of a vestigial claim to Stuart blood through my great-grandmother who had been a Graham of Fintry.

My father was a very good-looking man. Not tall, only about five foot eight, but very well and powerfully built. He had a cavalry moustache – walrus type, but fashionable then. His hair was grey as I remember it, but had been dark, and he was partially bald. His eyes were blue but could blaze as if there was a fire behind them when he was angry.

My mother had been a beauty and was still a handsome woman. She too was dark with large brown eyes and rather heavy eyebrows. She was tall for her days when girls took very little exercise, played no games – and must have been willowy with an exceptionally small waist compressed by whalebone and steel stays.

Jim, my eldest brother, was in the Merchant Service. The next eldest, Lance, was in the Consular Service. Lovel lived at home in Paris and worked at Tiffany's. Eric was also in the Merchant Service. Ronald was articled to a solicitor in London and lived there with my mother's parents.

Because I was an only child, or rather a child alone, animals came to mean more to me than people. Only on one occasion did my mother have all her six sons together under one roof. Lance was back on leave from Persia, Jim was home from the sea and so was Eric. Ronald came over for a few days from London; Lovel lived with us. I was about five. Jim gave me some sharks' teeth which I put into my collection cupboard and Eric gave me a big blue stamp album. I stole a number of Lance's ties because I liked their colours and the feel of silk in my fingers. I was spoilt by them all, a kind of human pet.

My mother was presented at Court when she was seventeen and married my father in her first season. This was the rather curious procedure of those mid-Victorian days. Girls 'came out', hatched like chickens from the shell of the schoolroom and finishing school. Deemed marriageable, they were presented at Court, if they belonged to the privileged classes, with fanfare and panoply of white dresses, long white gloves and white ostrich feathers in their hair. They curtseyed to the Queen and retired backwards, kicking the trains of their long court dresses as they did so. All this had to be taught them. The manners, the procedure, the orders of precedence. These young ladies, the cream of England in terms of breeding, wealth and looks, guaranteed virgins – since none of them had ever been alone with a man who was not a close relation – were then thrown on to the marriage market. They were married for their money, their looks, their social connections and position. There was, I suppose, some love, attraction anyway. But since few girls knew the facts of life it must have been a rather curious concept utterly lacking in realism. Most girls married the man their father told them to. In fact a man addressed his attentions to a girl's father rather than to her since she could not marry without his permission. Every girl hoped to get married in her first season. And her parents made every effort to get her off their hands, giving balls, dinner-parties and dances in which, like a filly in a show-ring, she could show off her paces. This was a period of big families and the thing to do was to market the girls as they ripened so that they made room for the next in line. The coming out, début, could only occur once. The chick could not be put back into the egg of schoolroom ignorance again. After the first season the girl had come down in value and her parents might have to settle for second or even third best.

After her marriage, my father took my mother to the Cape of Good Hope which she did not like much. I think she found his family difficult and she did not like the Cape coloured servants. What she liked best, she told me, were the hedges of blue plumbago.

My eldest brother was born at Rondebosch when she was eighteen. All my five brothers were born at the Cape of Good Hope but after some years my father moved back to London again where he was very successful as a financier or what was known in those days as a company promoter. He had a house in Queen's Gate, a racing stable at Newmarket and a yacht at Cowes. He was one of the first men to see the future of oil and obtained concessions from the Shah of Persia. He then over-extended himself, went bankrupt and made a new start on the Continent. All this took place before I was born, so I knew nothing of these past glories except by hearsay. Before her death my mother told me more about this Victorian London period where she appears to have belonged to the fast or swinging set. Baths in champagne. Meeting her friends at a fashionable abortionist's office. Dancing till dawn: waltzes, polkas, the lancers. My father playing a banjo and singing while she accompanied him on the piano. The old lady was over eighty then and still a fascinating companion. She was delighted to tell me on returning from a week in Brighton that a nice-looking man had remarked on what good legs she had. 'How old was he?' I asked. 'Oh, a young man,' she said, 'about sixty.' According to today's standards she had no education. But she could talk French, German and Italian. Play the piano, sing and paint. She knew how to run a house and raise children. She never lost one, which was a rare occurrence in those days. She read rubbish. Her favourite poet was Ella Wheeler Wilcox. Her favourite authors Ethel M. Dell and Elinor Glyn. She seldom looked at a paper. But she had character and became, in her old age, a character.

My father on the other hand was brilliant. He could cast up three columns of figures at one time – pounds, shillings and pence – by just running a pencil up the paper. He was a good bridge player, good at billiards, a good shot and a fine horseman. He played tennis, cricket and football in his youth. He was a strong swimmer. He was a very good-looking man, extremely sociable and social, a fine ballroom dancer. There really seemed nothing he could not do well. My mother and father were, even in late middle age when I was old enough to appreciate them, a distinguished-looking couple, but they quarrelled continually about money. Their only real income came from my mother's settlement – the sum put in trust for her at her marriage by her father which was meant to give her dress- and pin-money. All my father now had was what he could make out of a few French agencies, which was very little as he never mastered the language. He reported racing for the *New York Herald* and so had a press card which entitled him to get through the police lines at any disaster and enter all museums and most theatres free. I think my father added to his earnings by playing snooker and bridge. He was far above average as a player. He also got commission on any saddle horses he sold for Goldschmid, the job master. A quite ordinary horse looked splendid under him as he trotted or cantered it in the Bois. But it must all have been a terrible comedown for him, the ins and outs of which I did not understand till much later. These financial difficulties which worried my childhood have, I think, had a great effect on my behaviour by making me afraid of poverty and causing me to be over-careful with money, always making sure my expenditure never exceeded my earnings.

My mother's day, after her breakfast in bed, began with giving orders: about meals, about laundry to be washed, about me. What I was to wear when I went out, if it was cold or hot or wet. She might then go shopping accompanied by a maid with a big basket to buy vegetables, bread and flowers, or send the maid alone. Before dressing she had her bath. The tub, a large, round, flat tin one painted white inside and brown outside, was carried into the bedroom and filled with hot water carried from the kitchen boiler and later emptied by hand into slop pails.

There were no labour-saving devices, no elevator to the back door. Everything, from groceries to coal, was carried up five flights.

My mother might go to the shops in the Rue St-Honoré where she bought her embroidery designs and silks. She was very fond of embroidering table cloths and cushion covers. May Volans, the governess I had later, did drawn thread work, pulling threads out of a piece of linen and making patterns that looked like spiders alternating with squares and crosses.

In the afternoon my mother might do more shopping or go calling on her friends. This was a ritual. Visiting cards, which had to be engraved not printed, were left. One woman's card and two men's, or vice versa, I forget which. If the top right corner of a card was turned down it meant that it had not been presented in person but left by a domestic. The cards were accepted at the door by a maid or a manservant who came with a silver salver in his hand. In the evening the mistress would ask for the tray to see who had called. If you wanted to see someone and not merely leave a visiting card – a phrase that now only seems to refer to male dogs and lamp-posts – you said: 'Is Madame X at home? *Chez elle?*' The butler, footman or maid would go off with your card on his tray to enquire, saying: 'I will see.' One could imagine him looking everywhere for his mistress. Naturally he knew perfectly well if she was in or not; in fact, if she was out he would generally say so. The going to see bit was to present your card and ask her if she wished to see you. If she did not he would return saying: 'Madame is not at home.' Madame, of course, was never at home to anyone undesirable such as a divorced woman. Sometimes cards would be left at several apartments and houses in one afternoon and tea taken in the last one. After tea came the

evening with preparations for still another change of costume –
an ordinary evening dress, or full dress with long white gloves,
fan, Parma violets and all. No men wore dinner-jackets unless
they were dining alone or with other men.

As a child I was dressed up and pushed into the drawing-room
for tea with my mother if she was home. After an hour or so I was
removed, given my bath and supper and put to bed. My bath had
high sides as, like all children, I splashed about. It was painted
white inside and brown outside, like my mother's. It had a
wooden lid and was used as a trunk when we travelled since in
those days one could not expect to find baths of any kind outside
the metropolis.

I began to drink wine and water when I was about four years
old. I was often given a *canard* to suck – a lump of sugar dipped
in coffee – by grown-up people when they were drinking it. The
procedure was to hold an oblong French lump of sugar in the
coffee till the coffee reached the fingers through capillary action
and then eat it before it melted. The servants would give me bread
and butter thickly sprinkled with brown sugar, of which I was
very fond. They also used to put a little milk in the bottom of a
jampot that was nearly empty, stir it up and give it to me to eat
with a spoon. My favourite jam was Felix Potin's cherry jam
made with whole cherries. I also liked strawberry jam, apricot
jam and Dundee marmalade and would eat them all out of the jar
if I got the chance. In fact I liked jam and liked it straight.

CHAPTER 3

FATHER AND SON

THE world of my childhood was active, seething, and from our point of view today, quite without fear. There would be no more wars. People were now civilized. They had learnt their lesson. The Boer War did not count. That was a colonial war.

There was the Great Paris Exhibition. I remember that. My father had something to do with its promotion. He had a finger in a lot of very small pies. We bought some Turkish carpets. I remember how they smelt and the smell of the chocolate we drank in one of the pavilions. Smells and sounds seemed very important then. The first sound I remember is the screaming of the swifts that nested in the walls of the next building. I know I remember this because no one would have told me about it, though there must always be some confusion in one's mind about what one actually remembers and the stories which are later told about one's cuteness or naughtiness in childhood. Another thing I remember is a liver and white spaniel being given to us, which I loved dearly but which was got rid of because as soon as I stood up he knocked me down and overwhelmed me with affection, licking me from head to toe. This was my first dog. Since then there must have been fifty or more. My life has been punctuated by dogs and horses; by animals in general. I have seldom walked alone.

But to return to the picture of Paris that I was painting. There were, as I say, the *nou-nous*, the *nourisses* (wet-nurses) in their variety of costumes. There were the beautifully dressed children, babies in long clothes. Then there were older girls with longer dresses, their hair on their shoulders, or tied with a ribbon. There were débutantes, each accompanied by a parent, a maid or companion – their virginity, a marketable product, had to be protected. Then the young married women, recent débutantes who had blossomed out, and the older married women with adolescent children, in the full flower of life; and the still older married women, and finally the grandmothers who dressed in black and, like Queen Victoria, wore white caps and little frills of lawn round their necks and wrists. Some of them cannot have been much more than forty, but life was over for them.

There were the officers in uniform who rode by on their showy chargers often accompanied by pretty women who rode side saddle. (Women did not ride astride till the First World War.) And soldiers – cuirassiers, dragoons, chasseurs, brilliant Zouaves with wide trousers and embroidered waistcoats; an occasional Chasseur Alpin with a beret, and the ordinary infantry soldiers of the line who were dressed much as they had been in 1870 – a red képi, a long blue coat and red trousers.

There were servants going on messages or taking the air – English butlers, parlourmaids, *valets de chambre* with wasplike striped black and yellow waistcoats, grooms, coachmen – cockaded if they were English and drove for an officer who held the Queen's commission. Footmen, flunkeys in the costume of another, pre-revolutionary age, with silk stockings and powdered wigs. There were barrel-organs, street singers, jugglers, and tumblers who spread a little carpet and performed upon it till they were moved on by the police. There were balloon sellers with big grapelike bunches of multicoloured gas-filled balloons. Sometimes a child would lose one and we would watch it getting smaller and smaller as it rose into the sky. There were pavement artists and men leading dancing bears who came from the mountains of Austria. There was a herd of goats from the Pyrenees that was driven to Paris every winter and marched back in the spring. They were led by a man with a bagpipe and women came to the pavement with little jugs and waited while his assistant milked the goats into their own receptacles. There were knife-grinders who operated their grindstones with a pedal while they sat in a little handcart with a roof. Women brought them their knives and scissors to sharpen. There were china-menders who riveted broken vessels together while you waited. There were women who with an apparatus of spikes teased mattresses of mixed wool and horsehair into renewed buoyancy. They usually operated in a courtyard by the *porte-cochère*. In the winter there were the chestnut-sellers who roasted their chestnuts in portable charcoal stoves. They generally wore round brown sealskin caps. They put the chestnuts into cones of newspaper and I used to like to hold them warm in my trouser pockets. Even the shops did not have paper bags, just cones of white paper. There were ragged beggars and women with crying babies, often not their own, holding out their hands for coppers. *Un sou. Deux sous* . . . There were children playing. Concierges sitting on chairs outside their doors, a fat cat or dog beside them, a canary singing in the window. The barrel-organs played as monkeys in red jackets and caps held out tin cups for money. Street children danced to the music.

A great deal of life went on in the streets. Carpets were beaten with wicker paddles, slops were emptied into the gutters, people made love and quarrelled, women slapped children. Drunks leaned against lamp-posts. Dogs lifted their legs and yellow powdered sulphur was scattered on the corners of doorways to discourage them.

Hygiene, baths, hot water, that was all English and American nonsense. Cows' milk was delivered by means of a great metal churn on a cart and ran out through a shiny brass tap into measures which were hung on hooks on its side. Everywhere there were horses and horse dung; small boys disputing it with sparrows as they loaded it on to little carts made of boxes mounted on old perambulator wheels. It was sold to market gardeners. There were practically no cars.

The world was filled with colour and variety. And this was not in Paris alone. The whole world was in fancy dress. The Chinese still wore pigtails. There was no uniformity – no standardization, no mass production of clothes or ideas or men.

I was taken to see Santos Dumont – a Brazilian – make an ascent in a balloon. He drifted with the wind. To gain altitude he emptied sand out of one of the little bags he carried to lighten the basket in which he sat. To come down he allowed the gas to escape from the bag above him. It was very exciting, very modern. This was about as far as man would go in his conquest of the heavens. But I got a stiff neck watching him and was against progress. My neck was rubbed with Elliman's Embrocation – one of the medicines that has survived. Elliman's Embrocation, Chlorodyne, Scott's Emulsion, Wincarnis are others which can still be bought.

How much did I know at this time? That I loved my Elsa. I loved my mother too, but I seldom saw her. She was beautiful in evening dress when she came to kiss me goodnight. She smelt wonderful. She wore bunches of Parma violets at her waist and long white gloves. I loved dogs but could not have one yet. I recognized the cry of swifts. In addition I had long golden curls which were washed with yolk of egg and done up like a girl's in screws of rag and paper every night in order to make ringlets by day. I wore girls' frocks, mostly of broderie anglaise with ribbons through them and a wide blue sash (blue for a boy, the only masculine touch) and a sort of floppy Ascot hat. I was pretty. So pretty that people stopped in the street to speak to Elsa or Mother about this lovely little girl.

There remain two events of some importance in this broderie-anglaise-little-girl period. They must have occurred when I was about four or five and have had a profound effect on my life. The first was due to my beauty and charm of manner. Every first Thursday of the month my mother was at home. A vast company of women smelling of perfume, furs – and probably of themselves, for in those days very few houses had bathrooms – used to come for afternoon tea. Some of the older ones had hair on their faces. This hair usually grew like a small plume out of a raised mole. I was always brought into the room dressed in my best and made to go round the company on a hand-kissing expedition. But that was not enough for these abominable women. Oh no, they had to embrace the dear child. I was kissed and hugged, prickled by bearded woman, sunk into the billowing doughlike breasts of others. Wet kissed, dry kissed, all but raped in the strokings and pattings of these eminently virtuous guests of my mother's. I suffered. But one day it occurred to me that I could get something out of all this. Some reward greater than the single cake my mother gave me. And the cakes in Paris in those days were something to be remembered. Chocolate and coffee éclairs bursting with real cream, cakes covered with a rich mixture of coffee and butter that melted in your mouth, cream puffs, *babas au rhum*, *mille feuilles*, little tarts filled with every kind of preserved fruit in syrup.

My plan was simple. For the first time, but not the last, I was about to prostitute myself. The beautiful child was going to demand the reward due, not to his beauty but for the maulings and messings about he had received because of it. I wonder if there is not something of this feeling in the gold-digging of the showgirl hired to strip at stag parties? Anyway, I went up to the first lady, smiled beautifully into her eyes, stood shyly on one foot and then on the other, allowed her to put an arm round me and said: 'Do you think my mother would mind if you gave me a little piece of cake?' 'Of course Mother would not mind,' the lady said, patting my behind and chucking me under the chin. But this was the price I was prepared to pay. I got the cake. Since ladies all talk and never listen, her neighbour had no idea of what had been going on and she, too, fell for my charm. There were a lot of ladies. And I was a very small boy. I was sick for three days. They had to get a doctor. I was purged and enema-ed. And I have never eaten anything sweet since. No cake, no sweets, no pudding.

This was an interesting example of an orgy, a childish orgy. A cake shop to a child probably corresponds to a brothel in a man. There must always be danger when unlimited desire is presented with the possibility of surfeit. It is against nature. But I should never have thought of it if I had not been inspired with a fury of revenge, with the intent to make someone pay for the indignities I had suffered. Of course it was I who suffered.

The second event took place after a dinner-party. In those days everyone dressed; the men wore white ties, tails and white gloves, the ladies full evening dress and long gloves. It was all very formal, rather like a ballet, like the courting dance of a turkey or a peacock. The couples paraded, bowed, scraped, kissed hands, exchanged compliments and remarks about the weather, the theatre, the health and progress of their children, the defects of their servants, and where they would spend the summer. Then they marched in to dinner, two by two, the ladies on the gentlemen's right arms to leave the spiritual sword that still hung on their left hips free. It was not so long ago that they had worn swords. The dinner had an endless number of courses: soup, fish, three or four choices of meat or game, sweets, fruits, coffee, liqueurs and, naturally, several kinds of wine. Sherry with the soup, white wine with the fish, red with the flesh, or champagne right through. Then came Port or Marsala, and finally liqueurs: brandy, crème de menthe, kümmel, curaçao, benedictine. So there were glasses, many glasses, all beautifully cut, their prisms shining in the candlelight. At the end of dinner each glass held dregs like multicoloured jewels – scarlet rubies, orange topazes, green emeralds, dark red garnets. A baby does not know about jewels but he knows pretty things; he wants to possess them and the best way to possess anything is to eat or drink it. This I did when everyone had left the dining-room and when I had done I felt pretty good, but a little sleepy and vague about the direction of the nursery from which I had escaped. However, being a philosophical child, I abandoned my search, crept under the long white tablecloth and went to sleep with the pleasant dusty smell in my nostrils of my friend the blue and red Turkish carpet that had come from the Great Exhibition. I was very happy.

After dinner, people did not play bridge then, they talked, they sang, they recited, they did simple conjuring tricks and, in a decorous way, made each other improper suggestions and assignations where these suggestions could be carried out. But as usual, before the evening was over, my mother wished to show me off. Her Benjamin, her baby, sleeping like a fair-haired angel in his cot. She led the cooing covey shushing each other with fingers raised to lips. But baby was not there. Baby had gone. The crib was empty. The bird had flown. He was safe, and drunk as a lord under the table. Out of it all.

What a fuss! It was an hour before they found him and then only because Elsa, who slept in the nursery and should have heard him escape, pointed out that all the glasses on the table were completely empty. She was a country girl and very observant. 'He could not have drunk them, not my baby,' Mother said. 'Not the dregs. My little golden-haired cherub.'

'By God, if he has he won't be far off,' Dad said. Someone raised the cloth and I was discovered. I did not mind how many people kissed me or messed about now. This was the secret of social intercourse. The anaesthetic that I was eventually, many years later, to employ as an escape mechanism. But I did not get drunk again, except accidentally on three or four occasions, until I was past middle age. From a moral point of view I suffered nothing. I was not sick and had no hangover. I suppose I just drank enough to last me forty years and then began again.

Another curious thing happened to me about this time. I

always carried my mother's breakfast tray into her room – she breakfasted in bed. One morning I dropped the tray. Mother said: 'How did you do that?' I said: 'I forgot I was carrying it.' I remember this quite clearly, still. I thought: what are my hands doing out in front of me like that? So I put them down to my side and let the tray fall.

The next event of importance was my seduction – I am assuming that seduction has importance. I owe it to my mother who wished to improve my French. At that time I spoke only German well. A very beautiful young French girl of seventeen called Katerine was hired to instruct me. She was slim and blonde. She wore lovely underclothes and was much nicer to sleep with than the coarse-figured but virtuous Elsa. Elsa was still with us but had been promoted to parlourmaid. She stopped nursing me when I bit her. She said to my mother: 'Madame, I do not wish to be employed suckling a cannibal.' So I was weaned on to Dover sole and sheep's brains. I have often thought that when men in strange lands decide to go home to die it is due less to patriotic nostalgia than to a desire once again to taste the food on which they were weaned.

Elsa's sister, Caroline, was now the cook. So as both my mother and the servants spoke German and I associated with very few other people, both my English and French required polishing up. Naturally I was not supposed to sleep with Katerine but when she picked me up, took me to her warm fragrant bed and petted me, I was delighted. She allowed me to explore her girlish body. I had had no idea till then that breasts served any other purpose than a dairy function or that they were capable of changing shape. All this was most interesting and instructive I am inclined to think that what Katerine taught me has been most valuable. Her conversation was about boys, bigger boys than me, *bien entendu*, but constructed in a similar fashion; about her father who used to whip her naked on his knee. Evidently a sadist and possibly an incestuous old man. But gradually some of this leaked out. I dare say I was abstracted in my manner, confused by the glory of the new world this lovely girl was showing me. However, when my mother discovered what was going on it ended abruptly. The pretty bubble was pricked. And sex was out for another twelve years or so. As a boy, later, I was very interested in girls but hardly kissed one and never touched one. Not that I didn't want to – I did. But I was afraid of the hiding I would get if I was caught. I still maintain that fear is an excellent deterrent in the control of morals and crime. My beautiful golden daffodil, Katerine, was replaced by a governess. A Yorkshire woman of great virtue, honesty and limited talent. Her name was May Volans.

Before she came I went to a dame school. I do not know what I learnt there, if anything, but I mixed with other children. I cut things out of coloured paper, drew pictures, and fell in love with a big dark girl of fifteen called Léonie Rideout. This was a very one-sided affair but that did not deter me though I had other girl-friends – the De Bries and Kippings – with whom I used to play Happy Families, Snap, Draughts and Dominoes.

I was still at this time a miniature transvestite dressed as a girl and wearing long golden curls. My pursuits, too, were girlish. I had been taught to sew and tried to do embroidery. I made a cord out of silk to edge my mother's cushions which I worked through a cotton reel that had four nails in it with a crochet needle. I played with dolls but would have nothing to do with teddy-bears which had just appeared on the toy horizon.

May had previously taught two of my abominable Swedish cousins, Kitty and Percival Quensel. I say abominable because they had been, according to May, paragons of virtue. Intelligent, obedient in their habits, simply delighting in washing their hands before meals, and so willing to brush their teeth that one had to keep snatching the toothbrush out of their rosy clean-nailed fingers before they wore their gums away. May stayed with us for about six years but she never took kindly to Paris. It was too shocking. It was not like York where her father and brothers had clerical positions in a chocolate factory – Rowntree's, I think.

But neither in York nor Sweden were there waist-high urinals in the street where men, if a lady passed whom they knew, raised their hats to her. There were no enormous and embarrassing, in every way, white stallions dragging great blocks of building stone through the city streets. These horses always enthralled me. So strong, so big, so white, with their great wooden collars decorated with sheepskins dyed red or blue. It is typical of the

French that they kept the mares on the farms to breed and sent
the stallions to work in the towns. Hardly any of their horses
were gelded which, since the French are such a logical race,
confirms my opinion that an entire horse is better than a gelding.
That even supposing, as the tests have shown, there is nothing to
choose between them in performance, they can live on less food,
pick up more quickly if they are let down and are more intelligent.
There are naturally difficulties. They are less tractable, they tend
to fight and can be dangerous.

I must have been a great trial to May who was very virginal,
very English and aged, I suppose, at that time about twenty-five.
One thing that disturbed her occurred when we were out for a
walk one day. I became very upset because one of the horses
pulling a waggon had his penis out of his sheath. It was a big
horse and its penis was about as long as I was tall. I stopped May,
whose face had turned scarlet at the sight, and asked if she thought
he was ill? Were his insides coming out? Should we tell someone
about it? A policeman, *par exemple*? I thought she was upset for
the same reason as I was when she dragged me on, still protesting,
and it was a long time before I grasped the twin facts of equine
anatomy and English middle-class prudery. But my May was no
person to instruct me in the characteristics of entire Percheron
horses which are, to employ a euphemism, exaggerated in all
directions.

Then there was Nellie, the smooth-haired fox-terrier bitch – a
real beauty – who belonged to Mr Chinery who was head of the
His Master's Voice Gramophone Agency. Gramophones had
begun to come in, though so far I had never heard one. He was
a tall, thin, rather deaf man, which may have assisted him in his
business. When he went to America he left Nellie with us. We
were inseparable. I thought her the most lovely thing in the
world. Better even than Katerine. Then my father, at Mr Chinery's
request, bred her. This was another shock for May. In cathedral
cities it is evident that dogs do not breed, that bitches do not have
pups, that little boys do not witness the various processes or
question respectable governesses about the sequence of events.
But I did. This was Paris, not York. Not Uppsala. Poor May! She
taught me my alphabet very badly, with labelled bricks, so I
never learnt the order the letters go in till much later and still

have trouble with a dictionary. She taught me to read with the aid of a primer entitled *Reading Without Tears*. I do not think any child ever wept more than I over his letters. I have an idea Winston Churchill was instructed from this same book and detested it as much as I did. She taught me to write in copybooks where I drew line after line of copperplate, pot hooks and hangers and then graduated to words and finally to sentences, mottoes and moral precepts such as: 'Honesty is the best policy,' and 'A stitch in time saves nine.' I am inclined to think that the copying out of these precepts when one is learning to write with much suffering may impress them on the unconscious and have some effect on one's subsequent behaviour. May also taught me my tables, so badly that I have half forgotten them, and some elementary arithmetic. A middle-aged Frenchwoman, who smelt as only such a woman can of virtue, old black clothes and funerals, with a touch of vinegar, garlic and naphtha balls, came to teach me French. We read *Les Malheurs de Sophie* – what silly little sins she committed – and similar books of the *Famille Rose* library.

My mother said: 'Do you like her?' 'Oh yes,' I said. What was the good of protesting? 'But I should not want to get into her bed,' which made Mother laugh.

The books I really liked May to read to me were *Black Beauty*, *Wee MacGreegor* and *Froggy's Little Brother*. I cried and cried when May read them to me and fell asleep on a pillow wet with tears. But I never tired of the stories. Was this masochism? Or is it good for a child's heart to be wrung? I do not think anyone really knows. But I think that Grimm's and Hans Andersen's fairy stories are far better for a child than the comics or the books that are now considered children's fare. The figures they portray exist – sleeping beauties, giants and giant-killers, witches, were-wolves. Don't we know them all? We could each make a little classified directory listing them. Wolves – male and female. Sleeping beauties that only I can wake. Prince Charming – what you hope you are. Witches – the mothers of the sleeping beauties and those you have waked up. Fairies – we know them too. Some of my best friends are fairies.

An event now occurred that upset me badly. I saw from quite close up a street accident. Two traps collided, the shaft of one of them penetrating the chest of the horse pulling the other, which went down screaming in a welter of blood. There is no more horrible sound than the scream of a horse in agony. Blood has always upset me. This may have been the primary cause of my dislike of it or it may have been a goose that my father decapitated when we were in the country. When its head was off it slipped from his hand and flew, spurting blood, straight into my face. Later on, in a move which would shock the psychologists of today, my father, in an effort to get me used to blood, used to take me to the abattoir in Geneva to watch animals being killed. I remember oxen being slaughtered by having a spike driven into their brains. It was set in a slot in a leather mask that covered their faces. But I still did not get used to blood, no matter how much ran in the gutters. It is difficult to imagine today a father being allowed to take a child into such premises. But I never got used to the sight of blood or its smell, and I have always been amazed at people who are attracted by blood and like to watch operations or gather like vultures round the scene of an accident. The first accident I remember – I must have been about two at the time – was when Elsa was sewing and drove the needle of the machine through her first finger, nail and all. She screamed. I screamed. My mother came running, gave the wheel a half turn and the needle came out. Elsa began to cry; I cried, and we both precipitated ourselves into my mother's arms. Elsa, although she had been a mother, was not much more than a child herself, possibly eighteen years of age at the most. My mother kissed us both and told Caroline to make some tea. This personal relationship between master and man is something inconceivable today. It was very often one of reciprocal affection. They were part of the family. Was this better or worse? All I can say is that it was different and as I have said before, our servants sang at their work.

This must have been about the time of what I now call the revolution. The day that I rebelled. I forget where we were, somewhere in the Bois, the Pré Catalan, I think. It was Sunday and I was dressed in my frightful best. I watched the cows being milked. I drank milk, foaming hot and smelling of cow. Naturally homogenized, the way God meant it to be supplied to calves and children. I was beginning to like cattle. I liked the smell of the place. I liked to smell the cows' breath. No woman's is as sweet. And I saw other things. Splendid cow-pats behind the cows.

Rich, dark brown, glutinous. I watched a man come and collect
them in a barrow. I slipped away after him and saw the manure
heap. My first manure heap. My first conscious one, anyway.
Here at last was the way out. Here was the door of escape into
boyhood. With great deliberation I approached the heap, climbed
it, lay down and rolled. It was very soft, beautifully warm and
quite fragrant. They would never dress me as a girl again. No,
never. And if they did, I'd do it again. I had found a method to
defeat them. No more broderie anglaise frocks, no more Ascot
hats, no more lace-edged drawers. God damn it, I was a boy! I
wanted trousers. A suit, and my hair cut. I got what I wanted.

On the way home my mother told people there had been an
accident – her dear little girl had fallen into the *fumier*.

My hair was cut off. After my mother's death I found a ringlet
in an envelope with 'Stuart's Hair' written on it in her hand,
among her papers. People of my mother's generation still
treasured glass-fronted lockets with the hair of dead relations
woven into intricate patterns of flowers or lovers' knots. Hair has
always had a certain mystic significance, being a living part of an
individual that could be detached in life or after death. It was said
to continue growing on corpses. It was the quality by which
women were described: blonde, dark, redhaired. Only whores
dyed their hair. When women wore their hair up, the day she put
her hair up was a significant day in a girl's life; taking it down was
a kind of undressing. It was something men asked girls to do.
'Will you let me see your hair down? I want to touch it.' The hat
came off, the hairpins came out and the hair fell in a mane about
her shoulders. It was an act of intimacy in front of a man. A
promise. Part of a courtship ritual which had a slow, minuet-like
beauty as the figures were performed. Even the removal of tight-
fitting kid gloves was a kind of preliminary undressing that
stimulated the imagination. I have always loved long hair. As a
child I used to like to see it flowing like a horse's tail behind little
girls as they ran. I used to like watching Louise brush my mother's
long, dark hair. I have never outgrown my liking for it and have
what I suppose is a long-hair fetish. I also like high heels, lace,
silk, satin, taffeta – and their synthetic equivalents – underclothes.
What a fetish really amounts to is a personal taste with particular
reference to sexual relations, an idiosyncrasy which, carried to

extremes, could end in vice, but which in the ordinary way is no more than wanting or not wanting to wear a buttonhole.

In the same drawer as my lock of hair I also found a picture of myself in a suit. Black and white checked like a bookmaker's, and a pale-coloured tie. I remember it well. It was Cambridge blue. But I don't think that was the first suit. I think I was forced to go through a Little Lord Fauntleroy period. But I had learnt something: the way to deal with a problem is the *fait accompli*.

CHAPTER 4

SOUND AND COLOUR

IN 1960 when we visited Cairo the Pyramids and Sphinx were illuminated with alternate floodlights of rose, pink, mauve, green and blue while a taped loudspeaker told us of the wonders of ancient Egypt as we sat in folding wooden chairs on the sand. This was progress – *son et couleur* – something as far as I was concerned utterly unreal and unrelated to history. But it set me thinking of the old days in Paris at the turn of the century and up to the First World War, and it is the colours, the smells and sounds that come back to me. In the windows of the chemists' shops there were great flasks of red, blue and green liquid. In the sidewalk cafés one saw children drinking red *sirop de grenadine* through straws, and women pale green *menthe à l'eau*. There was cassis (blackcurrant) brandy, a purple that was almost black. Byrrh, an amber apéritif. But colour, always colour. Red wine, white wine, Pernod cloudy as an opal or a moonstone. Dubonnet, dark as blood.

In the spring there was the young green haze of the trees, the pale underclothes that were the forerunners of full summer dress, and later the white and red of the chestnut candelabra that illuminate the Parisian avenues in June.

Soldiers, house servants, grooms, girls, children and women. Top-hatted men. All colours and textures. Silks, satins, linens, cotton, floral muslins, broadcloth, tweeds, leather. Ostrich feathers, furs. The perfume of women, the smell of stables, of flowershops, of bakeries, of butchers' shops, of rotting vegetables. All blended into a single odour, that of a great metropolis. A capital city. What a place to be brought up in with its museums, its whores and artists, its horses and dogs, its trees, its views, its street scenes.

This is the overwhelming impression of my childhood. Beauty, variety, colour, contrast. Beggars and millionaires. The starving horses of the *chiffoniers*, who were sorting trash for bottles and bits of rag, and the splendid oat-fed pairs of matched carriage horses high-stepping down the fashionable streets.

It is curious how sounds have changed in the twentieth century, most of the old ones being lost for good. Brass bands, barrel-organs, street singers and musicians, the cries of hawkers selling their wares. The sound of horseshoes and iron tyres on the *pavé* of the roads. Of blacksmiths hammering red hot iron. And the smells that went with all these things: the smell of burnt hoofhorn as a shoe was fitted, the ammoniac smell of horse manure, the smell of human sweat, of excrement, of a *pissoir*, of raw meat. Of roses – for roses were scented then; much less perfect in appearance but a bowl of them would scent a room.

The world was less deodorized, homogenized. Everything was stronger, more differentiated. There was no problem in deciding on the sex of an adolescent. The food was less processed and more highly flavoured. There were no battery eggs or mass-produced broilers. Food was grown on family farms. Farming was a way of life, not an egg, broiler, pork, veal or milk factory. We all lived much nearer to reality. Nearer to the earth, and the wonderful muck of it. The rich muck that is the basis of life – the *fumier* (manure heap) which existed in front of every peasant's house and was taken in wheelbarrows through the kitchen to be spread on the *potager* behind it. Babies were born and people died in their homes among their neighbours. Bodies were not whisked anonymously away.

We were aware of death, even as children. Again, I have no idea how good or bad all this is; all I wish to record is the difference between *then* and *now*. I sometimes feel that if what we have gained in comfort and luxury were to be measured against what we have lost, the scales would be fairly level and possibly even favour the past.

Frenchwomen went into deep mourning even for the death of a distant relative. Draped with black crêpe, using black-edged handkerchiefs and writing letters on black-edged notepaper, they were part of the sartorial picture, punctuating it with this public demonstration of their loss. From black they graduated to white, purple, mauve and grey. Older women – grandmothers – always wore black since they were always mourning someone in the vast ramifications of their families. On their heads they wore lace caps or jet embellished toques. Jet was much used to ornament black clothes. Artists wore velvet berets and wide silk bow-ties. Actors wore cloaks and large sombreros. There was an immense difference of dress according to age and class. Men wore top hats – *chapeaux de haute forme* – and morning coats. In fashionable streets street-cleaners performed their never-ending duty of collecting horse droppings almost as they fell. In the winter they steamed with heat from the horses' bowels. House sparrows searched for undigested oats. Sparrows have almost disappeared today; they went with the horse and the gentleman (*chevalier, caballero, Ritter*) a curious symbiotic trio that had been associated for centuries. There were more dogs then. Pet dogs of all kinds, and big mongrels in harness pulling costers' barrows.

The quality I am trying to capture is one of colour, sound and smell: of reality. This was a world of absolutes, of good and bad. The values may have been all wrong but they were probably easier for the human spirit to cope with than the world of today where the whole spectrum has been blended into a democratic grey.

My father taught me to split and sharpen a goose quill into a pen. That was all he had as a boy. There were no pen nibs then. Just feathers. We had goose quills at the Guards Club in Brook Street till 1930. The method of fixing them was simple enough: the quill, a strong pinion from the wing, is shorn off diagonally with a penknife (hence the name) and then split upwards for half an inch or so. The most popular metal pen nibs at this time were Jay and Relief.

I called my father 'Daddy' when I was small. Then I was made to call him 'Dad'. I remember this affecting my relationship with him; I should have come round to it on my own if left alone.

My mother was wonderful. All my life she was always there when I came home or if out left a note for me. But once even she betrayed me. I showed her a secret nest I had made hidden among the rhododendrons in the garden. But one day she showed it to some of her friends, saying how cute I was hiding away like that. I never used the place again and after that my mother always complained about my being secretive. I think I was, having learnt very young to keep my mouth shut.

Many years later at Hardelot a Christian Scientist practitioner

called Miss Drake bought a cottage. I dug her garden and fenced
it for her. I was then twelve or thirteen and quite a good gardener.
I expected some praise – it was a good job – and a small cash
reward. I got neither and since then have been prejudiced against
Christian Scientists.

These things are interesting. If one has either liked or disliked
a boy or a girl with a certain name, or even certain coloured hair or
eyes, one tends to remain prejudiced, either in favour of or
against anyone having them in later years. This is grossly unfair
but there is no such thing as justice. I tend to like people who are
good-looking, though they may have nothing else in their favour.
Some people like, or conversely hate, redheads, Negroes, Jews,
cripples. But there are men who like hunchback girls or girls with
one leg, and girls who like only fat men. There seems to be no
defect which is not in certain circumstances an asset. How many
mothers have deplored something being wrong with their sons
only to find that when war came they were left safely at home
while the strong straight boys were called up.

I believe a child's character shows when very young. Even at
the age of four or five I disliked parties and after what seemed to
me a respectable interval would find whomever had brought me
– a servant, usually – and ask to be taken home. I thanked my
hostess very politely as I had been taught to do and got to hell
out of it. This dislike of parties has remained with me, as has my
love of animals. I have never been a man's man. I have never
understood anyone being really interested in any game. It was
always a matter of complete indifference to me who won the
Boat Race or an international football match. Shooting I used to
like, but I was a bad bird shot except over dogs. I remember once
in Scotland being out with a colonel of the Black Watch who
commented on my bad luck with driven birds. I had, however,
shot a number of rabbits and hares, so I said: 'Yes, sir, I'm not
lucky with birds but I'm hell on rabbits and lions.' I had just come
back from Africa and had never shot a lion, but he was not to
know that.

Even as a child I never liked Christmas, though we had a
candlelit tree with presents round its trunk and buckets of water
and sand to put out the fire if it caught alight. I was not impressed. I had more or less everything I wanted – I never wanted

much – and I disliked having to be grateful to people I did not like for presents I did not want. I liked books and lead soldiers and money. I did not like clockwork trains or Meccano sets.

When I went out, even at school, it was always with one or two of my friends, never a gang. Later, with a brother officer or a girl. I have always liked to talk and for conversation there cannot be a crowd. I think psychologists would try to find some deep-hidden reason for my love for animals. I do not think there is one beyond the fact that I am good with them, and we always like what we are good at. It is very pleasant to have the love and trust of an animal, to create a field of understanding as one does with a good horse or a working dog. I am sorry for people who miss this, as I am for those who miss the beauty of women. I suppose I am visual and tactile; I like to look at things and touch them. A dog's wet nose, a woman's breast. The feel of a horse's neck. The perfection of a rose. To some people this must sound like nonsense; perhaps it is. After all there is no money in it. It does not help anyone to get on.

There is no longer the summer buzzing of insects in clearings in the woods that I knew as a child. The bees, bumble bees, wasps and darting, hovering flies have gone. There is no longer the sound of a horn from an occasional coach and four. No crowing cocks, nor the cackle of a hen which has just laid an egg.

There used to be smells of drains, of manure, of garbage. They may not have been pleasant but they were part of reality. Mankind had smelled them for millennia. Their sources were not dangerous except when they contaminated the water supply. Less dangerous, certainly, than the carbon monoxide and hydro-carbons we breathe today. There was in those days a far greater incidence of infant and child mortality but mothers expected to lose some children, and the law of the survival of the fittest operated so that those who were left developed a great resistance to disease and hardship. Water was often impure, meat unhygien-ically handled, milk unpasteurized. It was impossible to keep flies off food. But adults live no longer now; the improved life insurance statistics are due to the reduction in infant mortality.

It was a bright, gay world, at least for me. A world of variety and paradox, with very rich people and starving paupers. A colourful stage on which I stood, a wide-eyed, middle-class little

boy, knowing neither the very rich nor the very poor. I played
with a few children of my own kind. There were distinct classes
then. I had friends among the servants, grooms and coachmen of
the neighbourhood. Among local artisans: house-painters,
cobblers, carpenters. Blacksmiths, wherever we were, always
fascinated me, handling red hot horseshoes, beating the iron on
the anvils and dropping them to hiss in a water trough. Big men
in leather aprons, the sweat cutting furrows through the grime of
coal dust on their faces.

But it is the variety of what I watched that comes back to me
now. Horses were much more varied in type, breed and value
than cars are today. From a purely artistic point of view, a
Rolls-Royce cannot compare with a matched pair of well-bred
carriage horses. Since early childhood horses have been my
passion. Whenever I could I spent my time among them and the
men who worked with them. My father, in some ways, treated
me as if I was grown up and taught me to be a good judge of a
horse or a woman. He taught me to watch how women stood,
moved and spoke. He thought good fetlocks and ankles a sign of
breeding. He taught me to look for the 'bad 'uns', equine and
human. Horses that showed the whites of their eyes and laid back
their ears. People who did not seem trustworthy. He said once
they reached a certain age people's lives were written on their
faces. He said you could tell brains from a person's eyes and
character from their mouths. I understood very little of it then
but it stayed with me, and perhaps due to what he taught me I
have been lucky with my friends.

There was a great deal of cruelty to both animals and children.
Overloaded carthorses were beaten by drunken carters. Sometimes horses lost their footing on the slippery roads. When a
carthorse went down someone had to sit on its head to prevent it
struggling while the harness was removed.

It was a world of essentials, a primary world. Children's toys
were very simple. I had a Jack-in-the-Box in the form of a snake.
The snake was made of a spring covered with green material. It
was compressed in a small square box which I would ask my
friends to open. When they undid the lid the snake jumped out
and I became hysterical with laughter. They knew something
would pop out at them but they were just as amused as I. Imagine

kids of five or six getting fun out of something like that today!

Little girls all had dolls that they wheeled about in tiny prams. They varied from great big expensive golden-haired, blue-eyed beauties with waxen faces who closed their eyes when they were laid down to rag dolls with flat painted faces that leaked sawdust if roughly handled. I had about two hundred lead soldiers. Infantry of the line, Guards, cavalry. They came in flat boxes, six to a box, and I bought them at Porter's, a toyshop in the Old Brompton Road. I had a Household Cavalry band. I had Blues and Life-Guards. Lancers and Hussars. A box of Greys on white horses. I had Highlanders. Marines and Blue-Jackets. I enjoyed playing with them very much. I had a rocking-horse, a painted dapple grey with a real horsehair mane and tail.

This was the atmosphere, the background, of the world into which every afternoon Elsa had taken me out in my pram or toddling. She had cleaned my ears with a bit of cotton-wool on a matchstick. Today parents take children to a paediatrician for such jobs, but then it was simpler. It was assumed that any young woman could take care of a child; after all, they had always done it. When my face was dirty Elsa wetted her handkerchief with saliva and wiped off the spots. A cotton handkerchief wet with spit has a smell of its own. Oddly enough, after a gap of fifty years a woman at a New York cocktail party asked me why my eyebrows grew as they do. I said: 'Madam, it is because I wash my face anti-clockwise which leaves one eyebrow up and the other one smooth.' She then wetted her handkerchief and smoothed down the upstanding brow. I was astounded. How dared she smell like my beloved Elsa? That, as far as I was concerned, ended the party. I found Tiny and said: 'Come on! We're off. Some bloody woman has just spat in my eye.' Perhaps it was a sexual advance? Perhaps a perverted sense of humour? Whatever it was, it left me amazed at such unwarranted intimacy. Little incidents such as this assume a psychic importance quite out of proportion to their true value, which is nil. But it helped to confirm my view of American women: they tend to despise men. I once heard the recently divorced wife of a friend say: 'Oh, he'll come back to Momma. Men are all like little boys.' How could he go back to her after that, even if he had wanted to? Men are not like little boys. In their rivalry with men, American women have de-sexed themselves and it is not surprising so many soldiers stationed abroad marry foreign women simply because they are women.

When I was small my mother spanked me with a slipper or the back of an ivory hairbrush. When I was older my father used a hunting crop and my schoolmasters a cane. I think I deserved every beating I ever got. They were fully expected if I were caught. I always worked it out on 'a game being worth, or not worth, the candle' basis. I was a normal, high-spirited boy who needed beating as a horse needs a bit, or a dog a chain, to limit my activities. There was no psychiatry then, no Dr Spock. Kids were brought up as their parents had been, by rule of thumb. A method that had produced such men as Wellington and Nelson in England, and Lincoln, Washington and Franklin in America. The hard way. But the world is a hard place. It has always seemed better to me to be trained in a hard school young, than be pampered and then pitchforked into a hostile and competitive world. For that is what it is, no matter how much it is democratically disguised with first name goodfellowship.

If some children were ruined because they could not take it they were probably less in number than those who fold up today when half the hospital beds are occupied by mental cases. This is of course an archaic point of view but one which was valid at that time and may yet prove valid again. The race was to the strong. This corresponds to the laws of nature which we now defy on humanitarian grounds.

On Sunday mornings the grown-ups walked in the Bois *endimanché* – in their Sunday clothes. My father always took me, also dressed in my best. I looked forward to it all the week – my promenade with Papa. By the time I was six I knew some scandals about married ladies and came out at a party one day with the information that the Marquise of X was the mistress of the Duc de Y.

On these, and indeed on all occasions when I went out, I wore horrible knitted gloves of white silk. I hated the way they creaked as I drew them on. I hated the way they felt so I walked with my fingers extended like little white starfish in an agony of aesthetic discomfort. Gloves were a status symbol. All respectable people, that is to say people who did not do manual labour, wore them.

Cotton gloves, silk gloves, kid gloves, doeskin, reindeer, chamois. Footmen waiting at table wore them. Gentlemen in evening dress wore them so that they would not touch the bare backs or arms of their partners, such flesh being theoretically inviolate outside of matrimony. Gloves, walking-sticks, umbrellas, parasols, fans, and muffs in winter were the paraphernalia of fashion. A pretty woman could look very coquettish with a fur muff raised to the eyes, or peeping over the top of a fan; a man very dashing, swinging a gold-topped malacca.

To look at the women no one would have imagined that butter could melt in those lovely unpainted mouths, or that so many of the women had lovers or the men mistresses. It was a period when hypocrisy reached its most decorative and fantastic peak. Everything was a matter of appearance, of form, of outward show.

Perhaps the most honest of them all and the most worthy of respect were the *grandes cocottes*. Famous then, as film stars today. At least here there was no deception. No subterfuge. They sold their favours openly and formed a hierarchy of their own. They had style and wit, more important even than beauty, and much more rare. They had salons where they entertained noblemen, artists, writers and politicians – the intellectual cream of Paris. Their expenses were fabulous and some men were only known by the women they kept. To be able to do so gave them a sort of fame. One even heard people say: 'Ah! Pierre Colin! Yes, he was ruined by La Belle Pouliche. She took him for all he had.' And the reply: 'Well, he knew what he was doing and he had a good run for his money . . . Ah, those women! They are witches who enchant a man.'

Even as a child I felt this although I did not understand it. I saw things and heard things as grown-ups talked, thinking I should not understand. From ladies' maids and servants I learnt of hairpins being picked up in a gentleman's bedroom. Of long hairs on his pillow. People often acted as if servants were not there, as if they were dogs or cats whose presence could be ignored, never realizing that they, Madame and Monsieur, supplied almost all the amusement their domestics could enjoy. The performances of the rich became the entertainment of the poor. Servants pieced together torn-up letters. They eavesdropped.

They looked through keyholes. They exchanged gossip and in the end very little was hidden from them.

My father took me bathing in the Seine. The bathers were fenced off from the main river but no effort at purification was made. I don't think anyone thought of it. Drains ran into the river, but *tant pis. Pis*, indeed. One was supposed to survive all these things and one did. Most of us, at any rate. My father swam breast-stroke and I sat with my legs round his neck, holding on to his hair. Sometimes I was taken to the lakes in the Bois where I fished for tiny sticklebacks. I caught tadpoles with a little muslin net, carrying home my catch in a jam-jar. I kept them in a basin at home and was much interested watching them lose their tails and grow legs. Tadpoles had a special smell.

There was always something to watch in the Bois, a moving panorama of people. Beyond the stream of carriages were the riders: officers in uniform, civilians in long-skirted riding-coats with striped trousers strapped under the instep, carnation button-holes, top hats. Women – side-saddle, of course – in top hats or tricornes, accompanied by bowler-hatted grooms. English, if possible, like the nurses. So there it was. Working backwards across the Avenue: the riders, the carriages and the children.

In the carriages beautiful women beautifully dressed reclined in their beautiful equipages. Lace-edged parasols. Long gloves. Wives, mistresses, actresses. The demi-monde. All out taking the air. Showing off their clothes, their carriages and their horses. Their fine feathers. Enormous ostrich plumes were *de rigueur*, feathers anyway. Birds of Paradise, small stuffed birds perched on hats the size of cartwheels. There were small exotic birds: African finches, South American humming-birds. There were even robins and swallows. Terns were popular but they were for the more severe tailor-made costumes. Egrets were often worn with evening dress. That was what birds were for, why else had God created them? To put on hats, into cages, and to eat. One saw strings of larks, blackbirds and thrushes in the shops. When I went with my mother to her *modiste* I used to watch the construction of these enormous hats that looked like chunks taken out of a herbaceous border or a selection from an aviary. I used to play with the flowers and the cottonwool-stuffed birds.

When I was about five some wealthy American friends of my

mother's – a Mr and Mrs Pick – wanted to adopt me. I can't
imagine why they thought my mother would let me go as I was
her Benjamin, the apple of her maternal eye, even though I had
disappointed her in my sex. Not that I should ever have minded
being a girl provided I could be a pretty one. I have always
thought a pretty woman got the most out of life. I remember
being disappointed that this adoption did not come off. I found
the idea exciting. This was the first of the many might-have beens
in my life, a crossroad over which I had no control but which
would, had the result been different, have turned me into something quite other than what I subsequently became. I was happy
at home. I loved my father and mother and the servants and the
dog. But I think I would have been equally happy in any other
good home I had been moved to. With young children love seems
to be very one-sided. The parents love, the child accepts the love
as it accepts its food. Much later at boarding-school, much as I
disliked it, I would have been relatively happy leaving home if I
could have taken my dog with me. This does not mean that I was
not attached to my parents, only that the gap of understanding
was greater between them and me than it was between me and
Flirt, my dog.

Is it imagination, the retrospection of old age, or were there
greater men in those days than there are today? Are there men
alive now who could fill the shoes of such eminent Victorians
and Edwardians as Darwin, Huxley, Gladstone, Disraeli, Dickens,
Pasteur, Shaw, Gordon, Kitchener, Roberts, Livingstone,
Stanley, Florence Nightingale, Zola, Renoir, Rodin, Freud,
Clemenceau and hundreds of others? Is the explanation, perhaps,
that then more men were characters, personalities, individualists?
And that today we have teams of men; specialists, often so
specialized that they are known only to each other? Another
factor may be due to a liberal approach which is anti-individual,
anti-leader. This may be an illusion on my part, but I do not
think we can list men today who can compare with those of the
relatively recent past.

I was brought up with the heroic ideal. I read G. A. Henty's
books for boys. Stories of heroic adventure. I had books with
titles like *Boy Heroes*. Magazines like the *Boy's Own Paper*. I read

Carlyle's *Heroes and Hero Worship*. This was the trend of the time. Kipling, Captain Marryat, Conan Doyle, Jack London, Sir Gilbert Parker, Rider Haggard, Cutliffe Hyne, Nat Gould were the authors I enjoyed.

The *belle époque* has never been pin-pointed in time but I suppose it lasted about forty years, from the war of 1870 to that of 1914. It certainly ended in 1914 but it may have begun earlier and included the period of Napoleon III and the Empress Eugénie. The Victorian era was one into which the profligacy of the Regency merged till driven underground by the good Albert, the Consort. A bourgeois world, if ever there was one. It was a terrible but fascinating period into the end of which I was born, too young to profit from its licence but old enough to observe what went on around me.

This was the time of the Fauves. The Impressionists affected me profoundly as a boy. The reason I wanted to be a painter is easily understood if one can imagine the variety and beauty of the Parisian scene. Many carriages had coats of arms or initials on the doors. Snobbery was accepted as normal. The horses were often so cruelly curbed with bearing reins that their lips foamed and they looked as if they had shaving soap in their mouths, so much that some of it spilt over on to their chests. The varnished spokes of the wheels and panels of the carriages shone in the sunshine. There were coaches and fours with a groom blaring his yard of tin from the boot, the horses tossing their heads and jingling their chains. Smart women driving hackneys in high-wheeled dogcarts, a little uniformed tiger (boy groom) with folded arms sitting with his back to her, ready to jump out and hold the horse's head when she stopped.

Although much more restrained than it is today, there was an atmosphere of sex, *sub rosa* but implicit and omnipresent. Apparent even to a child. It was the age of feathers and fans, of frou-frou, of accordion-pleated taffeta petticoats, of heavy perfumes: Patchouli, lilac, tuberose, violet, jasmine. Of glimpses of a well-turned ankle and the flash of lace-edged petticoats. All underclothes were decorated with handmade lace. No lady would wear anything machine-made, not even machine-sewn. Handmade lace was easy to check. If you got a loose thread and pulled, it unravelled itself. Camisoles, chemises, corset covers, drawers and nightdresses were all threaded with baby ribbon, pink, blue or white. Women's drawers were often divided into two separate legs joined by a waistband. Drawers themselves had only come into use in the 'sixties. This revolutionary idea was due to a Dr Tilt who believed that wearing drawers would preserve women from certain feminine illnesses. This was in 1852. The innovation was resisted as being immodest and contrary to the biblical prohibition of women wearing men's clothes, and so they were not worn by respectable women. 'By 1859 drawers were the latest fast fashion among the aristocracy,' according to Peter Fryer in *Mrs Grundy*. They were probably considered fast because previously they had only been worn by ladies of easy virtue, presumably as a temporary deterrent to their customers.

The hooped crinoline with nothing but several petticoats beneath it presented a perpetual risk of intimate exposure, which encouraged the spread of drawers. It is therefore not surprising that the courtiers of France as depicted by Watteau and Fragonard enjoyed pushing swings for young ladies. Even when I was a boy, fishergirls, wives and peasants wore nothing under their petticoats and often just spread their legs like mares to urinate over a gutter. But the drawers, at first a *fantaisie* of fashion, seeped downwards into the middle and working classes, becoming knickers, bloomers and finally the panties and bikinis of today.

Ladies used no make-up. A little *papier poudre*, perhaps. This came in sheets bound in a small booklet, rather like the paper used by men who roll their own cigarettes. Each sheet had a sprinkling of face powder on it. No lipstick, no eye pencil, no tinted hair except for the demi-monde who had everything and used everything. They looked like ladies in every way, aping their style and manners but in a vastly exaggerated way. Their hats were much bigger, their feathers larger, their trains more superb, their perfume more profuse. No wonder men liked them. They ranged from the *poule de luxe*, to bedizened worn-out old hags who hung about near the railway stations willing to take on all comers.

It was the age of the brothel, of kept women in apartments, in discreet little love-nests in St John's Wood or the Parisian suburbs. Many of these ladies were famous, or infamous, according to the point of view of the speaker. They were known as pretty horsebreakers. Aspasias. Traviatas. Anonymas. Demireps.

In Paris I knew many of the more famous by sight and had even been kissed by one or two to whom my father had spoken, bowing hat in hand with the greatest respect, for these women might be light but could not be treated lightly.

There was a kind of musical comedy atmosphere which was helped by the variety of costumes worn. We, the audience of this never-ending play, knew that the good-looking *valet de chambre* probably slept with both his mistress and her maid. One knew that many men, masters of even small establishments, exercised a kind of *droit de seigneur* over their maids. There was a comedy here, the men trying to hire pretty servants with their wives firing them at the first possible opportunity. One heard of these stories from grown-ups who had no idea of the perspicacity of children, from servants whom it amused to tell children the facts of life and even to demonstrate them. I was very interested in all this. Even at an early age it was quite clear to me that men wanted to get into the beds of young women. The question that exercised me was, why? In winter I could understand it. It must be nice to cuddle a young woman. But why in the summer? But since they did, then there must be a reason. This was before Katerine had initiated me into the arts of love.

There was peace and order in the world. But above all there was hope. Certainly the working man is better off today. Better off even if he does not work. But that is not the world picture. The destruction of the colonial empires has not brought happiness or prosperity, or even food to the liberated millions. Two atomic bombs have been dropped, thus establishing a precedent for their use. Never in the history of the world have there been so many people enslaved, so many displaced and homeless. Never have so many people – scores of millions – been liquidated. Two-thirds of the people of the world are suffering from malnutrition. There is less food now than there was even ten years ago and the population is increasing explosively. Where there was law and order there is now chaos. Though the colonial possession of the old empires have been liquidated new countries have been brutally taken over by Russia and China.

There is today a complete lack of panoply. Military parades, brilliant uniforms, variety in civilian clothes have all gone. There are no national costumes left. But it is my belief that mankind requires panoply; that it is a psychological necessity. The mounted parades of the Western States with their palomino horses and silver-mounted saddles, flags, bands and drum-majorettes tend to prove this thesis. So does the dressed-up masquerade of the New Orleans *Mardi Gras*, or the Carnaby Street clothes. Kids dance naked in front of the New York stock exchange. Adolescents in revolt dance African war dances to neo-African music. They sit in, lie in and preach love, not war. Communist agitation may take advantage of these feelings but they did not invent them. They are, as I see it, the outcome of too much conformity, of a computer-run society functioning in a concrete jungle. These events are a side-effect of boredom, the newest world diseases born of a dull, permissive, colourless yet affluent society. It is possible that mankind in general cannot take affluence; that fear is a necessary ingredient of life. There can be no freedom from fear – one of Roosevelt's four freedoms. A man who is free of fear would be killed the first time he crossed the street. And over us all is the terror of the bomb. This is denied; it is not discussed but it is there.

CHAPTER 5

LOST AND FOUND

—————

I HAVE discovered that there is a certain recapitulation in the life pattern. Girls whose mothers have been divorced several times appear to want several husbands on the what's-good-enough-for-Mum principle. Both men and women who come from large families want large families. The noise and disorder, the toys, potties, high chairs, babies' bottles, drying clothes are what make a home for them. I do not like small children and attribute this to a lonely childhood. Although a sixth son, I was to all intents and purposes an only child and very happy that way. I was much loved, spoilt up to a point, but also punished. Then a baby came into my life: my brother Lance's son, and therefore my nephew. I was about five and he was a year old. He got the attention which I considered my due. His parents, my brother and sister-in-law, neither of whom I had seen before, put this infant on my bed and he proceeded to wet it. This was the last straw and I burst into roars of rage. The baby was removed, the bed re-made, but I never forgave him. I do not think I ever saw Gerald again. Lance's next appointment was Vice-Consul in Algiers and our paths never converged till just before his death. But years later in the 'forties I met Gerald's divorced wife, Alice, in New York. Gerald had followed his father into the consular service and she was full of stories about China. A pretty woman of thirty-five or so. I told her I was entirely on her side because her husband had wet my bed. She looked astonished and I did not elaborate on my remark.

My relations with my parents were curious, or would seem so today. I loved my mother but she always embarrassed me. Making too much of me when I was a child because I was pretty, and being almost in love with me when I was grown up. She just loved me too much and I had to be careful she did not spoil me, by giving me everything I wanted. Somehow I knew, even as a child that I must not have everything. That things must not be too easy.

My father is another story. As a baby I loved him. He liked babies. Old songs which have recently been revived on the air bring him back to me. Later, as I grew older, I respected and feared him. Later still, I did neither but by that time it did not matter. My character was formed. I am thinking now of his friends, and mine, inevitably the children of people my parents knew. They were almost all of them Americans and many of them Jews. I knew nothing about anti-semitism until many years later though I remember the vague vibrations of the Dreyfus Case.

Among my father's friends were Slesinger who had a sports-shop, and Gaiger, an enormous man who ate a whole chicken for lunch. I watched him do it on several occasions. He had two beautiful collies. Then there was Russek of Russek's Department Store, I think. He had an invalid wife and was a fine musician. And Chinery who owned Nellie, the smooth-haired fox-terrier bitch I liked so much.

There were the Rusts whose son, Fillmore, was one of my friends. They were Americans. His father had the Napier Agency and we used to go rides with them. I think this gave me my first mistrust of motor-cars. It seemed to me that we were always breaking down, which meant we had to sit in great discomfort and hunger in some uninteresting place while the car was repaired. I have never got over this feeling about internal combustion engines.

Mrs Rust was a very small, very chic American woman. She took a size two shoe. One day I was to marry an American girl who took the same size. Fillmore was an only child and both he and his father were terrified of Mrs Rust.

My greatest friend was Gerald Sinclair, whose two aunts – Miss Sinclair and Miss Choate – were his guardians; he was, I believe, the heir to a large fortune. Years later we met again when I was in hospital in Reading. He had a house nearby and introduced me to some charming girls. He was in the Black Watch and was later killed leading his company in action at Passchendaele.

Then there were the Comtesse de Brie's (I always associated her with the cheese) two daughters. Dark girls, much too old for

me, being groomed for the good marriages they would undoubt-
edly make. And a girl, also too old, called Nina Bessel, who later
became a close friend of my brother, Lovel.

There were others: Perceval and Léonie Rideout. I met Léonie
again after the war when she was married to a stockbroker. And
the two Kipping girls, both blondes with long hair. Joyce, the
younger, was very sweet. She had a deformed left arm; it was
much shorter than the other and the hand had only three fingers.
Dulcie was prettier, harder and, I imagine, made a success of her
life. Their mother was a fashion artist and was divorced. This, it
appeared, was better if you were an American. I remember going
to their flat and seeing coloured sketches of ladies' costumes in her
studio. Divorce was still a terrible word. I do not remember when
I heard the word first whispered. I do not know when I first
heard of women making up . . . that was for actresses and whores.
The two were then almost synonymous in the public mind.
When my father took me walking with him in the Bois we were
continually bowing and raising our hats to people. Among them
was a splendid-looking man, an absconding President from
Brazil, I believe. He stood about six foot two, always wore a
buttonhole and had his tophat cocked over one eye. A real *vieux
marcheur*. He was said to have got away with millions and it was
not hard to guess where they ended, since he was always accompanied by a pretty woman.

My dislike of crowds may be due to my having been lost in one
when I was about five years old. I was with my father among
thousands of people watching some parade or other in the Bois.
Missing him, I knew what to do. I had been taught that should
this ever happen I was to stand quite still and wait for his whistle.
He had a special five-note whistle for me. So I stood, somewhat
comforted by the presence of Nellie, Mr Chinery's fox-terrier
bitch, who was on a lead sitting beside me. Still, being lost in a
seething mass of people is a frightening experience for a small
child. It can see no faces, the people are too close together – only
a forest of legs and skirts. I stood for an interminable time that
was probably not more than five minutes. Then I heard him. I
knew, too, what he would do – he'd go to the place where he
thought he had lost me and stand there whistling till I made my

way to him, which I now did, moving through a forest of cloth towards the sound.

Later on I must have got over this fear because I enjoyed mingling with the *Mardi Gras* and *Mi-carême* crowds. Perhaps because everyone wore harlequin masks or masks like clowns, or Chinamen, or Negroes, or big noses. They were no longer people but mythical creatures blowing trumpets and throwing confetti.

As I grew older my dislike of crowds returned, this time for a different reason. I felt they had an entity, that the crowd absorbed people into it and that, ceasing to be an individual, one became capable of anything – in French *capable de tout*. The fear was now psychological rather than physical. I also disliked the pressure of strange bodies against my own. This I think is a very primitive instinct which has remained with me to this day. A fear of being absorbed into an undisciplined mass bears no relation to its opposite which is becoming part of a regiment, also an entity but one which has organic growth with its roots in history, whereas a crowd is a mob which collects, often fortuitously, round the scene of an accident or disaster and can be dispersed by a factory whistle indicating the lunch hour or the arrival of the police which recalls them to reality.

When I was seven I nearly died, having bronchitis and whooping cough simultaneously. My chest was always weak and the remedies in those days were mustard plasters and linseed poultices, the seeds being boiled, put into a linen bag and put on to the chest. It felt terrible, hot and soggy, and they smelled.

I had a machine which was supposed to produce ozone in the room, and a little lamp under a powder that produced a smell that was said to help the lungs to take in air. My father bought me a cage of lovebirds – they are called budgerigars now – and some white mice. I was nursed by my mother and the servants day and night and pulled through, but I believe it was a near thing. I was taken to recuperate at Houlgat in Normandy and found on the beach at low tide a rusted and shell-encrusted dagger, about a foot long, that had probably lain there since some of the Spanish Armada ships had been wrecked on this rocky coast. It could still be drawn from its scabbard but there was no blade; all that was left of it was the top part of the knife where the blade had been thickest. Or perhaps it was a stiletto of some kind. At any rate it was Romance. It was History. It was glory, once again.

I played on the sands and among the rocks. I helped my mother collect mussels. I was given a little net and caught shrimps on the edge of the sea. I liked to see them turn pink when they were cooked for tea. I made sand castles and waited for the waves to destroy them. This was one of the Normandy beaches of World War II.

Back from the sea were the orchards of cider apples for which Normandy was famous. They had a special, rather acrid taste. The farmers had wooden presses and each made his own brew. Sour-sweet stuff of great potency. In the lush fields were the Normandy cattle, white-spotted and blotched with black and brown. So the country had a character of its own: grey Percheron horses, Normandy cows, cider apple orchards with their old gnarled trees, and the Normans themselves – big, dour people who kept everything neat and clean.

In a loft in a farmhouse I found hundreds of large tortoiseshell butterflies sitting with folded wings almost as invisible as the autumn leaves they resembled, hanging on to the rafters of the roof. They must have been about to hibernate. I have never seen such a thing again.

In the country the farmers wore smocks; in fact the clothes of the French peasants – both men and women – had changed very little in four hundred years. Wooden sabots were common and very practical, since when the workers came into the house, their feet covered with the muck of the farm, they simply left the sabots on the threshold and walked in their stockinged feet or put on *pantoufles* – the felt slippers worn by most domestics going about their work or even out shopping if the streets were dry. The women wore shawls rather than coats, and scarves over their hair. In general the country people looked like those one sees in old Dutch paintings. Sartorially, time had stood still for them.

What I am trying to describe, to give the feel of, is the slow tempo of life, its gestation as it were. Each thing in its appointed season. Something to look forward to, like duck and green peas in June, strawberries in July, pheasant in the fall. And look back on when it was over. Nothing was frozen, nothing instant. Very little canned food, though the canning process had been invented in Napoleon's time to facilitate the feeding of his armies.

Another summer we went to Château Thierry, later the scene of a great American battle in the First World War. The woman with whom we were staying, I presume, *en pension*, kept guinea-pigs in her chicken run, she said they kept away the rats. She ate them and said they were better than rabbits and easier to rear. I have never since heard of this being done but they were certainly very good roasted. I was delighted with them because they were born ready-made, mouse-size miniatures of their parents that ran about even the first day. Later on I bought myself a white, pink-eyed, long-haired so-called Peruvian guinea-pig at one of the pet shops along the Quais in Paris. I had it in a big box in the apartment but it was a dull pet and I gave it away in the end. But animal shops have always interested me with their goldfish, puppies, kittens, fancy pigeons, canaries and exotic birds. Sometimes there were whole piles of tortoises from Algeria, crawling over each other. Green lizards, tree frogs. One might find anything in these places and I often wondered who bought them and what sort of homes they got.

My father seemed to know everyone in Paris, or if he did not at least he knew about them. At a very early age I knew numbers of pretty ladies. They liked me. And I knew who was keeping them. This information I used to give to my governess, out of politeness naturally, because I had been socially trained to converse. Walking beside her I would take off my cap to a world-famous courtesan who smiled at me enchantingly and would tell May how soft she felt, how beautifully she smelt, how kind she was.

One night my brother Lovel took me to the *Folies Bergères*. How he got a child in I can't imagine, but he also knew a lot of people. I was incredibly bored and came back to my mother with a long story about how cold the ladies must have been. And as they were so beautiful why did someone not do something about it. Already I understood that things were done about beautiful young ladies. Worldly wisdom was not forced upon me, I grew up in its atmosphere. How Mother laughed!

I was never disturbed by the demi-monde. I had come in touch with it when very young. My brother Lovel was a great womanizer. He was one of the finest-looking men I have ever seen. He stood six foot three. A dark dashing young man of enormous strength. He played football for France, till he damaged his knee. He was a first-class tennis-player and for some years was the amateur heavyweight champion of France. He was badly beaten by Bobby Burns and deserved it. He never trained, but would just leave a girl and go and fight. Burns smashed him up properly, broke his nose and finally knocked him out. My mother loved him. He and I were her favourite children. Later, when I was seventeen, and we were both in the army, he used to pick me up and toss me in the air the way I could throw a child. Our apartment was filled with his prizes – bronze figures, silver trays and other ornaments much more interesting than the cups people win today. He was killed at Passchendaele with the Cambridgeshires. They were driven back by the Germans and when they counterattacked he was found dead with six dead Germans round him. They were driven back again and when finally the position was re-taken my brother had disappeared. The barrage had destroyed both him and the Germans he had killed.

Had he lived my life might have been different; twenty years later I still often saw him in my dreams. Lovel was young and full of life, his spare time filled with sport and women. At night he carried a brass knuckleduster when he crossed the Bois which was far from safe. The police in this area were accompanied by police dogs with spiked collars. That was the beginning of the police dog era. They were then called *chiens loups* or *bergers allemands*. It was only after the war that they became Alsatians, like the waiters and everything else that was German.

I saw my first pair in a wired-in kennel at the ratadrome near the Porte de Neuilly where I used to go on Sunday afternoons. Having seen them I determined that one day I must have one. I have had them, bred them, trained, shown and judged them. This was almost the first example of a fact that I have observed very often since then. That we get what we want if we want it enough. So much so that I have reached the conclusion that it is very dangerous to wish too hard. You get your wish all right but the timing may be wrong. I remember going to a shop that I dealt with in Fifth Avenue to buy perfume for my wife and the saleswoman being in a great state of depression because her son was going overseas. Oh, she would give anything for him not to go overseas, anything. The next week I went in and asked about him. He was dead. Oh no, he had not gone overseas. He had died of cerebrospinal meningitis in camp.

The ratadrome where I saw the Alsatians was an interesting place. I do not know if they still exist but I went there alone each week and spent all my pocket money buying rats for Flirt, my wire-haired fox-terrier bitch. I suppose this must present a curious picture. A small English boy of seven accompanied by a wire-haired bitch on a lead going into these really rather disreputable premises and asking for rats.

'*Combien, monsieur?*' They were very polite, even to a little boy. I reciprocated. '*Dix, monsieur,*' I replied.

'*Tous à la fois?*'

'Yes, all at once.' What did he think Flirt was? All at once, certainly. How happy she was! How she wagged her stumpy tail! How she looked up at me!

We went with him to a loose box where he kept the rats. They were caught in sewers and brought up each day. Fresh rats, as it were. He waded into them. There were hundreds and he put ten into a bag with his hands. They bit him but he did not seem to care. I was told this man was prepared to kill rats like a dog with his teeth, with his hands tied behind his back, for a wager. Now we went into the drome, a circular enclosure about fifteen feet in diameter. He tipped the rats out. I held Flirt by the collar and then let her go. 'Sah, sah!' I said. She was on them. She killed first one and then another. A man with a stopwatch said: 'One minute and fifty seconds!' She would never make a champion but she loved it. It was her Sunday treat. She loved to shake them. That was what slowed her up. The technical term is 'dwelling'. She dwelt on her rats. A champion does not stop. He never shakes a rat. He kills it and with one twist of his head throws it over his shoulder as he gallops after the next one. About a second per rat is tops, champion timing, there is no hesitation, it's so fast that all you can see is the rats in the air as they fall and the dead ones lying on the ground.

I have only had one perfect ratter, a mongrel fox-terrier bitch with a long tail, called Follete. I have seen her chase and catch a rat as it ran over a tiled roof. Looking back, I suppose the ratadrome was almost as low a place as could be found in the rougher outskirts of the city. It was obviously derivative of the cock and bear pits of the past. It had an aura of blood and brutality, of bull-baiting and dog-fights. In fact I think dog-fights were staged there sometimes. The main drome (there were several smaller ones) was tunnelled with a twisting ditch supposed to represent the earth of a fox. This ditch was covered with close-fitting wooden shutters which could be raised if necessary. The exits were blocked when it was used for rats so that they could not escape, but its purpose was for drawing foxes and badgers. They had mangy specimens of both in cages. When anyone wanted to pit their dogs against them, they were brought in, being handled with long iron tongs, and put into the earth. The dogs, usually a couple, were then turned in. I never saw either a fox or badger killed but I saw some terriers that had been badly bitten. Had I been able to save such a large sum, I think it cost five francs, I would have tried Flirt on them. She was keen enough.

Later when we were in the country and I was older I used to enjoy joining a crowd of men and boys with dogs when they surrounded a wheat field that was being mown. The machine went round and round. The uncut centre grew smaller and smaller and the rabbits and hares bolted, to be killed by men with dogs and sticks.

How cruel was I as a boy? I do not know. I loved to kill things, to hunt with dogs. It all seemed natural enough to me then. It was sport, somehow related to glory. Gerald Sinclair had a Boston bull-terrier of which he was very proud and wanted to try with the rats. So one Sunday we came with both dogs. But the rats bit the bulldog and chased him till I put Flirt into the ring to save him from further indignity. Gerald was much upset but I told him it was just because his dog was still young and inexperienced. But I don't think a blunt-faced dog is often a good ratter, although I once had a bull mastif that killed them in the open.

It is interesting the way the fashions in dogs change. In those days there were a lot of great danes, they were called boar hounds, and most of them were elephant grey in colour. They were far larger, heavier and more massive than the present show type.

There were numbers of little Italian greyhounds shivering in their high-collared coats. There were pugs and any number of fox-terriers of the old fashioned 'His Master's Voice' type. There were griffons, *papillons*, poms, collies, borzois and poodles. But no pekinese, airedales or chows. This parade of the dogs was part of the Paris show. You saw them with their mistresses, with servants; you saw them on leads and loose, playing with a ball on the grass. Sometimes running between the wheels of a smart dog-cart you would see a spotted carriage dog, as they called dalmations then. There were dachshunds, Aberdeens, Irish terriers, an occasional basset or bloodhound and French and English bulls.

It was a period of animals, of pets. The slow tempo of life, the many servants permitted it. Children had kittens, rabbits, guinea-pigs, white mice, lovebirds. At one time or another I had them all. I had an aquarium of goldfish. Rather before the rata-drome period, my father went to report on a copper mine in Brazil for some company in which he was interested. He was something of a mining engineer, having had experience both on the Rand and in Kimberley. The mine proved to be of no value but he came back with glowing tales of Brazil. The richest country in the world, he said. He talked of the mixed colour of the population and the complete lack of prejudice, which must have shocked him as a South African. I remember the story of his surprise when, having danced with a particularly lovely girl, she introduced him to her brother, an officer in the navy, who was coal black. Among the things he brought back was a bag of green coffee beans. They made the best coffee I have ever drunk. They were roasted daily in a frying pan with a little olive oil and ground just before it was made. He also brought a very fine green parrot which had been blinded to make it talk better. This upset me very much and though I loved it my mother got rid of it because it kept calling the servants in her voice. '*Caroline, Caroline,*' it would scream, '*kommen Sie hier!*' He also brought a tiny marmoset which the French call a *Ouistiti* and which I adored. Its cage was put on the kitchen stove at night but during the day it played about fastened by a light chain to a belt round its waist. One day it got away, ran out on to the stairway and, slipping on the polished handrail, fell five storeys and was killed. He also brought a panama hat which he said was woven under water and could last for ever and it still seemed to be in good order thirty years later.

Then there was a jaguar skin. Mother got rid of this too because such things got moths. Mother was a great 'get-ridder of things'. Later, when we lived in a house we had bought at Condette, near the Château d'Hardelot, and were digging a well, we dug up a large pot containing human remains, some rusted weapons and part of a horse's tail. But before these could be sent to a museum to be examined – and I think they would have been of interest as the castle's foundations were partly pre-Roman; it had been built to defend the village against the Norsemen's ships – Mother had tidied them up.

But some of the Brazilian things were kept. Six stuffed humming-birds like little jewels. A skinned troupial. How odd that fifty years later I should buy one in New York and see them for sale in the market of Caracas. These birds were the beginning of my collection in the museum cupboard. This was a white-painted glass-fronted cupboard which was bought for me to keep what I called 'my best things' in. And some odd things I had in it before I was done.

There exists some chronological confusion about this time – after a lapse of almost seventy years – but one outstanding event was my first contact with the police.

One *Mardi Gras*, parading by myself in the crowds of the Bois with my false nose and little bag of confetti, I found under one of the seats a ladies' handbag. Filled with importance, I proceeded to the nearest *sergeant de ville* and prepared to address him in the manner to which I had been trained. I clicked my heels, placed my hand on my stomach, raised my hat and bowed. Then I said: 'Mister Policeman, I have found the bag of a lady which has apparently been lost or abandoned.'

Equally polite, the policeman said: 'Young sir, this is a very serious affair. You will give me your name and address. I will take the bag. Its contents will be listed at the police station and then if in one year and one day it has not been claimed you will be notified and you can come and claim it as yours.' He looked in the bag and gave me some Métro tickets which he said would expire if they were not used. On that note we parted with bows, salutes and mutual good wishes. I have always found the French,

Italians, Spaniards, and Portuguese very easy to get along with. You cannot smile too much, bow too much, take off your hat too much or shake their hands too often. They do not care for '*le tough guy*'.

These manners were to create something of a sensation later when I used them in England. My habits were, and have to some extent remained, continental. I tend to be demonstrative, talkative, excitable, and to stare at women. Even looking back at pretty ones quite shamelessly. I do not pinch them – that is against the law – but I regard the pinchable parts with interest. Certainly most women are more beautiful from behind than in front. This is one of life's minor disappointments.

In Paris I was accustomed to buying fruit off barrows and eating it in the street. One advantage of a complete lack of hygiene is a resistance to everything that has not already killed you. But once, while with great and meditative pleasure I was eating a large bunch of grapes and spitting out such pips as I did not swallow while walking down the Strand, I met my brother who was articled to a solicitor in the vicinity. He was scandalized. I regret to say I have upset him many times since then.

I continued to bow to policemen but with less effect in London. They were so much larger that they embarrassed me. It was like prostrating oneself before a mountain. Besides they seldom understood what I said. My French accent was so strong. But despite everything my manners continued to be superb. Those of the *vieux boulevardier* in miniature. I wore my hat on the side of my head and swept it off, bowing from the waist, to any lady I had ever seen before. Those that I had seen before were never far from their accustomed beats and our mutual recognition gave us much pleasure. These ladies were the only ones in London who, to my Parisian eye, dressed correctly with chic and abandon, looked right, smelt right and smiled into your eyes.

But I liked my London visits. I liked the flowers in the parks, the people riding in Rotten Row. I had a boat that I sailed on the Round Pond. And above all I liked the meals at my grandfather's house, Number Three, Wetherby Gardens. The enormous table and sideboard were covered with great barons of beef, legs of mutton, cold tongues, brawn, corned beef. There were always two different puddings. The meals were served by a footman and a parlourmaid. It was all very exotic to me. Even the Grace before meals and the morning prayers when the servants all filed into the dining-room directly after breakfast and, after listening to my aunt read a chapter from the New Testament, knelt to pray with their elbows on the dining-room chairs. I prayed with my head buried in an armchair whose thick fabric smelt like our Turkish carpet in Paris.

I cannot now imagine how it was I was allowed to go about so much alone. I made friends with strangers quickly and in London as in Paris knew all manner of undesirable characters – servants, grooms, coachmen. I spent as much time as I could in the mews and stables of the city. I adored prostitutes because they were young and pretty. I was fond of old ladies who continually pressed small sums of money on me. This was insulting as I had no need of money. I had no expenses but I took the money to please them.

I suppose all this was permitted because I was what the French would call a serious child. I had no vices. I was careful crossing the streets. I did not pilfer from the shops. I was always punctual in my return to the house. When I was seven I took my first railway journey alone. I was labelled like a parcel. I was being met but still my mother was worried. She said: 'Suppose he falls out of the train?' Dad said, 'If he does he's not worth keeping.' My father had taught my older brothers to swim by chucking them into twenty feet of water over a pier. Then he dived in after them to see that they did not actually drown. When they came ashore they could swim. Mother would not permit such treatment for me, but I never swam as well as my brothers.

My father was a magnificent horseman and, having taught me the elements, would chase me back on to my horse with a hunting crop whenever I fell off. I became a good horseman because even he could not destroy my love of horses. But most other things he spoilt for me by being in too much of a hurry, and expecting too much of me. I was of an athletic build and had a good eye and good co-ordination, but he made me nervous of a cricket ball by throwing it too hard. He stopped me playing cards and billiards by shouting at me so that I threw down the hand and the cue and refused, even when he beat me, to pick them up again. He was very good at everything but had no patience. I liked to ride, to walk with my dogs and to read.

'Always lolling about, reading magazines. I don't know what's the matter with that boy.'

But in other ways and at an earlier period he was kind to me. He treated me as an interesting pet, a rather smart one who was liable to do or say funny things and make such *faux pas* that their repetition amused people.

So I led a sort of double life. Part of it that of a spoilt and pampered child, going to the office with my father and sitting on a cushion on the floor for hours, or going to the dressmaker with my mother where I amused myself collecting snippets of the lovely materials that littered the floor – silks, brocades, Lyons velvet. There were no synthetics then, no rayon, no nylon. I also liked the dummy, a curiously shaped woman's torso mounted on a single leg, which was used for fitting dresses. It bore no relation to the human form but the human shape, suitably compressed by stays, was made to conform to this arbitrary standard. The stomach was pressed in, the thighs confined almost to the knees and the breasts pushed upwards till they formed a kind of plat-form under the chin, by a corset constructed on a frame of whalebone and steel.

In those days dresses were fitted with dress guards. Double half-moons of waterproof material were sewn in under the arms to prevent perspiration from perishing the material. There were no deodorants. The cosmetic industry as we know it had not yet even been thought of. Women used homemade preparations of lemon, cucumber, rose-water and even milk for their complexions. Hair combings were saved in little jars which had a round hole in the lid, to be made up when enough had been collected into switches. These pots were part of the usual dressing-table equip-ment, standing beside a kind of little stubby branched china tree on which ladies hung their rings like fruit at night. Another article which has disappeared are the ivory glove stretchers. They were shaped like scissors and used to stretch the fingers of new kid gloves. There were also initialled hand mirrors of silver, ivory or tortoiseshell with brushes and trinket-boxes to match. Cut-glass scent bottles. Receptacles for hair pins. Manicure sets with nail buffers – nails were polished till they looked like the inside of small pink shells. There were no beauty parlours. But court hairdressers came to the house to do hair for great occasions.

It is almost impossible for a girl who today only wears a bra and panties to imagine the number of clothes her great-grandmother wore. A vest, corset, corset cover, camisole, drawers and two or three petticoats. There were no beauty aids, few tricks. If a woman was beautiful then it was real beauty, unassisted by cosmetics or other aids – hair-dyes, face lifts, contact lenses, wigs or any of the other things that are today accepted as normal.

I was a judge of laces – Honiton, Irish, Brussels, *Pointe de Venise* – through the dressmakers' assistants and ladies' maids with whom I consorted, just as I was a judge of horses through my father and the grooms with whom I was such friends. A passion for women's clothes has remained with me. Some women find this attractive, others have been furious because I did not like what they were wearing. But how can they have it both ways? and they are quick to complain if their clothes are not noticed.

I should like to have been a dress designer and have had some ideas which I have been unable to sell but which have been re-invented by other people. Long ago I made drawings of bathing caps that resembled hairdos. They were later put on the market.

I have always liked to watch a pretty woman dress and undress. They look particularly beautiful with their arms raised doing their hair or, oddly enough, bent over their feet cutting or painting their toenails. There are many paintings and statues that prove this point. On one occasion, watching my first wife, I decided that her breasts would look better if held and raised up. So, taking a piece of material I put a saucer on it and cut two circles. I then cut a piece out of each like a slice out of a pie and sewed them together again. I now joined them in front and put on two tapes to tie at the back. I had, and this was in about 1924, constructed the first brassière. If I had patented it I should probably have become a millionaire and also probably been dead by now.

I also thought of a white evening dress with black panels on the sides, which would make a stout woman look slim, many years before it appeared in *Vogue*. I designed the first fur hat for my wife that was ever worn in London, and had a lot of trouble getting it made.

It has always amazed me that women, who spend so much of

their time and a large proportion of their husbands' money on their personal embellishment, should make such a mess of it. How often does one see a perfectly turned out woman? A woman who has not made a mistake? Who has the right accessories, or who has not improved a carefully designed model by some little touch of colour somewhere?

And hats. It is unbelievable the way women go out and buy a hat. Because they are unhappy, because they are happy. Because they have gained or lost a lover. The answer to any problem is a new hat. This hat is bought regardless of anything else, as if it was a plant to put in the window. There is only one law about hats: a hat to go with each costume. A hat that goes with anything goes with nothing.

I have never liked nice, healthy, out-of-door girls who smelled of *eau-de-cologne* and wore tweeds and low-heeled shoes. No woman's legs can look good with low heels. I like artificiality, make-up, *maquillage*. Women have made up for thousands of years. Not to do so is either a sign of great vanity – they are perfect without it – or an expression of lack of interest in men. There are plenty of women who do not like men, just as there are plenty of women who do not like dogs.

Fashion, make-up and the rest may be a sign of decadence but it is also a sign of civilization. The caveman and his bride were not decadent. Is this then the ideal?

Perfume is another factor of dress, an accessory often based on the glands of animals where they serve the purpose of sexual attraction. When a woman uses scent she is, whether she knows it or not, prepared to be courted by someone. Or at least, if not courted, she wishes to be noticed and admired. What does a scent do but call attention to itself? What does it say but *Here I am! Just look at me!* Because it says it to the nose instead of to the eyes, does it still not speak? Children, since they do not drink or smoke, are very susceptible to scents of all kinds and almost certainly one's taste in such things, like one's appreciation of art, begins very young and is based upon the impacts to which one is exposed. I, for instance, never found the smell of clean sweat objectionable. The so-called body odour of well-washed young flesh is an aphrodisiac devised by nature to attract, a process now turned upside down by cosmetic interests in order to sell deodorants. We seem to have become afraid of so many natural things.

In an autobiography some digression is necessary. Thoughts and ideas must be developed unless it is to be no more than a chronicle of events. These are some of the impacts I received and their results. Perhaps I learnt some of these things a little young, on the other hand it all came very naturally. At this time I was happy, confident. I sometimes wonder at what precise moment in its life does a puppy or a child lose confidence? Cease to feel that everyone loves it: that no one will do it harm?

CHAPTER 6

ST BERNARD

At the dame school I attended I was made to write on a slate. The writing came out grey on the black stone and was cleaned off with a small wet sponge that was tied to its wooden frame with a piece of string. Writing on the slate made a nasty squealing sound which I disliked. Other things I disliked were the feel of cotton-wool in my fingers and the sound it made being dragged out of the blue paper packet in which it was wrapped. I also hated Scott's Emulsion which, because of my weak chest, I was given in large quantities. It had a picture of a fisherman carrying a large cod over his shoulder on the bottle. In the spring children were given a mixture of powdered sulphur and black treacle; and an abominable laxative – a pink powder called Gregory Powder which was supposed to be made acceptable by mixing it with a spoonful of jam. The jam did not remove the grittiness, which remained in the mouth for hours.

When my first teeth became loose my father tied a piece of thin string round the tooth and fastened it to the handle of an open door. I was then told to kick it. This jerked the tooth out and I was given fifty centimes for being a brave boy. I added this to my pocket money and used it to buy more rats for Flirt.

When I was very small my father made shadow pictures – men and animals – on the wall with his hands and a handkerchief. I enjoyed this very much. He also told me stories. One I liked in particular was about a hound called Gelert who was found covered in blood by a child's cradle and killed by the small boy's father, who then discovered that the dog had killed a wolf which had got into the house and was about to attack the child.

There are other memories of early childhood. The tiny drugged red-beaked African finches that Algerians hawked in the Paris streets. They sat utterly bemused in a row on a stick the man held. If they were taken home they refused to eat and died in a day or two. The *marrons glacés* my father would bring home in his pocket for me when my parents had been to a big dinner-party. A French bull pup called Tokio someone gave to my brother Lovel. I never liked him much. I rather despised French bulldogs. If we were going to have one I wanted an English bulldog; besides, I had Flirt. Tokio had been given to Lovel by some girl. When he went downstairs he always bumped his head, over-balancing at each step. I do not remember what happened to him. We gave him away, I think. French bulldogs were fashionable at the time and usually wore wide collars trimmed with badger hair (like shaving brushes) round both the top and the bottom in a kind of double frill.

Another pet we had in the apartment was a white rabbit. He ran loose and was remarkably clean, always going to one corner where we kept a newspaper for his use.

But above all our holidays in Switzerland stand out. There were hardly any tourists and few hotels outside the big towns. The peasants of the various cantons wore national costume. In some farmhouses the cow byre adjoined the kitchen so closely that the cows actually had their mangers along one wall of the room itself and watched everything that went on with big interested eyes. In winter their body heat helped to keep the house warm. It may not have been hygienic but it was very friendly and appealed to me greatly.

On one occasion we went up the St Bernard Pass and spent the night at the hospice, a large monastery. In the entrance hall there was a stuffed St Bernard that had saved over fifty people in the snow. I saw the kennels but was not allowed to touch the dogs as they were working animals, not pets. I saw some lovely puppies. I was shown the little brandy barrels that the dogs carried on their collars as they searched the snows, and was told that the monks, who worked the dogs, accompanying them in their search, could only live five years at that altitude and that they then descended to a rest home in the valley below to die. I was not very old then because I was carried on a guide's back in a long basket. I stood up in it with my head out.

I had some very undignified experiences in Switzerland. To get to some hotels one had to walk or ride mules over the mountain trails. The luggage went on mules and I was always attached in my basket by ropes to the saddle of the last one. The method of guiding these animals, since the path was too narrow and precipitous for them to be led, was for the muleteer to heave rocks at them. The mule, being a very intelligent animal, would turn away from the rock which was all that was required. To make the mules go to the left a stone was thrown so that it hit them on the right or off side. To make them go to the right they were hit on the near side. But I was much aggravated by this whizzing of stones past my head.

I was very surprised to find that these St Bernards were short-coated. They looked like enormous foxhounds in colour except that I do not think they had any black markings. I discovered later that long-haired dogs would have been useless because the snow would freeze on them. The St Bernard is a mastiff, related to the English mastiff, the Pyrenean sheepdog and various big breeds of mountain guard dogs in Central Europe and the Near East, and to the giant black mastiffs of Tibet. I heard some years ago that a St Bernard had savaged a traveller and that now, since so few people crossed the Alps on foot, the dogs had been sent overland to the monks in Tibet. If this is true, what an epic story!

We spent several holidays in Switzerland. I had many adventures and saw some strange and interesting things. The country was quite wild. The world was ours. I saw from a mountain top golden eagles, wide-winged, sailing in the void below us. This is the world's noblest bird. I saw them courting, playing with wild eagle screams. These are the birds whose pinions ornament the bonnets of the Highland chiefs and the headdresses of the Indian warriors. They are the birds that the sheiks in the East use for hawking gazelles. They are among the few birds that are beyond compare. Like the albatross, the peacock, the ostrich, the game-cock, the condor and the humming-bird, each in its own way miraculous.

I saw chamois leaping across a chasm a thousand feet deep and landing on a ledge no wider than the palm of my hand, to stand there nibbling some tiny mountain plant. I picked *Edelweiss* and wore it in my hat. Men have died trying to get this little flower that looks like a star cut out of cream-coloured flannel. I saw fields blue with gentians, and bright orange poppies piercing the snow. I listened to the cow bells across the valleys. Bells of all sizes, from miniature calf bells to giant bull bells weighing several pounds. I heard great storms where the sound of the thunder never ended because each clap was still echoing from mountain to mountain when the next one pealed. These storms sometimes start an avalanche. If the snow is in the right condition even the vibration of a human voice may be enough to start one.

It was in Switzerland that I saw my first death's head moth. The male will come for miles to find a female imprisoned in a matchbox. My father caught it and emptied its abdomen, which was very large and fat, stuffing it with cotton-wool. He also taught me to set butterflies on cork mats and fix their wings with little strips of paper so that they dried outstretched. I had a box of variously sized rustless pins with which to fasten my specimens. I saw swallowtail butterflies for the first time, and a large, almost transparent, butterfly with red circles on its wings which I think was called the Apollo.

Another, earlier, memory of Switzerland was of finding a very large old mulberry tree in front of an inn. The ground below it was full of fallen fruit, its crotch was fairly low and I was able to climb into the branches where I gorged myself on the fruit, which was delicious – like large, very, very sweet blackberries. When at last they got me down I was covered in black juice, face, hands, clothes and all. A very happy memory.

I bathed in rivers of ice-cold water that came from the melted snows. I climbed, I walked over glaciers – green and blue fields of ice – in small boots armed with spikes, a miniature alpenstock in my hand. I bathed in lakes and once found my clothes, which I had left lying on the short grass, full of snakes. Why had they come there? For shade, perhaps. It was a hot summer day.

On our first visit, when I must have been very small, I was seen at midday in the middle of the village street much interested in a snake that was curled up in the dust. I was about to pick it up when my father killed it. It was an adder. He obtained a glass bottle from the hotel cook which had contained stuffed olives, and put the snake into it, drawing it up, so that it was half extended, by a black thread which was held in place by the cork. The bottle was filled with brandy, the cork sealed with red wax, and we took it back to Paris when we went home. I had it for more than twenty years, together with other snakes and specimens in spirits.

I got bitten by very large, inch-long black ants when I was sitting in some pinewoods, and learnt to extract delicious kernels from pine-cones which I shared with the red squirrels.

There was another lake I remember well called *Blauer See*. This was very deep, very blue – *himmelblau* – and everything that lay on its bottom could be seen from a rowing boat. The woods round it were filled with *Regenmollies*, very attractive black Alpine salamanders that were easy to catch and cool to the touch. They did not have the beauty of the spotted salamanders that I caught later on in France, which were also black but the black was beautifully broken with large spots of canary yellow. Despite this warning coloration, it was harmless, a charming pet, and learnt to eat flies and grubs out of my hand.

My mother, much as she loved me, was never in full sympathy with my taste for zoology. There are one or two further incidents that I remember. A landslide had destroyed the graveyard of a small church and the bones were scattered everywhere. Nothing could have pleased me better. I spent as much time as I could collecting them. I liked the larger bones of the arms and legs, and the skulls. I collected several skulls which I was not allowed to keep. A skull makes a splendid toy for a child – round, smooth and almost unbreakable.

Once, on being taken to one of the village chapels which were bright with paintings, sacred statues of the Virgin dressed in blue and red, and Our Lord suitably bleeding in fresh vermilion, with much gold paint and tinsel distributed everywhere, I remarked: 'All is not gold that glitters.' I do not think this was particularly funny or intelligent. I do not think I was a prig. I am convinced that this was the first occasion I had found it possible to employ one of those maxims that I had transcribed with such care in a big round copperplate hand in my copybooks. When could I say 'Honesty is the Best Policy,' and to whom? And would Louise, my mother's maid, darning socks, have been pleased if I had told her that a stitch in time saved nine? Even if I had translated it into French it would have sounded no better. Louise had been with my mother since before her marriage and was part of the family, like an aunt.

As to skulls, I have retained my taste for them and have two animal skulls – a seal and a lynx – above my desk on a shelf as I write. Almost the first thing I cooked on our new Aga stove at Libris was the skull of a lynx we had hunted with foxhounds. A pair of them killed over fifty head of poultry on my farm. And I can certainly recommend the slow oven of the Aga for this purpose. The flesh came away beautifully and when I picked out the brain I decided to try it. I have never eaten anything more delicious. But I am omnivorous. I have eaten turtle, tortoise, zebra, elephant, horse, cat, lynx, porcupine, bear, rattlesnake, frogs, snails, hedgehogs, leguaan, mice, ants, ants' eggs, kangaroo tail, peacock, rabbit, guinea-pig, and will try almost anything.

Incidentally, the Aga is almost the only thing I have ever bought where the performance equalled the advertising copy.

There were a great number of snakes in Switzerland and my father would take me hunting them with a forked stick. He would put this over their necks just behind their heads and then pick them up. He taught me to kill them while he held them by taking the mouthpiece out of his pipe, getting a small twig or piece of grass and putting it into the stem to pick up a drop of nicotine. This I would smear on the lips of the snake and it would die at once. The black tongue would cease to flicker, the eyes would glaze and it was dead. My father said he learnt this as a boy at the Cape.

There were only two kinds of snake in Switzerland: adders, or vipers as some people call them, and grass snakes, which are quite harmless. The viper has enough venom to kill a child or a man who is in a poor state of health, but these accidents seldom occur. Actually in the wilds there are many less dangers than in a city. What animal is as dangerous as a taxicab, or another man? It was in Switzerland that I first saw hornets. I have never seen them anywhere else. They resemble very large fat wasps and three stings were supposed to be fatal. I do not know if this is an old wives' tale or not.

The finale of my Swiss adventures, as far as I remember them, was the accident on the Matterhorn. We were in a hotel which faced the mountain. There was much talk of the party which was making the ascent with guides, ropes, ice-axes and all the usual paraphernalia. Visitors watched the progress of the climbers up the mountain face through a telescope mounted on a tripod. I think the previous night the climbers had slept in the hut before attacking the summit.

Then the accident took place. Whether the rope got sawn in two by friction or what happened I have no idea, but a man fell and lay in a patch of snow on a ledge on the face of the mountain. I was held up to the telescope to see the body. I did not think much of it. It could have been anything – just something black on the white snow. Besides, I did not know him. Nor did I know death except very objectively through watching the funeral *cortèges* of Paris.

It appeared that the body was in a very difficult position. The man was dead. He had fallen several hundred feet, but the guides recovered the body. It took two days. I remember nothing except seeing them set off. Fine, nut-brown men with rucksacks, ropes, alpenstocks, ice-axes and spiked boots. They wore *Edelweiss* and eagle feathers in their hats. They were serious, mature men. Their honour as guides was at stake. They got the body down, lowering it on ropes, and came to the funeral. This was my first funeral and nothing could have been more impressive. Relations had come from England, there were the hotel guests and the people of the village. But above all, the guides. Guides had come from as far as twenty miles away. They wore their national costumes and carried the implements and ropes of their calling. They brought wreaths of wild mountain flowers: *Edelweiss*, gentians, harebells, wild pink tiger lilies and dwarf red rhododendrons.

Apart from my mother's, the other funerals I have seen affected me in no way except that I was bored. In war I have seen some of my friends buried but that was not the same; one was only glad to be alive oneself. They would have felt the same about me. They had died young and with honour. They had died with glory. I have all my life, since the war, that is, been much concerned with death. It is probable that scarcely a day has gone by without my thinking of it. It is like thinking of a country that I have nearly visited. I had been on the frontier with my passport in my hand. Once I set foot over the border. A country where so many of my friends now live. I thought of death then the way I think of America today. One day, perhaps, I shall see my friends again in both.

I remember seeing quite a number of people in Switzerland with goitre, due I learnt later to lack of iodine in their diet. I was also struck by several families of real albinos in a mountain village. One girl in particular was very beautiful with her long silver-white hair and large, pink, white-mouse eyes.

But now more about my father. That man whom I had loved, feared and finally was sorry for. He died when I was in Africa and although in 1938 I was within a mile of his grave at Condette I did not go to see it. What should I have done there?

I think what I disliked most about my father was the fact that in the end he had made me dislike him.

My mother's funeral I attended in a daze. Today I do not know the name of the cemetery in which she is buried, though we have a family vault there and it is in one of the big London cemeteries. I do not know the date or the month or even the year of her death. Nothing except that it was just before the war began. Freud would have an answer for this. Wilful forgetting. Perhaps he is right. That thing they put away so quickly, that was whisked through London in a Rolls-Royce hearse, was not my mother. That was her body. My mother lives and is still with me, as are my friends. As are my dogs and horses. How can they die while their memory lives? Nor have we any proof of death's finality. My contempt for the shell of the body may be due to having seen so many of them. There is no dignity in death. Not at least until the undertaker has done his work. The treatment of the dead in America is something I find completely revolting as, dressed in their best, painted like harlots, they lie bedded in satin in their caskets. Nor do I understand Americans wanting to bring back their warrior dead from the lands where they fell. I have often thought of the Zulus' treatment of their killed. They ripped them open with an assegai to let their spirits free and then left them to the vultures, the jackals and hyenas so that their mortal remains would continue to roam the veld they had loved, or soar in the currents of the mountain air. I have seen no dignity in death. The blood pours out of the wounds, spittle dribbles from the slack jaws, the bowels and bladder empty themselves, flies sit on the glazed eyes.

I found my mother dead in her room, lying on her face, the white medicine powder she had been trying to swallow spilt on

the apple-green carpet. I did not go near her. I never saw her
again. I called up her doctor. I told him to arrange for Harrod's,
where we had an account, to send their undertaking staff, and
went to my club. I did not cry. I did not cry at the funeral. But
I could have killed the miserable parson who rushed through the
service. That was his job – burying people on the assembly line
of a great London cemetery. This man of God was hired by a
corporation which made its dividends out of the sale and upkeep
of graves that held the nation's dead. There were more coffins
waiting outside the chapel before we had done. And this no
pauper's funeral. I should have assumed that we had paid enough
for at least the illusion of dignity. But I was wrong. That miserable
man was doing a job, striking each body with the solemn words
of the burial service the way a hog-killer in the stockyards of
Chicago sticks the pigs that hang head down on the slowly
revolving wheel of death. When my mother died something was
ended. The one person who, whatever I did, would always
believe I was right, had gone. Yet while I live she can never go.

The sentiment, mass-produced by advertisement and fear on
Mother's Day, is shocking. Mothers do not require gifts like
children. A mother is quite obviously beyond all sentiment. How
can there be sentiment about the womb in which you spent
the first months of your life, about the breasts you sucked?
It's all much too big. A mother is more than life-size to her
son.

For the war dead I have a special feeling. That is, that they
should lie where they fell, buried in their own blood so that there
the grass will grow a little greener, the apples ripen a deeper red
above them. That is the way a fighting man should lie unless he
can be buried with the panoply that is his right, under a flag on a
gun-carriage, with his boots reversed in the stirrups of his
favourite charger, led by his groom with his dog beside him,
with marching men, with the bugles that so often sounded in his
living ears blowing him into heaven, while his men stand round
the grave with bowed heads, their arms resting on their reversed
weapons, the muzzles of their rifles on the toe of their right boots.
The Last Post, the fired volley. The regimental band playing the
funeral march, as it may once have played the wedding march
for him. The same band because a regiment, like a corporation,

cannot die. As long as one man is left alive the regiment is not dead.

In 1922 I saw the war dead still being dug up in France. The War Graves Commission wandered about with spades and picks and sandbags in which to pack the remains. They dug wherever the grass, or the corn, stood a little taller, a little greener. Some of the bodies in the clay of Flanders were well preserved. I went to watch them to see if my nerve was still steady. I was unaffected. I was at that time making a tour of the battlefields with my wife and my friend George Buchanan of the Household Battalion. We were looking for the places where we had fought and taking pictures of the graves of our friends for their wives and parents.

But to return to my father. I owe a great deal to him. He was brilliant but with a weak streak in his character. My mother was a beautiful but not very intelligent woman, who was incapable of hurting anyone. I owe my taste in pictures and objects of art to Dad. He used to take me to antique shops and museums, and explain things to me. He often took me to the big Paris auctions. He bought me my first picture at the age of five. It was not many years later that I staggered home with a large gold-framed picture of a black Arab stallion called Nizam which had belonged to Napoleon III. It was so large that I could only just get my arm round it. As it was much too big to get into a bus or to manage on the Métro I walked home with it. I think it took me four hours, including rests.

My father was fond of nude pictures and had a number of them in his dressing-room. Among them was 'The Rape of the Sabines', a reproduction of an old master, Rubens, I think, depicting a lot of pink, naked, very fat ladies being carried off, apparently with great pleasure, since they were all smiling, by Romans wearing bronze helmets and little else on very large, fat horses.

I remember a few pictures in the flat. A large oil painting of Oriental Poppies painted by Nina Biesel, one of my brother Lovel's girl-friends. Two small water-colours, portraits of foxhounds in full cry, by my grandfather. They were part of the pack he kept at the Cape where they were used for hunting jackal.

My father told me of how on one occasion, finding the hounds baying round a bush, he rode up to see what they were barking at and a leopard jumped on to the withers of his horse. Dropping the reins, he picked the leopard up and threw it into the hounds which were now surrounding the horse. They fell on it and broke it up.

My mother had a hunter called Tiger Neck when she was in South Africa. As a foal he had been clawed by a leopard. Leopards or tigers, as the Boers called them, were a nuisance at the Cape a hundred years ago. Even today three or four are killed there every year.

My grandfather bred racehorses. The family had imported English blood horses since the eighteenth century. He never wrote a letter without a tiny sketch of a horse on it. A great horseman who, I remember my father telling me, would never allow a metal-pronged pitchfork in his stables for fear of injury to one of his animals.

My father belonged to the voluptuous school. A man's taste in women seems to depend entirely on his period. My father liked the Flemish mare type, if one can be imagined with an hourglass waist – what the French called *une belle pièce*. I went for the polo pony or the herring-gutted, greyhound-like, blood horse type. Girls who looked like beautiful boys. Looking at the average woman seen in a streetcar or on a subway, it is impossible to believe that she can ever have been any man's heart's desire. That this shapeless, pudding-faced creature had once inspired a passion of love in someone. The same naturally applies to men. Yet each man has his own standard of beauty, each some special feature that he considers admirable which appears to cancel out the rest. For my part a woman's figure, her legs, hands and arms, the set of her head on her neck and the way she moves are more important than the beauty of her face. I have seen women much admired because of their lovely faces whom I considered practically deformed. I prefer what the French call *une jolie laide* to classically beautiful women. The beautiful woman is always the same – like a statue, without variety of expression. Being brought up in France has, no doubt, influenced my taste. For there, charm and figure and style – chic – count for more than anything else. The fact that each man admires certain feminine features – face, breasts, legs, eyes, hair, and is prepared to take the rest as it comes, tends to prove that each man is, to a greater or lesser degree, a fetishist, and here we come to the analysis of the film star, international beauty and showgirl. She is merely a girl who has all the features that all men desire. The face of the man who likes pretty faces, the breasts of the bust-fancier, the legs of the leg-man.

This taste for nudity in my father was transmitted to me and I created a certain scandal at the age of ten by buying 'September Morn', a very sentimental picture of a nude, long-haired maiden meditating on the edge of a lake. I imagine she thinks it will be cold and I know now that it is not a very good picture. But my other picture was less innocuous. It was called 'The Bookworm'. I question this young woman's virtue. She has a complacent cat who has swallowed, or is about to swallow, the canary, look. And she is in colour – an aquatint. She is lying on her stomach on a bed, reading. Hence the title. But she is quite naked, and beside her is a vase of red and yellow tulips. Who sent her the flowers? Is she just reading to pass the time till he comes? Though these ideas did not occur to me when I made my purchases. The two pictures were taken away from me. But when I pointed out that my father had many pictures of naked ladies, and that they were much fatter, that is to say more naked, they were at last returned. Justice.

My father was a very quick-tempered man. He used to fly into rages (they were called 'his passions'). His blue eyes would flash, his face become flushed. It was what would be called a tantrum in a child. But a tantrum in an adult, powerful man, is a dangerous phenomenon. I think he would have been capable of killing someone when in this condition. He was quite without dignity and seeing him in this state cured me of temper. Mine was as savage as his own but I have always managed to control it. An example of his temper is illustrated by one occasion when we were nearly run down by a cab in Paris. Before I knew what had happened, he had pushed me out of the way, jumped on to the box of the cab, knocked the astonished cabby into the street with a blow of his gold-topped umbrella and pulled the horse up, back on to its haunches. A *sergeant de ville* rushed up waving his white truncheon, his short sword banging against his thigh. What was this? Certainly there would be a *procès verbal*. It was a scandal, an outrage! My father pointed out what had happened. He described the event with a gold coin on which was depicted the profile of the Emperor Napoleon III. It is remarkable how much such things will explain. In the end I think the cabby was arrested. True, he had almost run us over. Or had we walked under his wheels?

Among his other activities my father reported the racing in Paris. It was his optimism which made me put my total fortune, some ten francs, at the time, on a liver chestnut horse called Jack o' Lantern, an outsider that he said was sure to win at twenty to one. He finished last and I was cured of betting. I was now cured of betting, cards, all games of chance, sweet cakes, and hard liquor. Truly a fortunate child. I still liked racing but let the suckers bet. I saw a lot of races. I saw Pretty Polly, the English mare, run in the Grand Prix. She finished third, I think. All England had backed her. She was excused for not winning, the blame being put on the journey, French weather, French oats, French water, on anything in fact except that there were better horses running against her. But she was a very pretty chestnut.

I was taken to the *Nouveau Cirque* each year. And I loved the performing animals and the two clowns, Auguste and Chocolat. I always hoped that the animal tamer would be eaten. I was evidently a brutal child and was much upset when I was not allowed to accompany some friend I had made in the underworld to see a public execution. He had arranged it all. I think he was a friend or assistant of some kind to the executioner. Yes, I should see much blood and the severed head would be held up. I might even be splashed with it. Imagine that, *mon vieux*! Of course it may have been a hoax but it had a terrible reality to me. That was before I became afraid of blood.

But I loved zoos and circuses. Since this interest goes back to pre-Roman times, it must be lodged fairly deeply in the human psyche, and seems to have a particular bias towards the predators, the big cats, the lions, tigers and leopards that once menaced our ancestors. Certainly more people go to see them than the other animals. It is possibly titillating to see something so dangerous, so close, only separated from the public by iron bars.

It is therefore interesting to speculate on what makes people want to train circus animals. There must be some brutality and cruelty involved, so that a trainer must be exhibitionistic, sadistic and courageous at the same time. Exceptions to this are such animals as elephants and seals. The elephants are too dangerous and valuable to treat badly and the seals simply sulk. Dogs and horses can certainly be trained by kindness, so can birds and cats. The animals I should like to see in the circus ring would be cows. Twenty liberty cows wearing brassières. Or pigs, which are among the most charming and intelligent of animals.

I went with my father to see Buffalo Bill's Wild West Show, which was certainly instrumental in making me come to America so many years later. Dad knew Colonel Cody and introduced me to him. I remember him in his fringed buckskin shirt, big hat and long, yellow-grey hair. A showman, but a fine one. And what a show he gave! All the rodeo stuff that I was not to see again till I saw it in Jackson Hole and Cheyenne and many times in Madison Square Gardens, the climax being an attack on a stage-coach by yelling redskins. A terrific fight put up by the driver and the guard till they were rescued by cowboys, who charged the Indians and swept them off the field. I remember the Indians well, very nice red men sitting with their women and children outside their tepees. I was introduced to Sitting Bull. And Colonel Cody gave me a buckskin cushion with a picture of Sitting Bull burnt into it with a poker. It had fringes like Cody's shirt. I became so attached to this cushion that I sat on nothing else. I wore Sitting Bull out and Mother threw him away. I burst into tears.

I was taken to Bostock's Circus. This was the only circus where I have seen such a variety of savage animals in the ring at once. There were lions, tigers, leopards and polar bears, which are said to be almost impossible to train and are very dangerous. There were also black bears and black panthers, a Himalayan bear, and some Harlequin danes. These dogs could have done very little to defend the trainer, but they were beautiful to watch. The trainer was a pretty girl in a hussar's uniform. I must have been sexually attracted to her because she was the first animal trainer I had not wished to see devoured. Evidently I was growing up. The other circus I remember was Hagenbeck's, where my father held me up to look at a hippopotamus in a big cage. At that moment it yawned, opening its enormous mouth that could easily have engulfed me, showing its great teeth. I let out a yell of fright but soon recovered, such was my fascination for all animals, wild or domestic.

But all this was soon to end. My childhood, though I did not know it, was over. There had been family consultations. I was being spoilt. I was too precocious. I was too French. It was arranged that I should go to a boarding-school in England.

Part Two

THE BOY

———

CHAPTER 7

THE PRISONER

Now the picture changed. Happiness departed. I became a prisoner. I cannot understand men who say the happiest days of their lives were spent at school. I cannot see how being incarcerated, beaten, bullied, starved, driven and badly instructed by second-rate athletes can be considered pleasant. Naturally one develops a technique of resistance, mechanisms of escape. One learns dissimulation, stoicism, cynicism, masochism and sadism, which are described in the school prospectus as the arts of leadership.

I was in several schools in both England and France. I ran away from none of them. I learnt almost nothing in any of them but ended up, outwardly at least, that peculiarly English product, a public school boy who could be relied upon to play his part in the Empire to which he was, in those days, still the heir. These boys belonged to a class which is supposed to be privileged and which does, or did, hold most of the important positions in both civil and military government and business. By and large, with notable and important exceptions, even today these are the generals, the admirals, the ambassadors, the cabinet ministers, the bishops and the directors of the greater companies. But to achieve these ends boys are torn, when hardly weaned, from their homes and broken to their work as a gun dog is broken by a keeper. I do not say it is bad. I think it is good. If I had a son I should put him through it. But I cannot see how anyone can call it pleasant. Perhaps the best proof of this is that when I left school I went straight into the army, and though I was wounded first when I was nineteen and again when I was twenty-one, I preferred war to school.

Possibly I was a misfit. But I think I have always been a misfit, out of my environment, because I never really had one. In France I was an English boy. In England I was called Froggy because of my French accent. In South Africa, though of South African ancestry, I was an outlander as I did not speak Afrikaans. In America I was a resident alien. I do not think till recently I have ever remained in one place for more than five years although I have, on occasion, tried to settle permanently and send down roots into the soil.

Had I been able to remain at my preparatory school, Bilton Grange, and to have gone on from there to Rugby, the story might have been different, but I had to leave on account of my health. Warwickshire was too cold for me and I was always ill. In fact I was always ill with colds and bronchitis until the war, when I was never dry. I slept in wet blankets in damp dugouts and led a semi-nocturnal existence, all of which seems, as it did not kill me, to have cured me.

I went to Bilton because Mr Hill, who was the English chaplain in Paris, had become a master there, and Mrs Hill, who had taught dancing to a group of children of whom I was one, became the matron. I was therefore among friends, or at least in a place where I knew two grown-ups.

The house was beautiful. A big country house with magnificent grounds. The headmaster was a parson called Earle, who hunted two days a week. He rode a very nice brown mare and I remember seeing him coming home, his black clothes splashed with the mud of the shires. His father – also a parson – who had started the school was still alive, lived there, but was retired.

I still remember the names of two masters: Mr Cherryton, whom we called Cherry, and Mr Russell, an enormous, very gentle, red-haired giant who had played rugger – centre forward, I think – for England. I remember his English cap. It was made of dark red velvet decorated with a golden Tudor rose and a golden tassel. He was my hero. I went football mad and if I had stayed at Bilton might have been good at it.

There were two other new boys with whom I made friends at once. They were Claude Chevasse who was later to serve in the Navy and then become a priest, and Evans Freke who went into the Rifle Brigade. Only later when Lady Carbery, Evans Freke's mother, came over from Ireland and gave him a party at the Dun Cow – the local pub – for his birthday and he asked Claude and me to go did we discover that our birthdays were not only on the same day but that we had all been born in the same year –

July 23rd, 1897. This was the first example I had of there being something in astrology and the influence of the stars on personality. There have been other people to whom I found myself immediately attracted who had the same birthday or birth sign. It is something which makes no sense but which I find hard to deny, any more than one can deny clairvoyance or palmistry. In fact I now deny very little. Christian Science, the miracles of Lourdes, the curious powers of Yogis and Eastern mystics cannot be laughed off. Science cannot explain such phenomena so science denies them. But what can science explain? Only things that can be weighed and measured. Can a soul be weighed? Can love be measured? Can life or death be mathematically represented? These things, however, did not concern me then. Only football in the winter and learning to swim with water-wings in the summer in a swimming bath under the trees that had no purification plant and whose water was a lovely dark brown colour from the rotting leaves. I still think I should have been left at Bilton in spite of the colds I caught.

There were a few other boys whom I remember. A boy called Grayson whose father owned a shipbuilding yard in Liverpool. Freddy Selous, the son of Frederick Courtenay Selous, the famous African elephant hunter, was another friend, and two Swiss boys whose name, I think, was Bolliveau. Their father had a car – they were still very rare. I found it parked by some trees near the games field – a match was going on – and I got into it and succeeded in starting it. I was eight years old and have never been more frightened. I leapt out and hid. The car ran into some bushes and stopped. But this event confirmed my mistrust of internal combustion engines. My first experience with Mr Rust's Napiers in Paris made me think they always broke down. My second was that they ran away like horses, but were harder to control since they were machines and had no brains. One could have a pretty good guess at a horse's reactions but machines of all kinds were unpredictable.

Mr Selous gave us a lantern lecture on South African game and hunting, the hunters wearing only a shirt, hat and shoes. He said he could run faster that way and might on several occasions have lost his life if he had been wearing trousers. He lived almost entirely on buck meat but said he sometimes shot lion for a change of diet. His earlier hunting had been done with muzzle-loading guns. Elephant guns that fired bullets weighing four ounces each with a charge of black powder. He told us how Boer boys were sent out with one bullet to hunt buck for the pot and got a hiding if they came back empty-handed. This is what accounted for the marksmanship of the Boers in the Boer War. It so impressed Lord Roberts that he improved the musketry of the British Army to such an extent that the Germans, when they encountered the British Expeditionary Force in 1914, thought they had six machine-guns per battalion instead of one, so accurate was their rapid fire.

There were many lovely trees in the grounds at Bilton including sequoias at least a hundred feet high. These are the giant redwoods of the American West. And great yews whose red berries we used to eat. I think that is where my love of old trees began. I remember them as if they were people. Copper beeches, walnuts, oaks a thousand years old in the Great Park at Windsor. Three marulas on a farm I nearly bought in the Waterbery, a yellow wood in the Knysma forest, a wild olive near Naboomspruit, baobabs from the Transvaal to Nigeria.

I have few other recollections except of birds' nests and eggs. A whitethroat's nest, beautifully constructed of twigs, roots and horsehair. A greenfinch's nest with its eggs beautifully marked with scribblings that looked like Arabic. A chaffinch's nest in the fork of a tree that might have been made of felt. Other eggs in my collection were pale blue starlings', bright blue thrushes' eggs with black spots, mottled blackbirds' eggs, sky-blue hedge sparrows'. The tiny eggs of tits and wrens. I had them all nestling in beds of cotton-wool – a small boy's treasures.

I had a traumatic experience when I went to stay with a boy called George Thomson in Somerset (Thomson was not his real name). He had a sister, Esther. A flashing dark girl of about twelve who kept getting into bed with me and her brother, which made me nervous. Though this was nothing compared to the time she got me to come into her room and I saw on the floor a white cloth covered with blood. I almost fainted at the sight as she jeered at me. 'Oh that,' she said, 'that's just my month rag.'

Thomson's father had tried putting down golden and silver pheasants in his coverts but they would not flush, so were useless for shooting. In addition they killed the ordinary ring-neck pheasants. So in my mind ever afterwards golden pheasants became mystically associated with my experience with Esther Thomson. George had some beautiful bantams. Silver and golden sea-brights which I should have liked to have.

When I left Bilton Grange the boys gave me a leaving present – a volume of Shakespeare's Plays on India paper, bound in soft maroon morocco.

There was a farm near the school where my parents sometimes stayed, which seemed to me the last word in romance, with its cows and bulls, its immense work horses, its pigs. A calf died and I remember its being fed to the boar. Till then I never knew that pigs were omnivorous. The scene came back to me later when my friend, Mr C. G. Danford, told me of a swineherd on his property in Hungary who had fallen asleep and been eaten by his own pigs.

I found out later that Mr Selous, who had given us the lecture on African game, was a great friend of Mr Danford's. They had hunted together. I never saw him or Freddie again after I left. Both were killed in the war, Freddie in the Royal Flying Corps and his father while scouting for the British forces in East Africa.

I spent my holidays either in London or Paris. I remember driving with my mother and grandmother to change library books at Mudie's. Going to Harrod's. To visit her sisters, my great-aunts Helen and Sarah, 'the Miss Fairleys', as they were called, who lived in Notting Hill Gate which was then a very respectable neighbourhood. Also to see an old pensioned maid, Emma, whose greatest worry seemed to be her gigantic rubber plant that had reached the ceiling of her parlour. 'And what shall I do now, ma'am?' she asked. It certainly was a splendid plant.

I liked the flowers and flowering shrubs in Kensington Gardens and Hyde Park. The French did not do this sort of thing so well. Their lawns were not well kept; their flowers, when they had them, were symmetrically planted in circular or oval box-edged beds called *massifs*.

England might be politically the freest country in the world but that did not interest a child. Compared to Paris and France, it was dull. Even the light was different. When there in the autumn I often thought of the Bois when the leaves of the sycamores turned colour. A beautiful red, or ochre spotted and blotched with black. As a child I used to take the leaves home and press them. They soon faded but I still brought more. In winter I used to like to scuff through the rotting brown drifts to smell them.

The chestnut leaves turned a lovely amber and crackled into powder in one's hand, and I loved them in summer with their flowers and spiked green fruits, the chestnuts lying in their white beds of kid. Smooth, white and brown. Skewbald. Sleek as horses' necks to the touch.

One summer we went to Maidenhead and a hired Shetland pony ran away with me. He galloped along a low walk that was overhung by a holly hedge. I managed to stay on his back but he did not endear me to Shetlands. They are not, I think, the best children's ponies for though small, they are strong enough to carry a man and their short thick necks make them hard to hold.

Another holiday I spent with my aunt and uncle in the shires. My uncle, Joe Cundy, an Australian, had married my mother's sister, Cass, and was the agent for several large estates in Nottinghamshire. He lived at Linby. He had a big chestnut hunter, a dapple-grey cob for the trap, and a Shetland pony for my cousin, Tom. One place he looked after was Pappelwick Hall, a deserted mansion with an immense kitchen and a spit on which a whole ox could be roasted. It was, I suppose, built in the eighteenth century and was surrounded by a park with great trees and whole coppices of giant rhododendrons. I did a little shooting while I was staying there and killed a very pretty tufted duck, some Mallard, pheasants and partridges. The head keeper taught me to kill a wounded bird by biting it in the head with my eye teeth, and to tame a dog by spitting in its mouth. When he was given a young gun dog to train this was the first thing he did. Years later I was told the same thing by a man who was demonstrating gun dogs at the Sportsman's Show in Madison Square Gardens. I have tried it with great success on dogs, cats and birds and have a theory that girls in the past were warned against being kissed for this reason. It tamed them to the kisser.

My uncle also had, besides Flo, the black cocker bitch that he gave us, a collie and a black curly-coated retriever, a breed that no longer seems to exist. He lived what appeared to me an ideal life – hunting, shooting and fishing. His only work was over-seeing the properties in his charge and collecting rents, and most of it could be done on horseback. The keeper had a bull mastiff, the first I ever saw, that he used at night when after poachers who often showed fight. He also had a very small sealyham bitch that could kill a cat holed up in a drain. These half-wild cats did a great deal of harm to the game. It was here, too, that I saw hundreds of pheasant chicks being raised under hens in coops in a field near the keeper's house.

It was at Linby that I heard my first gramophone record – it was Redwing. The records were wax cylinders that came in cardboard cocoa-tin-shaped boxes lined with flannel. The machine had a large horn.

When I left Bilton Grange I was sent to Yardley Court in Tonbridge. Kent was warmer than Warwickshire. This was a good preparatory school but it made a very small impression on me. It had not the quality of Bilton. It was a red brick modern building with a wooden gym. Bilton had been a magnificent private house. One of the stately homes of England. I think the boys and the masters at Yardley Court impressed me, or rather failed to impress me, in the same way. Everything was all right but a certain snobbery had already been inculcated in my childish breast. Tonbridge was not in the same class as Rugby, and they played soccer. The house was not so grand, there was no chapel, no swimming pool, no real grounds. Only a playing field and an asphalt-covered playground. The masters seemed second-rate and not even athletes. There was no Russell with his English cap. And the boys were not the sons of peers, soldiers, shipowners, magnates, famous barristers or explorers. They were just the sons of ordinary men, some I believe even the sons of shop-keepers. This disturbed me. I was a real little snob, happy only with the rich and artistic, or with peasants, servants, grooms and criminals. There was nothing middle-class about me, no middle road. Though it is evident that this was the class to which I belonged, if one is thinking of classes as people did then. We were, I suppose, upper middle-class, landed gentry more or less, with some connections in the lesser aristocracy and some in the upper brackets of finance and industry. All good enough but not that good. Like many children, I had fantasies about being a prince in disguise who had been sold to my parents. I think many children feel like this. They feel so vastly superior to their environment that this is their only conceivable explanation.

I remember some of the boys at Yardley Court. There was Twyford, a Jew with poppy eyes, black curly hair and a big beak of a nose. He was my particular friend. I never really realized that others thought there was something wrong with Jews till I came across anti-semitism in South Africa and the United States. Like so many others, I can only say that some of my best friends are not only Jews but always have been. My father's friends in Paris, Twyford at school, Telfer and Jacobs in the army, Bob Nathan, Sarah Gertrude Millin, the South African writer, and many others. I do not like all Jews, but then I do not like all Englishmen, Frenchmen or Americans.

Another boy I remember was called Meek, a fair weak boy. Then there was Cave, of whom I was frightened. He bullied me. He had something wrong with one eye, which was larger than the other.

I have always liked women whose faces were asymmetrical, whose eyes were not quite level or who had something which, if it were any worse, would be called a squint. Such faces are to me much more interesting than the regular features of the classic beauty. The rest of the body cannot be too symmetrical – nipples at different levels are disconcerting. I am more interested in legs, bellies and bottoms than breasts. The back and carriage – the way of walking erect – is most important to me, but all men differ in their tastes. The bust men do not mind legs like a piano's and I had a doctor friend who only liked women whose front teeth were separated by a small cleft. He thought I was sadistic because I wanted my wife's ears pierced for ear-rings, but it was just a matter of security. I like ear-rings and did not want to give her good ones if they were going to fall off, which shows the way motives can be misunderstood.

I have only seen really different-coloured eyes three times. A boy called Donovan had them at Lancing, and Eileen Renton, a very beautiful woman – she was Rosita Forbes's sister – had them, and so did a girl in Africa, Elise ban der Merwe. I personally think this very fascinating because on the left-hand side you have a blue-eyed woman and on the right a brown, or vice versa. At least you have variety. I have seen green eyes once – Elinor Glyn had them. In her novels all her heroines had green eyes. I met her at a Curtis Brown cocktail-party. Really violet eyes I have also seen once. An Irish girl called Farthing, whom I met at Wimereux when I was a small boy, had them. And my cousin, Reneira Stanley, had the pale golden eyes of a Weimaraner flecked with brown. I think these are the most beautiful and remarkable eyes I have ever seen.

At Yardley Court we kept our pets in the gym – mice of all colours, squirrels, lizards, grass snakes and caterpillars. It was here I had my first silkworms. We bought the eggs – they were reddish brown – on a card from a shop in the Strand, by mail. When they came out we used to move them from one mulberry leaf to another with a camel-hair paintbrush. Later they were easy to handle and nice to touch in their cool grey segmented bodies. We used to try and spin our own silk, soaking the cocoons and unwinding them on to little bits of wood. We bred our moths in special boxes that we made with perforated zinc sides, and produced our own eggs. We also got puss moth caterpillars from a tall poplar hedge. These caterpillars are very odd, black when small, with ears like a kitten and two tails. These tails are hollow tubes and when annoyed the caterpillars shoot out a sort of red tongue from each. As they grew, they changed colour and became black and green, very fat and attractive.

I also got privet and poplar hawk moth larvae. I have always liked hawk moth caterpillars, with their decorative marking and spiked tails. The moths are beautifully coloured – bright in a muted way – but their great charm is their hovering humming-bird flight.

At one time on my farm in the Transvaal I had a large bed of purple salvia on the edge of the stoep. The hawk moths loved it and the noise of their wings – they were there in hundreds one year – could be heard in the house. There they hovered, flitting from flower to flower or stationary in the soft light of evening as, with long curved black watch-spring tongues, they sucked the salvias' nectar.

We found tortoiseshell caterpillars, spiky, not very attractive, in colonies on nettles. I found other insects, stones, fossils and objects of vital interest to a small boy, while I was being slowly tortured into comparative literacy. I was a poor pupil because I was bored, and only waited for the holidays which would take me out of this abominable place and return me to France, my actual and spiritual home. I can still remember my joy when I heard French again, and the wild shouts of the blue-bloused French porters as they swarmed on to the boat, strap in hand. I have never understood why other porters do not carry straps. They would thread them through the handles of half a dozen suitcases and, dividing them more or less equally into two groups, sling them over their shoulders.

After the age of eight I made the journey to England unlabelled, being put into the various trains and met in London. The boat I managed alone. One could hardly go wrong since every passenger went on the boat train and I was shepherded up the gangway with the rest. Naturally I was well looked after. Strangers did all they could for me and I accepted their help with gratitude and charm.

I had a gunmetal watch with a strap that fastened on to my waistcoat. I was very proud of it and consulted it all the time. Later on I was given a silver watch and a silver chain with big links. I had a little leather suitcase with my initials on it, of which I was also inordinately proud. It was about as big as a sheet of foolscap and six inches deep. I also had a leather stud box for the back and front studs of my Eton collars. That, too, was initialled. My trunk, when I went to school, was sent on in advance. All I needed for the journey was in my suitcase – pyjamas, toothbrush, clean collars, stud box and handkerchiefs. The essentials. On the boat I got myself a red wooden deck chair and if it was lashed to the bulkhead indicating a rough passage I fetched a white enamel tin basin which the sailor in charge of such things dealt out like playing cards from the stack at his side. I was a bad sailor till middle-aged.

When I was a small child the Channel boats were paddle-steamers. The wheels went round like great water-wheels in a millrace. One still saw sailing ships – fishing smacks, trading schooners, brigs, Thames barges and sometimes those great full-rigged ships that were the queens of the sea and, artistically, perhaps one of man's greatest masterpieces. I still love to see a sailing vessel or even a rowing-boat. Just as I love to see a saddle horse tied to a hitching post, or a two-wheeled cart rumble by. These things belong to the past, to the ancient realities. They have been in use for thousands of years and are the last survivors of those vanished eras.

These things are of particular interest to me since the umbilical cord of history which tied today to yesterday has been severed by science and technology; they give me a sense, or perhaps an illusion, of continuity in this new computerized world of synthetics. Yesterday is dead. Atomized. And God belonged to yesterday.

After a few terms I left Yardley Court for the same reason as I left Bilton. I was always ill. Evidently the English climate did not suit me. I also think my mother wanted me at home.

One other thing I remember about the school is that I learnt to play conkers there. A conker was a horse chestnut a year or more old. You made a hole through the middle and threaded a piece of whipcord eighteen inches long through it. At the bottom you tied a knot to prevent its coming out. Then turn and turn about you sloshed at your opponent's chestnut, going on till one of them broke. The winner then became a one-er, a two-er, or three-er, being numbered according to his victories. Some far-seeing boys kept chestnuts two years. These were very hard to break. It seems probable that this was a very old game, possibly even medieval.

I was now sent to a *lycée* in Paris. I wore a black cotton pinafore like all the other boys but did not have my hair cropped like theirs. This made me stand out, as did my habit of fighting. I had fought my way through two schools; in the end even Cave was a bit careful what he did because, although he could lick me, I always marked him up a bit. If I was annoyed or insulted at the *lycée* I attacked at once, and since no French boy fights, I bloodied the noses of boys twice my size with impunity and sent them home in tears. Naturally this could not last, but while it did my French improved still more. I learnt a number of obscene words that I had not picked up from what my mother called my lower-class friends, and got my first insight into the untruths and distortions of history by learning the French side of such battles as Crécy, Agincourt and Waterloo. I learnt the basic fact of French history: the French have never been beaten. They have always been betrayed.

I believe there is the same discrepancy in the history taught in the United States when it comes to dealing with the Civil War, or the conquest of the West from the Indians. And certainly much of the hatred of England that is apparent at certain times stems from the false teaching about the Revolution. Actually a great mass of English opinion was on the side of the revolutionaries, who were Englishmen like themselves, and against the army which was very largely composed of German mercenaries who were serving the German King of England. There might be more hope for world peace if every history book was destroyed. What are they but lists of kings, few of whose lives would stand close examination? And of battles which served no purpose but the aggrandizement and enrichment of the winner.

The *lycée* was the first school I was asked to leave. I was not expelled. It was simply suggested that I might do better elsewhere. Then came a tutor, Mr Stoddart, who taught me well. Among other things he taught me to learn history by reading historical novels about the period I was studying. He had a small book which listed the novels in one column with the dates and periods in another.

My parents now decided to leave Paris. They wanted a country place as more suitable for a growing boy. And their choice was Condette, which was part of the newly developing pleasure resort of Hardelot Plage.

CHAPTER 8

NUMBER THREE

NUMBER THREE WETHERBY GARDENS was a halfway house
between heaven, which was home in France, and hell, which was
school in England. Purgatory. A Limbo where I was alternately
possessed of despair when outward bound and delirious with joy
on my way back for the holidays. I had been going there with my
mother since I was a baby. All my infantile associations with it
gave me a sense of security when I was there. My brother Ronald,
who was articled to a solicitor, lived there with my grandmother
and Aunt Pim (Euphemia). Later when Granny died, they moved
to Number 8 Bolton Gardens, which was then known as Number
Eight.

My aunt was a tall, thin, plain woman dedicated to good works
in general and to the Barnett Cottage Home at Herne Bay, which
she had helped to found, in particular. This was a rest home for
Protestant women of the middle class who could not afford a
holiday. She had a companion secretary, Daisy Austen, who
came from Barbados, to help her with the letters, accounts and
interviews with applicants. My aunt and I had very little in
common. She called me Stu, a name to which I took great exception. Despite being well off, she did not dress well, used no
perfume and did not serve wine at meals; in fact she entertained
very little. The only people I remember seeing at her house were
parsons, church people and a lawyer – Oswald Norman – an old
friend of my mother's. He had, I believe, wanted to marry her.
He was a bachelor who kept three horses in London and used to
drive to his office from one of the suburbs every day in a dog-
cart. His coachman, John Leech, became a great friend. Oswald's
father had been in the Hussars and had married his father's cook.
I remember hearing this discussed one day. He naturally, after
such a *mésalliance*, had to resign his commission. What interested
me was that there should be a cook pretty enough for anyone to
want to marry – those I had come across were generally fat and

of uncertain temper, or religious and melancholic, like Alice, the cook at Number Three. Norman's hobby was breeding bulldogs and one day he arrived with six of them, a bitch and five nearly full-grown pups. Not knowing I was in the dining-room, he put them in there while he visited with my aunt and mother. I was about four and not used to English bulldogs. They advanced snuffling happily towards me and I, with great presence of mind, climbed on to a chair and got on to the table which was very large and sat there till rescued an hour or so later. I was then introduced to the dogs and have loved bulldogs ever since.

It seemed a pity to speak of a house by its number as if it was a criminal. But Number Three was my first experience of London. It had a basement where in dimly-lit, cockroach-inhabited dungeons the servants lived by day in a series of rooms known as the servants' hall, butler's pantry, store room, cellar (kept locked), scullery and kitchen. There must have been a lavatory too, somewhere. These premises were reached through a green baize-covered door and a dark flight of steps. It was the underworld which was only visited in the morning to give orders. One communicated with it by means of a series of numbered bells hung on semi-circular metal springs that were attached to jangling wires which ran through the walls to all the rooms in the house. When a bell rang someone ran to see which spring was trembling.

I spent as much time as I could in these dim, romantic and odorous surroundings. On one occasion I had to go downstairs to fetch something after the servants had gone to bed. I do not know what I was sent for but I did not get it. Candle in hand, I opened the green baize swing door and crept down the stairs only to find the walls alive with black beetles (cockroaches). They were so thick they almost touched each other. Whatever my project had been I abandoned it and retreated, thinking of a story my father had told me of how on one of his voyages from England to Africa the cockroaches had eaten his toenails. I now rather doubt this but still do not like cockroaches, particularly in battalions and brigades.

The drawing-room at Number Three was like all the drawing-rooms of the Victorian period: large sofas and low chairs made for women wearing crinolines. A grand piano, never played but covered with cabinet-sized photographs of men in uniform and ladies in court dress with feathers in their hair. The frames were of patterned silver set on blue velvet. There were some magnificent china jars three feet high on the floor. There was a big cabinet filled with most delicately carved Indian and Chinese ivories. The furniture was mostly covered in cut velvet. Some of the chairs had crocheted antimacassars on their backs. There were glass-topped tables filled with *bibelots*: snuff-boxes, ivory miniatures, ivory fans, little silver comfit boxes. The pictures were oil paintings of sentimental subjects of doubtful merit, interspersed with amateurish water-colours of the Bay of Naples or the Swiss Alps, painted by relatives. The taste of the time was for Landseer, pictures of Highland cattle and immense family portraits. The atmosphere was heavy but comfortable, cosy in the smaller rooms where pictures were often hung so close that they almost touched each other. Tablecloths of velvet had little velvet bobbles on them, resembling the seeds of plane trees. As the ladies' clothes were decorated with ribbons and frogged with cords, so the furniture was embellished with carvings and fancy cloths and cushions. The lampshades had little dangling frills of small white glass beads. Nothing was plain or simple. It was the age of the superfluous and the unnecessary. But for a child there was plenty to look at. To touch, to feel, if he was careful not to break anything.

There were two bathrooms: one for the servants upstairs and one for the main bedrooms, which had an enormous bath with a mahogany edge nine inches wide on which to sit. The toilets, or WCs as they were called, were separate. Night and morning the maids brought polished brass hot-water jugs shaped rather like small watering-cans to the bedrooms and covered them with a towel.

The front steps of all the houses were cleaned every morning by a scullery maid kneeling on a sack, with Monkey Brand soap and a bath brick. The scullery maid was the lowest of the domestic hierarchy and received five or six pounds a year in wages. A good cook got about twenty. The term slavery was not incorrectly applied. As a rule in a big house there would be scullery maids, a boot boy, a cook who held very high rank, two under housemaids or chambermaids, an upper housemaid, a butler, a footman and possibly a housekeeper. If there were children there were nurses, under nurses, nursery governesses and a governess. Outside there would be a coachman, grooms – one to three horses – horse boys; gardeners, under and head. In the country an establishment could have twenty indoor servants and as many men out of doors. In London from six to ten servants were considered sufficient. Ladies of fashion of course had ladies' maids, gentlemen had valets. There was often a sewing maid. Servants proliferated, each jealous of their position and privileges. They had a servants' hall downstairs, a kind of common dining-room/sitting-room, if they ever had time to sit. The butler and housekeeper had rooms of their own.

Number Three did not come into this class. My grandmother managed with about six servants, excluding the hired coachman who came with the horses and carriage in a contract package job.

Number Three was my London base as it were, for though we lived in France I got my clothes in England and went to an English dentist, Mr May, and I always spent a night or two in London between leaving school and catching the boat train.

Many things impressed me about this part of my life. As a small child I had confused my grandmother with the Queen. She dressed just like her – in black with a lace cap. The Queen ruled Number Three. The cook, Alice, who suffered from melancholia, was very religious, cried into the food and cooked without verve. There were two footmen, nice young men who spent much time caressing the housemaids, who were nice young girls and smelt of sweat and milk, like heifers. I can't imagine why, unless they drank it. The butler was a pompous man who spent much time polishing the silver with red powder and an old toothbrush.

Then there was the carriage. It was always called the carriage. I was much ashamed because it did not belong to my grandmother, though she could well have afforded it. Instead it was hired by the year from a job master, complete with a stout coachman. The footman who sat in uniform beside him was one of the two who worked in the house. It was his business to spread a big black bearskin rug that was mounted on dark blue flannel over Granny's knees in winter and a cream-coloured linen dust sheet over her legs in summer. There was also a foot-warmer that was used in the winter. A long copper container covered in some thick material. The horses were a well-matched pair of Cleveland bays who must have stood sixteen hands. This was the carriage in which we went to fetch the immoral butter every Wednesday. I think I resented Granny not owning the horses as, if she had, I should have had some sort of stable rights over them. I would have been allowed to groom them as high as I could reach, lead them out to water and perform some of the various other offices of a groom that were always my delight. I always wished Granny drove better, faster horses, or younger ones with a bit more life. This pair clip-clopping along bored me – almost the only horses that ever have. They had no character or personality. Perhaps belonging to a job master instead of to a private owner they felt the stigma of their position.

As a very small boy my visits to London were marred by my nightly terrors. These were caused by the screams, spittings and hissings of the innumerable cats that lived and courted in the square which belonged communally to all the houses that surrounded it. The children were taken here to play by their nurses for, fenced in by large houses and tall iron railings, we could neither be run over, stolen by gypsies nor meet undesirables, that is to say less well-off children. Though London did not equal Paris, there were compensations. There was Porter's, the toy shop in the Old Brompton Road. There was the Natural History Museum.

My mother had a faded snapshot of me in the square at the age of one. I am sitting very upright in my pram, wearing a satin hat ornamented with three vertical ostrich plumes, resembling the crest of the Prince of Wales. A child evidently in the great tradition. I am accompanied by the abominable Kitty Quensel, then a very pretty blonde of about sixteen, whose virtues were later to plague my first faltering steps in letters, and my beloved Elsa disguised as an English nanny and more self-conscious in her grey cap and uniform than she had ever been in the great black bow, velvet bodice and scarlet skirt of her national costume.

What else do I remember about London? Being taken up the Broad Walk in Kensington Gardens to play with my boat in the Round Pond. I remember the flowers, purple iris, yellow daffodils, some flowering shrubs that in the spring burst their way through the layers of soot that encrusted every growing thing. I enjoyed the excitement of the pea-soup fogs of November and December, when the visibility was nil and one had to feel for the kerb with

one's foot. But I was not in love with London. It was not Paris.
It was not France. There was too much order. Only one thing
appealed to me – the horses were better. More beautifully matched,
higher spirited, better groomed, and everything – coachmen,
footmen, the harness and carriages themselves – much smarter
and better kept. And I liked Rotten Row. The riders, both men
and women, in top hats with buttonholes, and small children with
their parents or grooms, their ponies on leading reins. But
though the horses were so fine, I missed the colour. There
were no uniforms. British officers when off parade do not wear
uniform. And there were no pretty ladies of doubtful virtue
wearing tricorne hats. It was very respectable. Whatever the
horses dropped was swept up by men wearing slouch hats, who
stood waiting for them before even the sparrows had a chance.
The Household Cavalry were wonderful. The Life Guards and
the Blues. But I preferred my Cuirassiers.

Other things come to my mind. The yellow straw spread in the
streets when someone was ill, someone rich, that is, to muffle the
sound of the hooves and wheels. I remember the butchers' two-
wheeled traps. The butchers wore striped blue aprons and straw
boaters, the uniform of their trade. Their ponies were of a special
type – small, well-bred and very fast. I could always tell if a
butcher's trap was going by without even going to the window
to look.

Then there were the hansom cabs, a splendid vehicle seating
two people, usually of opposite sex. They were covered to the
waist by folding doors that lay back at an angle of forty-five
degrees. A lot of preliminary love could be made in this dashing
conveyance, which was little more than a black box mounted on
two high wheels. On the top of the box there was a seat for the
driver. He had a little trap-door through which he communicated
with the occupants if they banged on it to call his attention. The
hansom cabs were very fast conveyances because they were
usually drawn by discarded race horses and hunters. This was
possible, as the height of the driver above the animal gave
him immense leverage on the reins which, running through the
hames of the collar, the turrets of the saddle, went up at a steep
angle into his hands. There were private hansoms belonging to
rich bachelors, their coachmen generally in buff-coloured uni-

forms with top hats to match, and a pink carnation in their buttonholes. There were horse-drawn buses which moved at a slow trot through the city. The horses were grey Percherons which moved faster than English draught horses. The upper decks of the buses were uncovered, but each pair of seats had a tarpaulin which came up to one's neck and clipped on to a stud on the back of the seat, so only the head of the passenger was exposed to the elements. The top of an open horse-drawn – or later motorized – bus was a wonderful way to travel and see the city. Another form of transport was the four-wheeled cabs, known as fourwheelers or growlers, which were used if more than two people needed conveyance or if there was luggage. When we arrived at Victoria from the Continent we always took a growler to Number Three. One of the common sights of those times was to see a man running beside the cab if he saw it was carrying luggage in order to be allowed to take it across the pavement from the cab to the front door. A man might run several miles to get a few pence. He might run several miles and get nothing. Even then this struck me as being wrong. Even then I was not satisfied with the *status quo*.

But there were glorious moments – such as fires – when the streets were cleared for the grey horses that pulled the red fire-engines at full gallop, with a fireman ringing a big brass bell. This has always been one of my greatest thrills, to see or to drive or ride horses at full gallop. I was taken to see a fire-station and watched a practice. The men slid down a polished steel cylinder on to the fire-engine. The horses were automatically released when the alarm bell rang and stood waiting while their harness, also released automatically, fell on to their backs and they then galloped into their positions on either side of the pole. A waiting fireman buckled the girths, adjusted the harness, and within three minutes they were out and off. Of course, for efficiency, such an outfit could not compare with the present motorized fire-engines. But it had a quality of reality which most things lack today. Just as the funerals of my childhood, which I was taught to watch standing at attention and hatless, had reality.

Both life and death were nearer to men then. One was aware of death when one watched the slow procession of hearses with black horses black-plumed and caparisoned, with top-hatted undertakers' assistants swathed with crape marching behind the coffin. One knew a child was dead when the coffin and caparisons were white. One knew that people died continually for one saw funerals several times a week. The horses' robes were dotted with silver stars. The coachman wore a cocked hat. As the cortège proceeded slowly, the crowded streets froze into stillness as it passed, the men removing their hats and standing to attention. They held up the traffic. The quick waited for the dead, and honoured them.

One of the remarkable things about life in Paris at this time was not only the brightness and variety of the street scene but the gaiety of the people. The painters sang grand opera as they painted houses. The servants sang. Our servants sang very loud and as soon as Mother stopped one of them, another began. Oh yes, there was much misery. *La grande misère*. Much wickedness and cruelty. I do not think there was even a society for the prevention of cruelty to children or animals in those days. There were few, if any, trade unions. Workmen were driven hard and were without redress. Children were forced to work, and terrible things happened. Strikers were ridden down by troops. There were innumerable abortions, as there had to be, before the general introduction of contraceptives. Unwanted children by the hundred were farmed out to be killed by slow starvation. Wet-nurses often lost their own babies, since they sold the milk that was their heritage to the children of the rich whose mothers either had no milk or could not be troubled with such things. The markets were filled with the bodies of little song birds hanging by their tiny legs. There were skinned frogs' legs pink naked, long-limbed like the legs of tiny show girls, threaded over sticks. There were butchers who dealt only in horse and donkey meat. They had a full-size cast-iron, gold-painted head of each very neatly executed to advertise their wares over the shop. Many of these horses were exported alive from England – as they are still. Horses that once had been the beautiful pets of lovely women who had stroked their velvet noses and fed them apples and carrots. Hunters, racehorses. I had Black Beauty in my mind.

When I was at the war my father sold my old roan mare, Gipsy. Something I never forgave him. For that is where she ended, brutally murdered in some knacker's yard. How could he boast of his son's exploits at the war, and then sell his pet horse for a few francs – not more than forty or fifty for that old bag of bones?

I remember gold sovereigns, half-sovereigns, louis d'or, Napoleons. Men wore sovereign cases on their watch chains. These little containers, made of gold or silver, had two flat platforms that fitted a pound and a ten-shilling piece. Under the platform there was a spring and they were loaded like the magazine of a rifle. In London I saw sovereigns made at the Mint. They were stamped out of a long flat golden ribbon and fell in a heap below the machine. I saw gold in the banks being scooped up in brass shovels and weighed as if it was sugar, instead of being counted. I knew that certain men rubbed gold coins together to produce gold dust which they sold – a crime whose name I have forgotten. This was a world of gold, of five per cent security, and above all, of hope. Perhaps that was why people sang. Things were bad but they would be better.

The death of song today seems to be due to a number of factors. People are filled with fear and fear does not promote gaiety. The radio with its professional entertainers has killed the amateur. In addition, by the time anyone has learnt a song it is already out of date. In those days people sang folk-songs, ballads, operas, comic songs, vulgar songs, and everyone knew them all.

What remains of Paris in my mind? The calendars issued by Spratt's Dog Biscuits that I used to look forward to each year with their pictures of different breeds of dog and game birds. I always kept them. A red book on horse and dog illnesses and accidents published by Elliman's (embrocation). The fat red Army and Navy catalogue. Then there was Felix Potin's grocery store, and a shop near the Madeleine where they sold exotic fruits where my father would sometimes buy custard-apples, pomegranates, coconuts and the like. When we went there he always got me a stick of sugar cane which I chewed and sucked all the way home. Nobody cares what you do in France as long as you are polite and annoy no one.

The England I was brought up in has disappeared. It may have had a lot wrong with it but it was beautiful, orderly and powerful. It had the tradition of glory. There were still men who had 'the will to rule' and believed in a Pax Britannica whose instrument was the British Fleet. This is what I was in a few years to fight for. Some American reviews of my novel *How Young They Died*, which is about the First World War, simply could not understand the patriotism or attitudes of our generation.

But if I were a young man today I cannot imagine myself fighting for England or the Commonwealth. This may be the greatness of England, to have had so bloodless a change. For hers is the genius of government.

The Magna Carta; the first successful parliament after Iceland; the first successful revolt against a sovereign that ended in the execution of the King; the forced abdication of another; the first socialist government: these are major political achievements. Even the American Republic – though most Americans would deny it – the greatest political success the world has yet seen, was designed and executed by English rebels. But to me the present situation of government by the blackmail of the masses – Labour, students, coloured immigrants – must end in disaster. It took a thousand years to create the English people, possibly the finest relatively homogenous race yet to be formed. What madness therefore to dilute these genes with those of people of alien tropic origin. Nor do I believe that the present components of the English population could withstand the hardships suffered in the Second World War.

Mr Enoch Powell's popularity seems to prove that I am not alone in this opinion. I do not believe that all men and all races are equal in ability, there is nothing in history to suggest that this is true, though it is the popularly accepted theory, and history is being falsified in an attempt to prove this thesis.

These views make me in modern parlance a racist. But racism and patriotism must be and are to a great extent synonymous. A patriot is a man who loves and serves his King, country and people. There can be no abstract patriotism. The Kenyans and people of Uganda are racist when they throw out the Asiatics. The Zanzibari were racist when they killed the Arabs and Indians on the island. Racism in India cost a million lives. In Biafra it cost two million. There is racial unrest in Cyprus, in Guinea, in Brazil where Indians are still being massacred, in Fiji, in Ceylon where the Tamils are persecuted. In the Sudan where the Arabs are destroying the negroes of the south. In Ruanda and Urundi. In

Taiwan, in Canada, in Ireland, in Belgium. Racism in fact exists wherever two races find themselves in competition.

Racism appears to be a built-in characteristic of the human race and the complete integration hoped for by the social scientists of today a wishful dream rooted in unreality.

To return to Paris and my childhood memories. In the Place Victor Hugo there was a fish shop aquarium. Here one could see the fish swimming – carp, bream, trout – and people came to buy them alive as they swam. They were fished out with a net. I am not even sure if they were killed. I only know that they must have been very fresh when they came to the table.

I loved the Punch and Judy shows that were so common then. The *Polichinelle* was one of my treats, to be allowed to watch these dramas of love and passion, of crime in which the puppets sloshed each other with a wooden club. I loved the fox-terrier that sat with the traditional ruff round its neck watching the proceedings. I loved the two Paris zoos. The Jardin des Plantes was rather far to go to often, so most of my zoo time was spent at the Jardin d'Acclimation, which was reached by a little railway that ran through the Bois, the miniature carriages drawn by trotting Shetland ponies. When we had arrived, there were ponies to ride and carts drawn by splendid white-bearded goats. Camels to ride. Elephants. And a thousand caged animals to see. Later, my views changed about caged animals and zoos. But that was after I had seen Hagenbeck's Menagerie where the the animals moved about in liberty, in surroundings that simulated their natural homes, and were kept from attacking the public – the very natural desire of any sensible animal – by deep pits of great width.

Another thing I enjoyed very much was the horse show – the *Concours Hippique* – and the agricultural shows which took place yearly in the Grand Palais. I loved seeing all the magnificent livestock: beef and dairy cattle, the immense work horses – Percheron, Boulognais, Breton and Flemish. I also liked to sample all the foods exposed. The stalls were generally run by big clean farm girls in the costume of their departments. Strong, corn- and milk-fed girls who could have been on show themselves and were quite ready to give a little boy sample tastes of cheese, country cakes, sweet spoonfuls of honey, when he stood – open-mouthed as a young bird – in front of them.

What other amusements had I? Walking in the Bois and playing with my hoop. I could never manage a top or a diabolo and was always amazed at the dexterity with which other children played with them. Later when I began to roller-skate I used to go to the Luna Park and made friends with a beautiful Portuguese girl of eleven who went there with her mother. Her father had something to do with the Embassy. We skated and danced to the music with crossed hands and much delight.

Since those days some event that I have tried to trace has given me a strange horror of blood. I have had to deal with it in war and farming. I have de-horned cattle and been covered with blood. Yet the word itself or the discussion of any operation will even today make me feel queer. I have had to walk out of dinner parties when the subject came up, without any apology. I did this once when staying with Dorothy Thompson in Vermont. They were talking about an eye removed from an executed man being grafted on to a patient. The real facts I can face. The words and idea I cannot. My dislike of operations I can understand. I had so many and was so weak after my wounds that when I saw the dressing trolley I dissolved into tears. So the sight and rattle of instruments, of dressings, of white coats and the smell of a hospital affect me profoundly.

But the fear of blood. I can think of only four events that might have caused it. The first was when Elsa drove the needle of the sewing-machine through her finger. The other things were, respectively, the horse that I saw staked in an accident just beside me and the white goose which my father beheaded and which then flew straight at me. The fourth possibility may have been buried in my subconscious: the bloody cloth that Esther Thomson had used during her menstrual period. (The disposable sanitary towel of today is a relatively new invention that stems from the use of surgical material for this purpose by the American nurses in the First World War.) I am inclined to think that this was probably the culminative factor of my psychosis, for menstrual blood has a mystic quality, something rooted in the depths of humanity. There is hardly a race whose men have not feared woman's blood. It is perhaps something no man should see. It is not the blood of war, or death. It is the blood of life, which is not man's affair.

In spite of these fears I can slaughter, skin and dress animals when I have to. I can perform minor operations on them, but am still upset if a woman goes into those obstetrical details that appear to be a favourite subject of feminine conversation. It is remarkable how many organs can be removed from a woman's body with impunity, and even apparent enjoyment.

CHAPTER 9

THIS FREEDOM

———

THE times I spent at Hardelot were among the happiest of my life for I was relatively free. Looking back, I can see that this has always been my aim. To be my own master. I did not mind the army because I knew that I must learn to obey before I could command, and it was always my intention as soon as I had sufficient seniority to try for the colonial service and independent commands. I nearly achieved it.

However, here was the beginning of freedom – a new kind – no longer of the city streets where I had been free to wander only by using some subterfuges, and where I sought the less respectable sections of the vicinity in which we lived as a woman seeks her lover. I must in some odd way have been aware that in these areas people were nearer to reality. The poor only lie to the rich, not to each other. They cannot, for each knows the other's affairs. They are kind, too, not because it is their nature but because tomorrow they may require kindness themselves. For the very poor disaster is always round the corner. For the rich there is always the cushion of their wealth. This may have been the beginning of my neo-Communism and Socialism, which I was cured of later when I found the brutality and filth of the mass, the *canaille*, as abominable as the selfishness, greed and unbelievable stupidity of the rich.

There is nothing like making a little money to cure Communist tendencies and nothing like living at close quarters with the very rich to find that this, too, is an emptiness. One ends with the bourgeois ideal. For the middle class, with all its defects, is the backbone of our culture, the source of all, or almost all, invention and art. It is the womb of progress, producing few of the criminals that spring from the working class, or the decadents that are produced by the rich.

But belonging to this class prohibited another ambition of mine. The soldier dream had faded through lack of nourishment.

There would be no war. There was no money to support me and no future in the army anyway. But I now wanted something worse in the eyes of my family. To be a painter, an artist. Did I know how many thousand artists there were in Paris? How many were starving? I saw no reason why I should starve. I would be good, also I wanted very little. I had few desires, I was not greedy. Women, perhaps, though I certainly never mentioned it, were in my mind even before puberty. I never even then had heard of an artist who lived alone. But the reaction of my parents was not favourable, in spite of my talent for drawing. An artist – God forbid! It's not respectable! So I am a writer.

But the country suited me and, true to my form, I got to know some of the wildest boys in the village and began to talk a French *patois* that my mother could not understand. A few words I still remember. A cow was '*vac*', like the Latin. '*D'où quelle est la vac?* for 'Where is the cow?' This must have been the language of Gaul, talked by peasant and soldier for hundreds of years. In every country there are two languages. These friendships were broken, but not before I had learnt a lot about local birds and how to find their nests. I almost killed myself on one of these expeditions. Having climbed a high ash and found two magpie's eggs, I was coming down with one of them in my mouth when it burst. It must have been addled and the heat of my mouth expanded the gas in the shell. It went off like a bomb of sulphuretted hydrogen and I nearly fell out of the tree.

I had learnt from my peasant friends to tie young wood pigeons to the nest so that their parents would go on feeding them till they were quite big. Then I killed them and ate them half raw, cooked on a fire of twigs and brush. I spent much time wandering about the forest. There were several thousand acres of woodland. It was divided into thirty sections and one section was felled each year. Before the work started the government foresters marked all the valuable timber trees that were to be left to mature still further. They were, as far as I remember, oaks, beeches, ash and wild cherries. They also marked young trees and saplings of these varieties that were to be preserved. So the work consisted of felling all the undergrowth, small trees, poor, crooked specimens that were sold as fuel, and such monsters as were fully grown and ready for the axe. These were sold to the sawmills and used for furniture. Some were bought by M. Vasseur, the village carpenter. He was a very remarkable tradesman. He could build a house, make furniture, and was also a wheelwright. He built carts for the peasants and made wheelbarrows. He made the coffin when someone died and the cradle when a baby was born. He even made his own planes and other tools; Gobert, the blacksmith, made the blades. There is none like him today. Is it sentimental to regret a craftsman's death and the end of such skills?

Coffins were made of elm, which he considered the best wood for the purpose. In Vasseur's yard the trees that he had sawn up into planks were seasoned in the shade. He cut up his timber by setting the trees on a great horse on which he stood with a big cross-cut saw with an assistant in the pit beneath him. This is the way the planks were sawn for the Roman galleys. Like everything else of those days, it was in the tradition, it had history behind it. Today we are divorced from history. Machinery has separated us from our hereditary skills. This may even be the basis of much psychosis in the world where man possesses too much and makes too little for himself.

At first, before we had even bought our property, we stayed at a small château belonging to a family called De la Court. There was a boy, Léopold, and two girls. Mme de la Court was a widow who took in guests to help her keep the place up. It was grey and gloomy inside and out. It had a wall round it, iron gates and some splendid trees. This is where I first learnt to love and respect trees. There was an enormous weeping beech, a species I have seldom seen since, a very fine copper beech, horse chestnuts, sycamores and elms. At the bottom of the park, as they called it, was a stable where we kept Jack the pony my father had bought at Aldridge's in London, and the dark green governess cart that was our transport. Horses, foxhounds and greyhounds had been sold at Aldridge's for centuries. Animals that were not good enough for Tattersall's. Jack was a well-bred dark brown pony, standing about fourteen one. He was quiet in harness and very fast. The stable had no door – instead there were three slip rails that ran through iron half-hoops. The top one was about four foot six from the ground and one day to everyone's astonishment Jack jumped out. A very fine jump with no run, standing in a box. I could not ride him, he was too much for me, but we were very fond of each other and I spent much time leading him about the grounds while he grazed.

He had a tragic end. My father, driving back from Boulogne one day, let him down on his knees on a steep hill. I was profoundly shocked, first that he should be hurt, and next that my father had done it. A governess cart has no brakes. The horse takes the strain on his britching and the passengers sit as far back as they can. To let a horse down was an unforgivable sin. It marked a great loss of confidence in my father. We had the vet out several times but Jack never recovered. If badly let down, a horse seldom gets better. Knees are impossible to bandage and are very hard to treat, and even if a horse does recover the marks will always show as the hair on the scar will grow upwards, towards the chest, instead of downwards. So poor Jack went the way of most good horses, and all bad ones, to the slaughter house. What we got for him may have paid for a dinner or two, but it seemed to me it would have been better to have dined at home and shot him. This is obviously a sentimental reaction.

Once we got settled I had plenty of pets. I had crows, magpies and jays that I took from their nests. Some lived and some did not. I had one crow that lasted for some years and I learnt some crow language from him, so that I could attract or warn wild crows. There is no doubt about animals and birds communicating with each other. Partly by voice – though the vocabulary may be limited to variations of the basic sounds representing challenge, sexual love, maternal love, danger, hunger, rage and warning. But there is much more than this. Something on a plane that we do not understand. Some telepathy which we, in our pre-human days, may have possessed but have now lost. I have noticed this with all animals – wild, domestic and tame.

I had several owls and hawks. To keep them healthy their meat has to be wrapped in feathers and gravel so that they can throw up pellets of undigested matter such as are found round their nests. If they can't do this they die. Some owls I got from the nest, usually in a hollow tree, but one I caught in my hand. It looked like a ball of fluff on a low branch and was being mobbed by small birds. I climbed up and got him by one leg. He drove the claws of his other foot right through my finger but I brought him home and he became very tame, though at first he had a very bad

temper and would lie on his back clicking his beak and striking at
me with his claws. The hatred of other birds for owls is often
used to decoy them into range. A stuffed owl will do and in an
open glade it will attract crows, jays, magpies and many smaller
birds. Though it is a pity to kill owls, which live almost entirely
on mice and rats.

This part of France was very rich in birds. There were icterine
warblers which are very rare, golden orioles and hoopoes.
Nightingales were so numerous that in June it was often difficult
to sleep. The charm of their song has been exaggerated. If they
sang in daylight no one would think much of it as it does not
compare with that of a blackbird, thrush or wren. I continued
my collection of birds' eggs and now blew them properly with
one hole. I bored a small hole in the middle of the egg and blew it
with a little metal blowpipe. If the egg had a young bird in it I
enlarged the hole and picked it out a bit at a time with a crochet
hook.

Flirt came with us from Paris and had three pups – Whisky,
Brandy and Gin. Whisky we kept, the others must have been
given away. Then there was Flo, the cocker bitch my Uncle Joe
Cundy had given to us. She was no good as a gun dog. No good as
a mother, because she trod all the pups to death in her ecstasy.
But she was a sweet bitch. Nothing could have been more loving.

There was Betty, a bull bitch. She got mange so badly she had
to be destroyed. There was another Betty, a mongrel miniature
fox-terrier that I picked up somewhere (stole). Diana, a mongrel
setter, I also picked up (stole). As far as I was concerned, any dog
with no collar and alone was lost and needed a home. Then came
Zulu, Diana's son by Turk, the local gamekeeper's big blue and
black French setter. And Tim, the Irish terrier that I bought after
many negotiations in Boulogne. He had been left at Merlin's
stable near the port by his master, a British officer, who had
brought him from India and could not take him to England
owing to the quarantine regulations. He was going to write, to
send money, to make some plan, but he did none of these things
so I paid his expenses and he came home with me. He was a
remarkable dog, a great fighter. He lost his left eye in a battle and
never whimpered when I dressed it. He liked riding in the tram
and would go down to the *plage* or up to the Pont de Briques all

on his own. I had him several years but one day he just disappeared. He must have taken one ride too many.

Merlin's was a stable where horses crossing the Channel in
either direction rested while waiting for the boat train or boat. I
used to go there almost every week, which was how I found Tim.
I think I saw almost every famous racehorse that crossed the
Channel in those days, and many hunters, polo ponies and other
valuable horses. Sometimes if they were busy they would let me
help with the horses – watering, feeding and grooming. I also
saw hounds, mainly extra large foxhounds, too big for British
packs, which were sold to the masters of French stag and boar
hounds who wanted new blood.

There were wild boar in the Forest of Hardelot. I often saw the
spoor and found their wallows. I found two small ones dead.
They were striped with white. There was a big fir tree on the edge
of the deciduous forest where it merged into the dunes and pines,
where they used to scratch their backs. Why just this tree? It had
a furrow worn two inches deep in the trunk with boar hairs
embedded in the resin. And round the base was the cup they had
trampled as they leaned inwards against the trunk. One year wild
boar dug up our potato crop. There were foxes, pine martens,
stone martens, wildcats, stoats, polecats and weasels in the forest.
There were also a few roe deer and many pheasants, rabbits, hares
and partridges on its outskirts.

The great *Forêt d'Hardelot* always fascinated me. A vast area of
deciduous trees that merged into pines as the character of the soil
changed and, towards the sea, gave way to sandy dunes, bare
except for patches of wind-sculptured bush that lay like cushions,
and sparse marram grass, which resisted the salt winds that
swept in over the Channel. Trees have always moved me
emotionally. The big ones seem to have personalities; they have
lived through history, gone on growing through wars and
revolutions, through the lives and loves of men.

I used to drive my mother into the woods to pick wild daffodils
and cherry blossom in the spring. White anemones grew in patches.
We dug up daffodil bulbs and planted them on a bank in the
garden where they flowered well. In the summer we picked
blackberries for tarts and jam. The peasants thought them
poisonous so there were always plenty on the sunny outskirts of

the forest and in the clearings. I used to unharness Gipsy, tie her
to a tree and give her a mixture of chaff and oats spread on a bag
while we picnicked. There is nothing nicer than to be sitting in
the open and hear a horse eating beside you. If we took a dog I
would tie it to the wheels of the trap as dogs were not allowed in
the forest. Those were very happy afternoons. Sometimes my
father came with us. We seldom saw anyone except perhaps a
woodcutter or a gamekeeper. Once we came across a man making
chair legs out of beech wood which he was turning on a lathe
operated by his foot. The treadle was fastened to a sapling which
sprang back and forth as he pedalled. This gave him his power.
We watched the birds and rabbits and saw an occasional roebuck
or fox.

I often wandered in the forest alone. I would have done so
more often if I could have taken my dogs. In the pinewoods of
the dunes there was no such restriction so I spent most of my
time there as I have never been happy without dogs.

The shooting rights of the forest and common were rented by
Mr Maxton, a lame Englishman whose family had had a lace
factory at Calais for several generations. He had a brace of
beautifully trained liver and white pointers that it was a pleasure
to watch working, backing each other up. It was rough shooting
and his bag comprised hares, rabbits, partridges, pheasants,
snipe, an occasional woodcock, wild duck, mallard and other
rarer kinds of duck, wild geese and coot. Sometimes he let me go
with him or the beaters.

The common that divided our lower cottages from the forest
was the village grazing ground – where every cottager was
entitled to graze two cows, one heifer and one horse. No sheep
or geese were allowed as they cropped the grass too close. Every
morning an old man, who was the herd, walked down the village
street blowing a cow's horn trumpet. The stable doors were
thrown open and the cattle and horses ran out as if they were
children going to school. Often in the evening one saw the girls
going to milk their cows on the common, with a milk pail in one
hand and a stool in the other. The cows were very tame and just
stood while the girls milked them. A pretty pastoral scene that
could have come straight out of a Morland print. I had learnt to
milk and would sometimes go up to a cow, not necessarily one of

our own, and squirt milk into my mouth, getting closer and closer till in the end I almost had her teat in my mouth.

The soil of the common was peat and very boggy. Sometimes a horse got bogged. I never saw a cow in trouble, the difference being due, I suppose, to a solid as opposed to a cloven hoof on soft ground. When a horse was bogged people were fetched by the herd, and a stable door, usually one of ours as we were the nearest house to the common, was lifted off its hinges and put in front of him. A rope was then pushed through the mud under his barrel and two men on each side pulled it tight. This raised the horse so that with a plunge he would succeed in getting his fore-legs on to the door and pull himself out.

Mounted, I have been bogged three times. A curious and frightening experience. Once during the war when riding a very nice hackney belonging to a gunner friend, I went down to my stirrups with no warning. Another occasion was in a bog in the New Forest, and I was once almost caught on foot in quicksands. To be caught and held, to feel yourself sucked down, is a most terrifying sensation and yet this is the way many cattle and big game animals die in Africa. When weakened by age or starvation they stick in the mud of a waterhole, a prey while still living to the hyenas and jackals.

The Château d'Hardelot had at one time belonged to a family called Guy. The song 'Roses of Picardy' by Guy d'Hardelot was written there. There was also a very nice long low bungalow called the Châlet Dickens. Charles Dickens was said to have written several of his books there. This house was bought by the Rusts after Mr Rust had retired from the Napier agency in Paris. Fillmore Rust, my friend, now became my companion as the only English-speaking boy for miles around. Both he and his father were dominated by Mrs Rust. Though he survived the war, he never got married. He suffered from barbers' rash which he caught from being shaved in a barber shop with a dirty brush. This was a kind of eczema that stayed with him all his life and for which in those days there was no cure. In the courtyard behind the Châlet there was a magnificent walnut tree that must have been a hundred years old.

Picardy, or the Pas de Calais, as it is now called, on the Channel coast had a kind of literary flavour. Oscar Wilde lived at Boulogne for a while. It had also been the home of English duellists who had killed their man, debtors, men who had run away with other men's wives, remittance men of various sorts, and soldiers of fortune. It was so near to England and yet at the same time spiritually and legally so far from it.

The *quai* was a forest of masts – fishing boats that went as far as Iceland or Newfoundland. The sailors wore red blouses dyed in ox blood and blue peaked caps. The fish was hauled out of the hold and taken to the market, where it was sold to buyers who sent the pick of the catch on ice to Paris. Many of the fishwives in their costumes – tight-girdled with swelling breasts and hips – were handsome in a greasy, fishy way. Their hair was slicked back. They had wooden sabots on their feet and in their hands knives with which they scaled and gutted fish with unbelievable rapidity. They were in every sense still medieval, untouched by modern culture. They fought among themselves. At Equien where many of them came from, some lived in overturned fishing smacks that were no longer seaworthy. They had been dragged up the cliff road and fitted with doors and windows. Inside they had bunks set in large cupboards, the last comer presumably closing the doors. This led to a great deal of TB, then called consumption.

Equien was a few miles along the coast. We often drove there over the sands in the trap to picnic and collect mussels from the rocks. The black wooden fishing smacks had dark red sails and it was a beautiful sight to see the little fleet come sailing in. There was a shop on the cliff top that sold everything from canned food to clothes and seaboots. The stock even included, hanging from a nail, a number of martinets, miniature cats o' nine tails for whipping children.

In the enclosed yards of the cottages one sometimes saw a herring or lesser black-backed gull pecking about with the chickens. The fishermen hooked them with fish bait, clipped a wing and kept them for two or three months, fattening them on household scraps. By this time, when they no longer tasted fishy, they were killed and eaten. This practice, like so much else in rural France, must have been very old; a trick handed down from father to son for generations.

The climate of Hardelot and its nearness to England were its great attractions. My father had become friends with a Mr John

Whitley, who had promoted Le Touquet and believed Hardelot had even greater possibilities. It had. It had more beauty, charm and greater features of interest, but Le Touquet had too big a lead. Too much money had been invested there and Hardelot was too near. Only fifteen miles away. The dream did not come off but a big hotel was built on the *plage* and a number of brightly painted villas sprang up round it. There were tennis courts, a good nine-hole golf-course and a tram that ran from the *plage* past the Château to Pont de Briques, where Napoleon had once had his headquarters in a long, low bungalow. This is a small town on the main Boulogne–Paris line, where you changed and took another tram to Boulogne.

The four peasant cottages my parents had bought in the village of Condette, about two miles from Hardelot Plage, were in pairs. One pair stood on the village street and the other at the bottom of the property. It was a rectangle of about five acres in extent and faced a common. Beyond the common was a large lake and beyond the lake the government forest. It was here I learnt my first lesson in real estate – to own my view.

Much to the astonishment of the peasants, my father immediately reversed the cottages on the street so that they faced the forest and backed on to the street. Then, as he needed a number of roofing tiles for the alterations, he made one of the local farmers the offer of a new roof for nothing if he would give him the old one. This man had always known that the English were mad but here was one even madder than usual. A madness from which he would benefit. 'Of course,' he said. Only a few months later when the tiles were used – they matched exactly – did he realize that my father had had to have old tiles and that he could have sold them to him at a handsome profit.

While the house was being converted Dad and I lived in the lower cottages, as we called them, on the common. Mother stayed in a hotel in Boulogne. I have never been happier. Dad was at his best. We cooked curries over the open fire in a big black pot to which we added more dried fruits each day till the curry was like plum pudding with a curry flavour. But I loved it. And we bought animals at sales: two red Flemish cows and a heifer called Rose. We hired a couple to work the place. We bought chickens and ducks; one of the ducks had a topknot on its head. Rabbits.

Dad bought me my first bantam hen. We bought pigeons. A cart, a plough, a harrow, garden tools, furniture, shrubs, trees, roses. At the sales we bought copper kettles and pots, old cast-iron firebacks, bellows and other fire implements, all for next to nothing. Today such things are only to be found in antique shops and are often fakes. I always felt a sale to be sad. A dispersal sale – lock, stock and barrel – means that the owner has died or gone broke, and these articles and livestock that had, as it were, lived together for so long are dispersed among strangers.

This all-male idyll of the first months could not last. My mother soon joined us and we had regular meals and I had to wash and go to bed at eight.

The brown English pony, Jack, had been replaced by a straw-berry roan mare called Gipsy who came from Goldschmid's stables in Paris. She became my pet and I really learnt to ride on her. During the holidays I fed, watered and groomed her. I learnt to harness her to the governess cart by myself and spent a great deal of time in her loose box or on her back. I nearly had an accident driving her in Boulogne when the wheel became engaged in a railway line with a train coming. Fortunately it was near the docks and the train was hardly moving, so I was able to jump out and lift the wheel out of the track and lead Gipsy off the line.

All the peasant cottages, including ours, had enormous open fireplaces, on one side of which was a deep oven. The peasants all made their own bread. Big flat loaves eighteen inches in diameter were put into the oven on a flat wooden tray at the end of a long handle when the oven had been sufficiently heated with a very hot fire of old pea sticks and twigs. The loaves rested on the ashes and the iron door was closed till they were baked. Bread like this with home-made salt butter was really the staff of life.

We found that the chimney of the cottage needed sweeping and to my astonishment Louis, the gardener, climbed on to the roof with an old hen under his arm. Reaching the chimney he held the hen by her wings and dropped her down. As she descended fluttering and protesting loudly, she dislodged the soot and landed a shower of it on the hearth. It seemed to do her no harm.

One night my father and I slept out in the sand dunes near the sea. This was my first night under the stars. In the morning my father took a shot with the 32 Winchester we had brought with us at some wild geese on the beach, but did not hit one. We cooked over a driftwood fire with the dogs, Flo and Flirt, beside us. We had driven down in the governess cart and Gipsy was tied to the wheel munching her mixture of chaff and oats. Dogs, a horse, a gun and the stars – what more could a boy want? My father told me stories of South Africa and his boyhood. How he had hunted big game and prospected for gold. How he had been chased by baboons on Table Mountain. Of horses he had owned and raced. Of how he once had exchanged a race horse for a farm in the Waterberg, and got another for a grand piano. Of how he had sold a plot of land in Pretoria to a man on Newmarket race-course for £500 – an immense profit – only to find years later it was the site of the new post office and is now worth millions. He told me of the Bushman boy he had bought from a Boer who was thrashing him for £5. He had later taken him to his house in Queen's Gate, in London, to do odd jobs, but my mother did not like him as he frightened the maids by hiding under tablecloths and biting their calves as they passed. Then Dad sent him to his stables at Newmarket, where he rode crouched like a monkey on the horses' withers. Probably the first man to use the modern seat of today. But he could not get on with the trainer, who beat him, so he ran away following the railway line and finally reached the Queen's Gate house which he knew from a tiny mark on the front steps. After that Dad sent him back to South Africa with a friend. Dad told me of a horse called Brian that he once drove in a dog-cart to the races, won a race on, and drove home. His colours were orange and black with a black cap. He told me hunting stories, including the story of a buffalo licking the flesh off the leg of a man who had climbed on to a branch that the buffalo could could not reach. Thirty years later I used this story in *Turning Wheels*. He was always telling me stories of travel and adventure.

These were some of the best years of my life. I was twelve when we came to Hardelot and lived here, apart from the time I spent at school, till I was seventeen and war broke out. This was for me what I have heard described as my calf country, like calf love. My first love, something I never forgot. I knew the country for miles round. I swam, I fished, I rode, I walked and I shot. As soon as it was light I was out of my bedroom window, called my dogs and was off.

It is here and at school that I went through the so-called difficult years of puberty and adolescence about which they make such a fuss today. I was in many ways a delinquent. If I was caught my father beat me, for which I bore him no malice. I took chances and often they paid off. If they didn't, it was just bad luck or judgement. I was beaten but never talked to. What was there to talk about? I knew what I had done and never lied about it. A lie would have meant a thrashing, something quite different from being beaten with a hunting crop.

In those years I fell in love with several girls but never even kissed one of them. I just liked to watch them and be with them. I had my dogs, my mare, my 6 mm. rifle and miles of commonage, forest and dunes with quite inadequate gamekeepers all round me.

The plan of our property was simple. The two top cottages were joined by a ten-foot passage at the back (there was nothing poky about my father) and a ten-foot verandah in front. Mother had a very large room at one end of the house. My room was next to hers. Then came my father's room and then a spare room; then the hall, the drawing-room, the dining-room, and finally the kitchen wing that ran at right angles to the main building. There were also some servants' rooms and two other spare bachelor rooms for my brother and his friends if they came up with him from Paris, where he had his own apartment. One of the two lower cottages was reserved for our use in the summer if we rented the big house. The other was used by the gardener and his wife.

At Condette the gardener's wife, Sidonie, fed and milked the cows, fed the mare and poultry, and made butter. She also helped with the laundry and housework if we had visitors. Louis did the garden, both flowers and vegetables. We grew all we needed for ourselves and he emptied the toilet buckets daily. The night soil was buried one spade deep in the kitchen garden and so what we ate was returned to the soil as it should be. It grew wonderful vegetables. It seems quite possible that much illness today is caused by improperly grown food produced on farms that are no more than factories. The mixed farm as I knew it has almost disappeared, except in parts of Europe where men still love the soil they cultivate and the stock they breed.

There was a prize given about this time by *La Vie à la Campagne* for the family that could prove they had lived on and worked the same land for the longest time. The winners, father to son, had done so for a thousand years. Men of the soil, indeed. Eating its produce and returning the residues so that year by year the land became richer. This was a way of life, a symbiotic association of man, beast and earth and not a business enterprise. Some of these big farms still exist; semi-fortified medieval structures built in a hollow square on to which the house, stables and building all open. Family concerns, vestigially feudal, which give one an idea of how things once were. The idea of a five-day week never occurred to such people. The great Percheron horses must be fed at weekends, the cows milked, the sheep tended. That is life as they see it. It is also as I see it. I would sooner work with fine horses, even if it is a lot of trouble, than a tractor. One cannot talk to a tractor. These agriculturists may have arthritis but they do not suffer from nervous disorders. The men are not impotent at forty nor are their women frigid. They have the immense satisfaction of knowing what they are doing. They are producing wheat, milk, butter, cheese, beef and wool. They see it in their hands. How many men today make anything? Make the whole of it? What satisfaction to man's creative urge does eight hours five days a week on an assembly line give him? If on the one hand these cultivators are brutal and uncultured, we on the other have refined ourselves into decadence. It is not only chickens that are mass produced in batteries without ever setting foot to the soil, it is also men. Some of the flavour has gone out of them too.

CHAPTER 10

THE MANTRAP

I REMEMBER that about the time we moved to the country the Catholic Church was disestablished in France and most of the church property seized by the government. Monks, and nuns were in flight everywhere. They were in no danger but they had been plucked clean. The accumulations of centuries had been reft from them. France had become very anti-clerical. The Dreyfus Case – much earlier of course – had helped to discredit the Church and the Catholic Party in the army. There were, too, I imagine, the beginnings of Communism, though I don't know if it was called that. Certainly I remember talk of the Commune and riots on May Day when the cobbles of the streets were torn up and used as missiles, and barricades were flung across some of the boulevards. One thing I remember about these conflicts between the workers and authority was that neither side was prepared to walk home. And that all hostilities stopped before the last Métro ran. Strikers, communists, police, troops and firemen all bought their tickets and went home on the same train. The French are a very admirable people, logical and civilized.

I remember, too, the great flood. Seeing the Seine rise and rise till the water swirled about the necks of the giant stone soldiers that were carved on the supporting pillars of the bridges. Cattle, even parts of houses, floated down on the stream. My father hired a boat and we rowed about the streets, staring at the poor people who had been driven into the upper storeys of their houses while they stared down at us. A handsome man in a top hat, accompanied by a blonde child, being rowed in a skiff by a waterman.

About this time my brother Lovel bought a pianola, a wonderful instrument that one could play by simply putting a roll of paper with holes in it into a slot and pedalling away. I always played it very loud.

There are no further Parisian memories except of the great fair at Neuilly. I think this festival dates from the Middle Ages. It was enormous and had every kind of booth and wonder. Carousels, wild animal shows, performing dogs and bears, acrobats, sword swallowers, bearded ladies, mermaids, dwarfs and other freaks, stalls that sold all sorts of food from gingerbread pigs to pork liver *pâté*. Everything was to be found there and, I think, many evil things. It was not so long ago that children were stolen by gypsies and made into dwarfs and monstrosities by skilful operations whose technique had been handed down from father to son for generations. Bones were broken, sinews cut. Boys were castrated so that their voices would not break, children prostituted.

The gypsies were poachers and tinkers, thieves of horses, dogs, poultry and children, who moved on the periphery of crime. They were the picturesque *apaches* of the countryside. They were procurers for the city sometimes, and it was at the fairs that they exchanged their wares for gold.

But it was noisy, it was gay, bright with sound, with music, songs and screams. It was old, it was dangerous and exciting. I saw things I should not have seen. A man catching a woman and flinging her down. I learnt things that are not generally known. I learnt that the dancing bears that were led about Europe were trained by being caged on an iron plate under which a fire was kindled, while the trainer played his simple wooden flute. By degrees the animal associated the sound with the pain, and the two became one in its mind and so when the flute was played the bear danced and suffered. I learnt that there are two ways of training anything: by love and by cruelty. I learnt that the outward results are not very different. The animal trained by love may, because it is not afraid, one day turn on its trainer. The animal that has been whipped into submission, burnt into it with hot irons, may one day overcome its fear and kill its trainer. I have been told that more respectable women have killed their lovers than prostitutes have killed the pimps who are their masters. Is there a moral here? It is possible that only the young can afford love – that the old must inspire fear. We reach the point where the beginning is also the end. Where opposites merge into a single whole, where the libertine poet is one with the ascetic monk. Each destroys desire as he seeks freedom from it, the one by surfeit, the other by celibacy. Which is right? Who thinks the most about food, the starving man or the *gourmet*? I knew none of these things but I was getting the feel of them. Had I learnt them even then in detail, I do not think I should have been much surprised.

I had in my wanderings even met *apaches* picturesquely dressed in their baggy corduroy trousers supported by wide red sashes. They usually wore a handkerchief knotted round their necks and a cap with a patent leather peak on the side of their heads. The scarves must have impressed me because I still wear mine knotted *a l'apache*. They always had a cigarette hanging from their lips and a knife in their sashes. Daggers, large sheath knives, Swedish knives in two parts, long clasp knives that flicked open when you pressed a spring. They lived in the slums but often slept in the bunkers of the old fortifications, which were considered danger-ous, and in the Bois where every now and then the police organ-ized a great *battue* and beat them out of it as if they were game, with dogs. The fortifications were a great ditch two hundred feet deep and a hundred yards across. The bottom, filled with small trees and bushes, made a fine hideout for criminals. The fortifica-tions were a feature of the city. The bunkers were used by lovers, by people in need of a toilet, and by *clochards* as sleeping accom-modation. The whole area was deserted, unpoliced, and had a bad name owing to rapes and murders which at times took place there.

My father had a big portfolio of marbled black and blue card-board that fastened with black tapes. Sometimes he would let me look at the pictures, an odd collection of prints, aquatints and engravings he had picked up here and there for a few sous as one could in those days. Among them was a set of large lithographs depicting the costumes worn in Turkey before the collapse of the Ottoman Empire. There were pictures of soldiers, wine sellers, dwarfs, palace eunuchs and officials of various kinds. They belonged to the Near Eastern world that Richard Burton wrote about. The world of Arabian Nights and Perfumed Gardens that has gone for ever. It is this colour and panoply, this variety, which has always appealed to me. A costumed world as opposed to one of uniformity in which people all over the world wear business suits or sweat shirts and khaki shorts or blue denim pants. Sartorial equality may be admirable but it is not artistic. The scene is no longer paintable. Uniform clothes seem to make for uniform people. The younger generation's Carnaby Street get-up and miniskirts would seem to be a revolt against this trend of dull respectability. That many of them go too far merely shows a lack of perspective. But behind them is a desire for personal recognition, to be different, and to be seen as themselves even if they are grubby, rather than as part of a mass.

Looking back, I can see that my father had the greatest influence on my life, both positively and negatively. After him came old Mr Danford and Dick Harris, who taught me English at Lancing, and finally E. Arnot Robertson, who encouraged me to write. Hundreds of other people must have affected me, as they do everyone in various ways. And then beyond them were the mysterious forces of heredity and circumstance which have led and driven me on. Women, naturally, though they fall into another category, have certainly turned the course of my life on several occasions.

When I was a boy money not only had real value – purchasing power and intrinsic value as metal – but it felt like money. It had weight and texture. There was no question about a silver five-franc piece – a *pièce de cent sous* – being valuable. It was immense. A cartwheel. In those days even a sou, five centimes, had importance. The French poor counted in sous. Twenty sous was a franc. A hundred was this magnificent silver giant. I bought a Napoleonic light cavalry sword for five francs. I do not know what it would be worth today. Oddly enough I still have it.

A golden sovereign or louis d'or inspired respect. It was a great sum to a child. When I was given a half-sovereign or a sovereign as a tip I was much impressed. I hated to break into it. It is easy to see how men become misers, playing with their little sacks of gold, pouring them out on a velvet tablecloth. They never tarnished and they were heavy for their size, heavier than lead. They felt greasy between the fingers. An English pound was worth twenty-five francs at that time – about 1912. I used to change my mother's cheques on London at a bank in Boulogne for gold louis, the odd copper balance I was allowed to keep.

In England there were not only sovereigns and half-sovereigns and silver but farthings too. Four to a penny. One could buy farthing buns, just like penny buns, currants and all, but a quarter the size. What can you buy for a penny today? Or a nickel

for that matter? We used to throw pennies wrapped in bits of
newspaper – so that they could be found easily – out of the
window to street singers, organ-grinders, German brass bands.
They fell from all the windows into the street – thrown like corn
for chickens – and were collected in a cap.

When I was a little older I used to take an unused stamp, stick
it on the pavement and watch to see how many people tried to
pick it up. I wonder who suggested this trick to me.

There were poor people then, really poor, hungry people. The
Russians were still serfs. But there were no labour camps. There
was no Berlin Wall. No villages being bombed.

A bachelor with £500 a year was rich. He could hunt, shoot
and indulge himself in every way. He could even get married if
he was prepared to live modestly. As late as 1930 one could get a
good meal at a London pub: a cut off the joint, two veg and
pudding or cheese for 1s. 6d. In 1937 in New York one could get
a very superior several-course meal, including steak and half a
bottle of wine, for a dollar. In 1914 a good horse was worth about
1000 francs or £40. A night spent with a very good class of woman
– pretty, well-dressed and with a nice apartment – cost a fiver, and
she gave you breakfast: tea, toast, bacon, two eggs, marmalade.
Now horses have almost disappeared and the price – unless they
are hunters, children's ponies or blood horses – is by weight. A
big common horse is worth more than a good little one. He
makes more dog food. And girls – today it's £10 for fifteen
minutes on the assembly line. That, I am told, is the price; the
time I can certify, having watched tarts in Nice and timed them
with their clients.

We did not buy food for our dogs. What was good enough for
us was good enough for them. Bones, scraps, bread, a few
spoonfuls of soup. And if that was not enough, a Spratt's dog
biscuit. Hard tack about six inches square with little bits of dried
horse meat in them. I was very fond of them. My mother was
always telling me not to eat the dog's biscuits but they fitted
nicely into my pocket and didn't crumble. Today the last brumbies
and kangaroos of Australia and mustangs of America are being
canned for dog food. Such is the power of advertising. Our dogs,
with our food plus a few butcher's scraps – déches – were just as
healthy and lived as long.

Like most small boys I liked castles, dungeons and torture chambers. I liked the Chamber of Horrors at Madame Tussaud's in London. This fascination for horror and abstract cruelty is not confined to boys and has never been given a psychological explanation. The torture instruments have now been removed from many castles such as Chillon, but when I went there as a child I saw them all – rack, thumbscrew, branding irons. The château at Hardelot had fine dungeons which one could visit with the guardian who had the key at the lodge gates. There were rusted rings and chains in the walls. There was an *oubliette*, a deep well into which the prisoner must eventually fall since there was no light of any kind in these deep cells and chambers. The foundations were said to be Roman, which seemed likely as there were Roman camps and earthworks in the vicinity.

This area had been inhabited since the early Stone Age. Mr Danford used to take me with him looking for flint implements. We found a lot: scrapers, saws, hand axes, hammers, arrow and spear heads. I always thought it extraordinary to hold these things in my hand and think of the men who had made them, perhaps ten thousand years ago. I got together quite a good collection, though it did not compare with Mr Danford's. The best time to look for them was after a thunder shower in a newly ploughed field. The worked flints stood out quite clearly if you knew what you were looking for.

We also found a kitchen midden in the sand dunes. These dunes move with the winds, and this midden must have been uncovered for the first time in two thousand years. Some of the pottery and rough silver jewellery we found, proved to be of Roman origin. We should have spent longer on it and gone through it with a sieve, but I had to go back to school and before I came back again the sand had covered it once more. In windy weather the dunes were hard to cross, the sand particles being driven into your face like tiny bullets.

I owe Mr Danford a great deal. He interested me in archaeology, he taught me a great deal of natural history. He taught me to paint in watercolour. He lent me books by Selous and others on game and hunting. At this time he must have been about seventy and I ten or eleven years of age. He was bearded and almost a hunchback. He lived with his wife and daughter, Beatrice, who

translated books from the Hungarian, in a smallish house near the
church about two miles away from us. He had been better off at
one time and had owned big estates in Hungary, where he had
hunted chamois, bear, wolf, red deer, roebuck and wild boar. He
gave me two pairs of chamois horns, a male and a female. The
female horns were a little thinner and not so wide spread. I was
very proud of them and hung them on little wooden shields in my
room. He told stories of werewolves, and of how he had tamed
a wolf bitch pup so well that she lived in the house with his
retrievers and other gun dogs. He said that in Hungary they used
to shoot lammergeiers from a hide by staking out a captive
eagle owl which the lammergeiers attacked. He showed me his
guns, and the skin of a Cape hunting dog. He took endless trouble
with me and he has been a great influence in my life. The hoopoe's
nest in the South Kensington museum was donated by him. He
also taught me to trap and collect small mammals for the museum.
He showed me how to skin and stuff them.

I had collections of shells, and rocks containing minerals, and
meteorites. One day I walked fifteen miles to the top of a hill and
picked up several. This was the highest point for miles around
and was quite bare of trees. But set on it were half a dozen poles
each with a trap on it to catch hawks, which like that kind of
perch.

At this time I was beginning to collect my first library. I had
Harmsworth's Natural History, a big work in three volumes.
Several books on birds, books on dogs, natural history books I
had picked up on bookstalls for a franc or two. I also had quite a
collection of Nelson's novels. Sevenpennies, they were called, in
hard blue or red covers. By Jack London, Sir Gilbert Parker,
Rider Haggard, and more serious books from the Everyman
Library that only cost a shilling. Darwin, the Koran, Huxley,
Malthus – a very odd and catholic collection for a boy of my age,
I suppose.

I had the run of my father's library and he had an odd mixture
of books, among them was Haekel's *Riddle of the Universe*, which
had pictures comparing a human foetus with that of a bear, of
hermaphrodites and other oddities. There was a book on famous
race horses. *Mr Sponge's Sporting Tour*, Jorrocks, Greek Myth-

ology, *The Life of John Mytton*, Nimrod's *Conditioning of Hunters*, Livingstone's Travels.

In the middle drawer of his desk he had some interesting things. A small lead model of Napoleon based on the *Mannequin qui pis* in Brussels. Coins of various countries. The reclining figure of a nude lady made of meerschaum carved into a pipe. It had an amber mouthpiece and was bedded down in a black leather case lined with blue velvet. He never smoked it. Sometimes I asked to see it.

Looking back, I seem to have spent my holidays riding Gipsy, swimming in the sea or, later, walking fifteen or twenty miles accompanied by my dogs, or lying on my bed reading or dreaming. In the summer when there were visiting girls I went out with them, utterly entranced but too shy even to attempt to kiss them.

I began to play golf and made friends with the pro, a big Scot called McDonald, who, like all golf pros in those days, made his own woods – drivers, brassies (baffies, as they were called) – and fitted wooden shafts to the irons. Balls I found. In the winter when there were no visitors I would go through the rough with Zulu, my half-breed setter, and find them. I repainted them and they looked like new. McDonald had an automatic. He was a splendid shot and killed rabbits on the golf-course.

The French were wonderful workers. I remember a man mowing one of our hayfields by moonlight. It was strange to hear him stropping his scythe and to see the swathes of grass fall in the silver blue of the night. I learnt to use a scythe, to set it by tapping the blade with a hammer on a little portable anvil, and to sharpen it with a piece of dagger-shaped wood with four sides that was dressed with a mixture of clay and water.

When we had been at Hardelot a few months I was given a black and white kid by a woman who wanted all its mother's milk. This goat became a great pet. I reared her with a bottle till she learnt to drink by herself. She followed me everywhere but had a tendency to go to sleep on my mother's bed. She reached her room by jumping through the window. After that she was tethered except when I took her walking with the dogs.

While I was at school in England I used to buy a grass snake from Gamage's which had a very good pet department and carry it in my pocket in a little canvas bag that I had procured somewhere. Once, by a fortunate accident when I was coming home from school with my snake, it escaped and popped its head out of my pocket. At the next station my carriage emptied itself and I lay down at full length on the seat and went to sleep. This discovery, like so many great discoveries, was entirely accidental, but after that I always brought snakes as travelling companions with the most excellent results. Snakes are nice animals. They get to know their owners and are reasonably intelligent, if not brilliant. They have grace and charm and are very pleasant to hold or have round the neck on a hot day. A snake is not slippery. It feels cool, like a beautiful piece of articulated jewellery. One objection to snakes is the necessity of giving them live food – frogs, mice – and for the bigger ones, rats, and rabbits.

On one occasion I caught a very fine specimen of a stag beetle, the only one I have ever seen. I had it in my room and was much concerned when I discovered that it had been able to push up the glass that I had put over its box. It was a very strong beetle. Two days later, while I was searching everywhere for my pet, piercing shrieks came from my mother's room. She was just getting up and had nearly trodden on my beetle, which had immediately attacked her and seized her big toe in his antler-like nippers. Mother was jumping about and I said: 'Be careful, Mother! Stand still! Mind you don't hurt him and I'll get him off!' I got him off without injury but then, acting under pressure, was forced to kill him in my killing bottle, from which he graduated as the prize specimen of my collection of coleoptera.

The local children were great torturers of animals and birds, destroying nests just for fun, catching cockchafers and fastening them to strings so that they flew about like living mechanical toys till they died. Toads they would blow up like balloons by inserting a straw into the anus. I was much upset by this kind of thing, though, when younger, I had been guilty of tearing the wings off flies and the legs off grasshoppers. I had been punished for this, and I think if I had not I should have continued doing it and worse. Cruelty seems to be natural in man. It is only kindness that must be taught, often cruelly, with a stick. That is the way I was taught it. There is some logic in this, as one gets some idea of pain with this eye-for-an-eye method of justice which a child, being primitive, can understand. Like the nurse threatening to give you something to cry for if you cry without reason.

I was, for instance, always beaten if I pointed any toy at anyone, not only a toy pistol or gun, but a stick which I was pretending to use as a gun. My brother gave me my first rifle when I was ten, a 6 mm., and I shot many small birds with it. I shot everything except robins and wrens which were protected by being God's 'cock and hen'. Later I got a .22 Winchester which came into two parts that I could shove down my trousers, and I used to go off poaching with it. I got a rabbit or two and one pheasant, I think, which, not daring to bring home, I cooked in the forest over a fire of twigs. My mother was allergic to cats and I had been brought up to hate them, though later I became a cat-lover and now have ten. The gardener, Louis, used to snare them and eat them. I have eaten them with him in a *ragoût* and they taste like rabbit. I skinned everything I killed and tried to set them up by following the directions in a small manual of taxidermy I had bought second-hand somewhere. I was always buying old books and prints. Things that my mother called 'that boy's rubbish'.

I was quite obviously of the material from which delinquents are made. Bold, imaginative and always planning new exploits. I was never caught. But suppose I had been, suppose my parents had not been in a position to use money, to pull strings, to extricate me – I should have ended in jail and begun a career of crime. It is a great error to assume that crime does not pay. It has paid many men very well. We are living in an era of successful criminals. It is the unsuccessful who are caught. But I'm sure that many of them started as boys no worse than I.

I believe, however, that there are bad strains of men as there are bad strains of animals – dogs, horses, bulls, that are killers from father to son. If a predilection for music, letters, art can be inherited, or a susceptibility to certain diseases, then so can the weakness that leads, given the correct conditions, to crime.

On one of my poaching expeditions I nearly got into serious trouble. There was a big estate a mile or so away that was carefully preserved and surrounded by a six-foot wire fence which had always intrigued me. I thought the business over for a week or two and then decided to cut the wire. I did this and got in. The property was alive with game and after a short walk I came to a large shallow lake in which there were several masked hides for duck-hunters. They were joined by a raised causeway, a very

narrow path, and as I went along it I sprang a man-trap. Had I
not been wearing football boots it would have smashed my leg.
It was an enormous gin a foot in diameter and armed with
spikes to catch poachers. Such traps are illegal in England but
were not so then in France, where they were called wolf traps –
piège a loup – though, except in the Vosges and on the Spanish
border, there are no wolves.

I got the trap off my boot and pulled it up. It was attached by a
chain to a peg driven into the bank. I threw it into the water.
Then out of revenge I waded in – it was winter and the water came
up to my belt – caught the tethered decoy ducks that were
swimming about and killed the lot by wringing their necks.
Except for the two drakes which I took home, I left them all on
the path. I had no right there and actually no cause for revenge.
The shooting-box belonged to a banker called Huret and he
kept peafowl. I loved their wild cry, which we often heard at
home if the wind was right, and I have since then, whenever
possible, kept peafowl myself.

The next phase of my education now began. I became a day boy
with a crammer in Boulogne. At first I took the tram from home,
changing at Port de Briques and walking up the hill to De
Gruchy's house. He took a number of English boys whose
parents were living in the vicinity. Eventually I was given a
beautiful bicycle, a Rudge Whitworth, with three speeds, and
rode to school and back each day. A matter of thirty miles the
round trip.

Opposite the Boulogne abattoir, which was the nearest tram
stop for me, there was an *estaminet* where the various cock-
fighting clubs of northern France brought their birds to compete.
Cock-fighting was illegal but was apparently winked at by the
authorities. The birds travelled in canvas bags with brassbound
eyelet holes to give them air. While the competitors were eating
lunch and drinking the bags hung on pegs above their heads.
When they had done the fights began. The cockpit was a fenced-
in area in the backyard. It had two small doors opposite each
other. The contestants crouched bent forward, holding their
birds in both hands, and at a given signal thrust them into the
ring. The birds faced one another, beak to beak, and then flew
upwards, striking downwards. There are few more beautiful

birds than game fowl. One kind in particular I liked was grey
with red hackles. Others had dark iridescent breasts and tails.
There was one white one speckled with brown. After the first two
fights I bet on the older, more experienced birds. They were easy
to recognize because their dubbed combs, instead of being
smooth, showed the scars of other battles. I won about 20 francs,
having started with a capital of five. I only saw one cock run
away. His owner went into the ring and wrung his neck. About
half the fights ended in the death of a bird. Sometimes both were
in a bad state. When a cock went down – either dead or beaten –
and lay panting in the dust, the victor would stand beside him,
raise himself on his toes, flap his wings and crow. I saw one cock
kill himself by driving his own spurs into the back of his head.
When a cock strikes having flown up, he flings himself backwards in the air and brings his legs back almost to the level of his
tail before driving his spurs downwards with all his force. This
accident occurred because the spurs were not properly adjusted.
Fighting-cocks have their own natural horny spur sawn off,
leaving a short stub over which the ring base of the needle-sharp
steel spur is adjusted on a pad of cotton-wool, the whole being
then bound in place with fine whipcord. The cocks when armed
have corks on their spurs; these are withdrawn as their handlers
put them into the ring.

There were cock-fighting clubs all over France. Our club, the
Boulonnais, would compete with the Lille Club, for instance.
The cocks were matched by weight, like boxers. A fighting-cock
is very strong. I had one that weighed ten pounds. He once
ripped open my heavy Bedford cord riding breeches with one
kick while I held him between my legs.

Game cocks are always dubbed. The comb and wattles are cut
off when they are very young so that they have the heads of
turkey buzzards. Their carriage is proud and their eyes red, wild
and fierce.

I agree with Hemingway about cock-fighting not being cruel
(as opposed to bull-fighting which, of course, was one of his
main interests). Game cocks have only one idea in their heads: to
kill any other cock within range. If they hear a cock crow they
will go and look for him. They are not tortured into fury like
bulls, nor are they irrevocably condemned to death. A successful

fighting-cock is given a harem of wives and pampered in every way.

The slaughter-house into which I drove myself almost daily was a strange experience. Like a Goya drawing. Bloody men seized a sheep from the group that huddled in a corner watching the murder of their friends, cut its throat and threw it to their collaborators, who began at once to flay it on the cobbles outside the killing-room. These rooms were large, three-sided and blood-spattered. Oxen were killed by being stabbed with a short knife in the vertebrae just behind the horns. It was remarkably skilful but how many failures had been required to learn this skill? One stab and the ox fell. It was very neat. Then men flung themselves upon the quivering carcase. Its throat was cut and the arterial blood poured out on to the dirty stones. A man brought an enormous bellows that he inserted into the belly of the beast through a small hole cut by an assistant. The ox was now blown up like a motor tyre. It looked bloated, like those animals that have been drowned and are filled with gas. Then the air was let out. This facilitated skinning by bursting the tissues that held the outer skin to the inner. But most terrible of all to me was the line of blood drinkers, women and girls, black-shawled, white-faced, all suffering from anaemia, who had been ordered by their doctors to drink hot blood. They held cups and glasses in their hands which the butchers filled, catching the blood as it ran out of the severed arteries, staining the vessels with the blood on their hands as the women stained their own through holding them. Their mouths and faces were bloody like those of vampires. As I had just read *Dracula*, this scene had a profound effect on me. But no matter how often I went, I never got over my feeling of nausea.

Pigs were stunned first with a big wooden maul and then had their throats cut. There were horses, too, but I could never bring myself to watch them being slaughtered. Nothing was clean, everything stank. There was, over the whole great factory of death, an aura of brutality which I have never forgotten, and a smell of putrid blood, meat – hot meat – excrement and urine, that rose from the blood-stained cobbles. There may also have been an odour of fear. How much fear had there been here from animals knowing they were going to die? I forced myself to go to the abattoir several times a week to try and get used to the blood. But I never did. I got over some of my nausea and did not faint, but that was about all.

It is curious now to think of nobody saying a word when a boy of twelve wandered in and out of an abattoir or attended cock-fights with a lot of men – mostly coal-miners – who were, I suppose, about as rough as they come.

Since that experience I have always hated to sell animals for slaughter. Between leaving the farm they know – their home – and their death in an abattoir there is great and incalculable agony. If possible, animals should be slaughtered at home, shot as they stand, between the eyes.

I do not remember many of the other boys whom De Gruchy taught. There was Charlie Black, whose father owned the Globe Hotel and who had a very nice brindle and white bull bitch. Bennet, whose father owned the Bennet Line of cross-channel cargo boats. And there was Read, an American, the son of a consul, I think, who had three sisters who were, from our point of view, very fast. It appeared they could be kissed. I was very much afraid of them. They were very pretty and though quite young, very grown-up. Very American in fact, with the sophisti-cated charm of all American teen-agers. But that was new in Europe then. John Read collected firearms and had a fine lot of them, particularly pistols and automatics.

CHAPTER 11

HARDELOT

THE memories of the three periods of my life at Hardelot tend to blur and merge. There was the time when I lived there, the time that I spent my school holidays there, and the five years I spent there after the war. There is also a sort of vagueness about those years. I do not know how true this is with other people, but with me, though childhood is very clear, the period of relatively intensive education combined with puberty and adolescence are both telescoped and distorted. Those times I can only see as in a mirror which either enlarges or minimizes them. I see no real chronology. Only pictures. Many of them of great beauty. For it was now that I really began to see beauty. And naturally wanted to capture it – to hold it in my hand. This may be why so many boys collect butterflies.

I shall never forget one small green dell, set like an oasis in the forest. There was a spring there that fed a pond surrounded by poplar trees and birches, but much of it was open and grew flowers that were particularly attractive to all the brightest common butterflies. Peacocks, red admirals, fritillaries, painted ladies, sulphurs and tortoiseshells were always to be found there by the dozen. I would sit in the sun watching them for hours as they drank the nectar of the flowers with their long tongues, as they fluttered, flew, courted and mated. There were, too, the great blue-green dragonflies as long as my finger, and on the lily-pads beautiful green and black striped frogs with golden eyes. These were the so-called edible frogs, though the French eat any frog. The water weeds were full of pond life and I could always capture beautiful orange-bellied newts by pulling some of the weeds to the bank. I swam in the warm water and lay naked in the sun, watching the butterflies and listening to the summer hum of insects.

On two occasions in the deciduous forest I saw the finest of all European butterflies – the purple emperor – flying high in the trees. I tried to trap them with a bait of carrion. They will come down to rotten meat to sip the juices, but they never returned or, if they did, I missed them.

Then there were the wild geese that used to pass overhead in winter and sometimes come down on the common. And once three wild swans, flying very low and close, against a dark grey winter sky over winter-killed yellow reeds and black water. Something I have never forgotten. There is much magnificence about a wild swan on the wing.

There were expeditions to the beach in winter with the two-wheeled haycart to pick up driftwood. Bulkheads and planks washed off the ships in storms. We found plenty of it. And this wood burnt well with wonderful green flames from the copper nails and fittings that were embedded in it.

There were the big flocks of crows that gathered in the winter – a mixture of carrion and hooded crows – that travelled the countryside in search of food and returned to roost in the pines of the dunes each night. There were hundreds of them and the rush of their wings as they passed overhead in the dusk made a noise like the wind and their droppings pattered like rain beneath them.

I used to collect glow-worms – only the female glowed – and wear them on my hat at night. The males were a sort of brown beetle and the females black slug-like insects whose lights came out of holes in their sides.

I generally rode alone but sometimes my father hired a horse to come with me from a peasant nearby who had been a Cuirassier. This horse was white with black spots – as if a bottle of ink had been thrown at his quarters.

About this time I got lice in my hair from leaning back against the seat in the tram. I was so ashamed that I told no one and got rid of them with kerosene and one of the small tooth-combs that were then sold for this purpose. Another embarrassing thing also happened: I got worms. But I cured myself with the powdered Areca Nut we used for the dogs. I had them once before when I was quite small and was terrified, thinking my inside was coming out. Elsa and my mother dosed me and got rid of them but this time it was a do-it-yourself job; the main problem being how to starve myself for twenty-four hours without causing too much comment. I managed it by feeding my meat to the dogs under the table.

I spent a great deal of time working with Louis, our gardener. An interesting man who bred canaries and mules, mules being crosses between canaries and goldfinches, siskins or linnets. These he captured by using decoy female birds to get them into traps and nets. The migrating goldfinches were the big brightly-coloured Siberian kind. He baited his net with their favourite food – the fluffy heads of thistles – which gives these birds their French name, *chardonneret*. He hung a small cage with a hen goldfinch in it beside the thistles. When the cocks passed overhead she would call them down. The net was about ten feet long, mounted on two sticks, controlled by a thin cord that looped through an iron peg in the ground. The end of the cord was about sixty feet from the trap and when Louis saw the birds were feeding on the thistles, he gave the cord a jerk which brought the net over the thistles and imprisoned the birds. Many trapped birds died, but some lived and Louis increased his income by their sale. I had a small aviary of wild birds he had caught for me, and it never occurred to me then that it was wrong or cruel. Louis taught me to set snares and to trap starlings by means of a line to which were attached black horsehair loops (pulled horsetail hairs) with slip knots. These were put on about a foot apart. The string was then stretched criss-cross on small pegs near a gate where cows had been standing and there were plenty of cow pats. The starlings, looking for maggots in the pats, caught their legs in the nooses and were easily picked up.

One of my most destructive amusements was to get into a plantation of young fir trees, climb one of them and then, holding the top, jump off. It bent over in an arc and broke with me holding on to it like a parachute. The tree of course never recovered. I was never caught.

Those were the days when men told stories. Radio, TV and night-club had not yet killed all conversation, and if I could remember some of the stories I heard from my father, my uncles, Mr Danford and others, I should be a richer man today. But there was no reason to suppose then that I should ever write though it was here at Hardelot that I met my first writers and publishers.

We lived in the lower cottage in the summer, and let the Châlet d'Hardelot, where we had some interesting tenants. A novelist whose name I forget. A quantity surveyor who had a blonde Alice-in-Wonderland daughter called Kathleen on whom Kathleen in *How Young They Died* was based nearly sixty years later. The Countess of Cromarty and her husband, Major Blunt-Mackenzie. Major Blunt-Mackenzie told me one day that he never used a toilet if he was in the country, and each morning he used to walk over to the forest a mile away. I thought this a very good idea and often emulated him. Hers was a title that descended through the female line, one of the very few in existence. Then there were the Spottiswoodes, the publishers, with their two children: Andrew, who was at Eton, and an older girl, Betty, a brunette, very sparkling and attractive, who did ballet and of whom I became enamoured though she never knew it. She married a stockbroker.

I was in love, then, all the time in a most inconspicuous manner, with a number of beautiful young women, all years older than I. Joan Smith was another. She was a lovely, willowy, brown-haired girl, with immense brown eyes and a scar above her lip where she had been bitten by a bulldog. Her father had bred bulldogs and she had been holding one under each arm and had been bitten as they quarrelled out of jealousy. Her father was a stockbroker but as a young man he had at one time been broke and hunted egrets in Florida. He told me about it and how he hated it because they only got their plumes when they had nestlings, and when the parents were shot the young birds died. But it was a way of making a living, the only way just then. Joan was on the stage. She acted under the name of Joan Challoner and married Harry Welchman, the musical comedy star. I met him early in the war. He was a very handsome, fair man, who at that time was a captain in the artillery. I was by way of courting Joan's sister, Eileen, who was about my own age – pretty, very intelligent and sophisticated. She was my girl-friend for several years, but I never got beyond holding her hand.

Condette was ideal for writing. A Mrs York Miller who wrote serials took a house there. Heath Hoskins and his wife who were both on the *Daily Mail* – she also wrote novels – came whenever they could get out of England. I was much impressed by them. They drank nothing but champagne. Mrs Miller had a son, Alderne, with whom I used to play. He was very intelligent. He knew the population of every large town in the world, or was it only Europe? I didn't even know the capitals. It made me very ashamed.

Blériot had a villa at Hardelot and I saw him set off for Cap Gris Nez to make his famous cross-channel flight. This was considered a great triumph. It was on this splendid beach that Blériot developed the sand yacht, which I think he invented.

I spent a lot of time at the lake. I used to fish for perch, roach and bream. I never caught much but it was pleasant to sit and watch the float bobbing about. I used to swim there, too, in spite of the dead dogs that one sometimes found in it. It was called the Lac des Miroirs – Mirror Lake – because of the way it reflected the scenery. Presumably because the water was almost black with peat. This peat was used for burning. It was made into bricks by an old man who dipped out the mud on the bottom with a bailer on a pole, and put it into small brick-sized forms which he emptied out on to a carpet of reeds that he had laid in readiness. When dried the peat-blocks were sold by the thousand and burnt beautifully with a red glow that gave off a lovely smell. They burnt slowly into very fine ash, almost without smoke. At one end of the lake there were white and yellow water-lilies and wild yellow iris.

At the age of about fourteen I had a strange experience which affected me as an unbelievable infringement of human dignity. In the train between Hardelot Plage and Pont de Briques a woman sitting near me addressed us, saying wasn't it disgraceful that a girl of her daughter's age – twelve – should wet herself. Whereupon she raised her daughter's dress and petticoat and showed her wet knickers. I was most upset and embarrassed for the little girl, who began to cry bitterly, and I was shocked that a mother could do such a thing. I have never forgotten the scene though it took place almost sixty years ago. Later, when I began to understand a bit about psychology, I often wondered what the effect must have been on a young girl. How deep would she bury it in her unconscious and with what result? Would it fester there and poison her life? I have never been quite satisfied that Freudian analysis is a good thing. It seems quite possible that the bones of disasters that we bury are meant to stay buried. But a public exhibition of this kind would probably have at least some effect on the character of the girl whose accident had obviously been caused by her modesty about relieving herself in the open. I had a parallel experience when I was four. A terrible thing happened. I had been given some laxative, and when I was almost home from my daily walk with my governess I had an accident. I know the exact place in the Rue Laurent Picha about fifty yards up from the Rue Pergolese towards the Bois. I had on a complete red costume, so it must have been autumn or winter. What an impression it made on me, the first really bad, shameful thing to occur in my life! It was not my fault but a lot of things that happen to us are not our fault. We are all the victims at various times of historic, social and sexual forces. Wars, illness, financial reverses, divorces, deaths. But it is curious that the really bad ones – earthquakes, cyclones, floods and fires – are so often described as acts of God.

I regard myself as having been very fortunate in being brought up in France. I spoke French as well as English, but most important of all, I learnt to work. The French people in those days really worked. At Hardelot all the cupboards built in our house were made at night by a carpenter who worked elsewhere all day. Often in the summer when I got up early to take my dog out I found all the washing, including sheets, already drying on the line by five o'clock. These industrious examples developed in me the ability to work hard and fast for long hours.

In France, both in Paris and in the north, I was always aware of art. I knew artists and watched them. Art and beauty in all its forms became an integral part of my existence; so did a sense of history. I liked old castles and Roman earthworks. I liked to walk where the legions had marched, to think of the men who had been before me, or, alternatively, its opposite – the wilds, the bush, the forests and the sea that were as they had always been, untouched, unaltered by man.

I was now considered strong enough to go back to school in England and for some obscure reason my parents decided to send me to an agricultural school – Carson Manor (not its real name) in Somerset, which catered for delicate boys. The boys did a lot of farm work: milked the cows, fed the pigs and poultry, weeded the crops. They had ordinary classes with the mathematics based on such practical things as the number of bricks needed for a wall or a building, or pipes to drain a field. I learnt carpentry and brick-laying. There were half a dozen horses I rode a lot. Naturally we groomed and fed the riding and cart horses as well as looking after the other stock. There was some rough woodland shooting and I often went out with a boy called Parr. The school had several twelve-bore shotguns and we were issued with cartridges that went down on the bill.

I quite enjoyed myself here once I had made it clear after a fight or two that I was not interested in homosexuality. What my parents did not know was that this school of about fifty boys ranging in age from twelve to nineteen was a place where boys were sent when they had been expelled or asked to leave other schools. They were either homosexuals or cheated or stole or had been caught in bed with a housemaid. An oddball school, in fact, with the pupils being given vestigial agricultural training to fit them for the colonies where, in those days, such misfits were sent farming, the idea being to get them out of England before they created a real scandal. It would have been hard to find a more representative collection of liars, thieves or perverts among the sons of the relatively well-to-do.

When my parents came to understand the set-up, I was removed and sent to Lancing. It is curious, however, that this academy for pederasts and upper-class delinquents should have taught me some things that were to prove of greater value than much of what I was later to learn at a public school. It was here that I learnt to kill and dress chickens, carpenter and lay bricks.

CHAPTER 12

THE SECOND STRETCH

LANCING was a good school. I was as happy or not happy there as I should have been anywhere else, except that they did not play rugby and spent too much time in chapel. I had no serious objections to it. It was something to be endured till I grew up and got away. That was always my dream – growing up, breaking away. Freedom to see what was over the next hill, and above all freedom from the necessity of explaining my actions. Elsewhere the teaching would have been no better, the games no more boring, the rules as foolish, the food as bad, the discomfort as great. Elsewhere I should have been beaten, as I was here by prefects and masters, the recompense being the knowledge that one day I would be a prefect myself and able to beat other small children for minor breaches of etiquette, such as putting their hands in their pockets in front of their jackets and pushing back their skirts over their hips before they were in the upper school. Also wearing coloured socks if they were not in the sixth form, and things of this nature.

It was all a very valuable experience, a part of that character-forming process to which all English boys of the privileged classes are entitled. If it doesn't break them, it makes them. It only breaks the weaklings and the artists. But, knowing all I do, if I had a son today I should send him to an English public school – to Eton if I could get him in, and I should put him down as soon as he was born.

The words public and private school have opposite meanings in England and America. A public school in England is a private school in America. There are various grades – Eton, Harrow and Winchester probably being the three best. And Eton to my mind the best of the three. Not only do they turn out a very special kind of boy, but it is a large school and the only one which carries a spirit of solidarity right on through the life of all old Etonians. Their tie – thin pale blue stripes on a black ground – is a passport to English society. I even doubt if there is any Etonian out of a job who is not a real wrong 'un. At one time most of the important posts in the Government were held by Etonians. This is less true now but the proportion remains very high.

I have had many friends who were at Eton and it would have been impossible to find men of greater charm and culture.

In the next grade I put Rugby, Wellington, Charterhouse, Repton, Shrewsbury, Lancing, Westminster and others whose names I have forgotten, and then the grammar schools. Many people would arrange these schools in a different order. Actually the variation is small, the main difference being the richness of the school's endowment, its age, and the social standing of the parents of the pupils.

Lancing was a church school. It was meant mainly for the sons of parsons, who paid a reduced fee. At least four of the masters were parsons – Bowlbey, the head, the others being the Reverends Bond, Fox and Lucas. Our great pride was the chapel, which resembled a cathedral. It was an immense affair that they had been building for about fifty years when I went there and I do not know if it is finished yet.

I created a scandal by refusing to be confirmed. This was due to a combination of my principles and natural idleness. I did not want to go to the confirmation classes. But as my father was an atheist or, if not that, an agnostic and free thinker, I had all the arguments. I was also very subtle. I said, when I was brought before the Head: 'I will do it if you insist upon it, but I do not believe in it, which will make it the act of a hypocrite acting under pressure.' I knew I had him. He wrote to my father, who said the choice was mine. So I was not confirmed. I cannot see that it has made any difference in my life as I seldom go to church. I was brought up nominally in the Church of England. As a child I said my prayers: 'God bless Mother and Dad and make me a good boy.' I went to Sunday School. I was baptized in the English Church in Paris. The war, which made many men turn to God, made others – like myself – deny the possibility of His existence. A god who permitted this holocaust was not for me. I am a hedonist, an agnostic, an atheist, or something of all three with no positive preference. That there is something, some force that governs the universe and everything in it, is certain, but also certain to my mind is the fact that this is no anthropomorphic God of love. It is a force, a mystery, which men, unable to explain by any logical means, have solved by inventing a God in their own image. As man is the only animal aware of death he had also to arrange for another life after this one ended: the Christian heaven, the Moslem paradise, the Viking Valhalla, the Indians' Happy Hunting Ground. But who has come back to tell of it? One day each of us will know the answer. That will be time enough. There would appear to be forces of both good and evil as inexplicable actualities with man balanced precariously between them as a social and political being. They are popularly represented by God or Jesus on the one hand and Satan on the other. They could equally be described in a mathematical formula as X and Y producing an insoluble equation. The force of X may be the human being trying to rid himself of the primitive and savage forces of Y which also exist within him. The important thing about any religion is its ethic: the morals of a good Christian, Jew, Moslem or Buddhist differ very little from each other.

At Lancing we wore a uniform of black jackets and striped trousers like miniature businessmen, with Eton collars and straw boaters both winter and summer. The boaters were decorated with a blue and white striped hatband, the school colours.

The old school and regimental tie joke is a never-ending source of amusement in America. And why not? All foreign customs are funny. Why, I have even been considered a homosexual because I used a large silk handkerchief and kept it up my left sleeve. Most soldiers do this as they cannot be buttoning and unbuttoning their pockets every time they want to wipe their noses. So here we have a symbol with a different meaning on both sides of the ocean. Homosexual or soldier, according to the point of view. But to the Englishman the tie seems a very good idea. By it you can recognize men who were at your school, or in your regiment, and if you do not actually know them you are still likely to have mutual friends. In America, a somewhat similar object is achieved by hanging a wild animal's tooth or examples of the locksmith's art on the watch-chain. The idea is the same but in many ways the tie is better as it is more conspicuous. Americans are very fond of our ties and one can hardly blame them as they are very pretty. The Household Brigade tie of dark blue and red stripes was originally popularized by the Duke of Windsor when, as Prince of Wales, he visited the United States. But this habit confuses the English. It confuses them as much as an Englishman wearing an elk tooth or Phi Beta Kappa Key would an American.

Certain things I did learn at Lancing. English from W. B. (Dick) Harris, a Cambridge soccer blue who almost converted me to the game by the grace and beauty of his play. He wore a Cambridge blue blazer varied by pink Westminster – two of the most attractive I ever saw. He called me Sandy, and gave me a soft leather-bound copy of De Quincey's *Confessions of an Opium Eater*, and I owe him a great deal. Curiously enough, after I left, he also taught Alec Waugh, who was there during the war. Dick Harris is the only master at Lancing who made any impression on me.

Sometimes Dick's brother, S.S. Harris, the English soccer international, came to stay with him; to watch the two of them practising with a soccer ball was beautiful, like a ballet. I was, I suppose, something of a favourite with Dick because I was one of the few who really took an interest in English.

I have often thought that all good schoolmasters must have a special affinity for boys – not homosexual – but men who under other circumstances might have become so. How else could they stand, much less like, so many little monsters, small boys being by nature idle, dirty, cruel, impertinent, liars and thieves – little savages till civilized by education and discipline?

In chapel the masters wore their gowns with variously decorated hoods. Chapel was a great feature of our cultural life, one which left me unmoved except that I liked to sing hymns with good tunes like 'Onward, Christian soldiers' or 'There is a green hill far away'. I did, however, learn from the Bible reading I listened to. It was later to have an effect on my writing. I also read the Bible during every service. I found the language enthralling and the subject-matter, particularly of the Old Testament, quite fascinating.

I made a few friends – Jackie Church, Philip Simpson, Hodgson, Kaffir Jackson, a boy with glasses who came from Gwelo in Rhodesia. I still have a battle-axe that I got from him – I forget what I swopped it for. I collected stamps and other articles and discovered that I got much better value for my money if I waited till nearly the end of term when all the boys were broke. We each took a pound to school with us which the housemaster kept and doled out as we asked for it. We also got sixpence a week pocket money. But I saved my money and then bought what I wanted – books, flashlight, knives, stamps and the like – at greatly reduced prices when the market was down. I spent a lot of my pocket money on stamps, buying them from other boys, swapping duplicates, and buying them from folders sent by stamp dealers, which just shows how honest we were. The prices were marked – sixpence, ninepence, a shilling, even half-a-crown. I think we signed for them and gave the money to a master who posted it back with the unsold stamps. I bought some high-value BSA used stamps (Rhodesia) from Kaffir Jackson which were very attractive. By this time the big blue stamp book my brother Eric had given me was getting filled up and my father suggested that I amalgamate my collection with his. I naturally agreed, assuming that one day it would be mine. That day, however, never came because in 1920 when I asked about the stamps he said he had sold all four of the big loose-leaf Stanley Gibbons albums.

I made a little money by eating live moths, caterpillars (not the hairy ones) and flies (but not bluebottles). More money was earned by exhibiting my bruises after I had been beaten. We all did this, receiving, I think, threepence a peep. We usually did it in the swimming bath so that we could not be accused of any monkey business. This was an obsession with the authorities. There *was* monkey business, as there must be wherever a number of young males varying in age from eleven to nineteen are incarcerated for months at a time. But I don't know if this is, in the end, much worse than what goes on at co-educational schools. At least none of us ever had a baby. Personally I had nothing to do with these things, not through any particular virtue but I just did not like to be messed around. There was one scandal in my time. A boy was caught doing something – we never found out what it was – and expelled. This was my first great drama, my first experience of society acting against a criminal. Having been caught, he was banished to the San, in charge of the matron. The dormitory saw him no more. The next day, before the whole school and all the staff, he was birched (not caned) in the great hall by the headmaster, the Reverend Henry Bowlbey. The scene took place on the raised dais. The school porter held the boy over a chair while the school doctor, Dr Lambert, stood beside him to resuscitate him if he should faint. It was a revolting and shocking spectacle.

I was beaten quite a lot with a pliable cane by Mr Smythe, my housemaster, for various sins, but mainly because I did not do the lines I was set. Lines were the accepted punishment, a hundred lines, two hundred, copied from some book. Or one line repeated, such as 'I must not be late for chapel' five hundred times. When these lines accumulated to such an extent that it was impossible to do them, they could be exchanged for a beating. Sometimes we tied two pens together and so managed to write two lines at the same time. More than two would not go into even a wide-mouthed inkpot. Most of us had stylographic pens, a kind of fountain pen that had no nib, just a point, like a ballpoint today, which was fed from the barrel. When fountain pens were invented they had gold nibs. The best was a Swan. But all pens had to be filled with ink which was extracted from a bottle of special ink with a fountain-pen filler (called an eye-dropper today). Swan ink came with an outer bottle of wood, coloured red, and was the easiest to pack. No wonder every little boy's hands were covered with ink, since he had to unscrew his pen and fill it every couple of days. Then came the Onoto, a self-filling pen – a great invention. This pen contained a pump. You stuck the nib into the ink and sucked it into the barrel. But we still got ink on ourselves, our work, clothes and desks.

One beating I think I deserved was due to a trick I played on the assistant nurse in the Sanatorium. The San was run by Sister Babcock. She was a stout woman with a hairy face. All she seemed to love was her big tomcat, a tabby Persian, which caught a rabbit almost every day. Boys she had very little time for, especially boys like me who only had bad colds and chilblains. However, I enjoyed myself in the San. The food was better and I had plenty to read. The assistant nurse, a tall dark-haired young woman whom we called Pop-Eye – a thyroid type – we all disliked; she was insatiably curious about boys and always tried to catch us dressing or undressing. One morning I decided to fix her, so I rolled my pyjama trousers up to my thighs, put on a shirt and waited for her to come in. As usual she came and instead of modestly turning my back on her I faced her and, raising my shirt, said: 'If you're so keen to see sights, take a look!' She said: 'You horrible dirty boy!' and ran out of the room. She reported me and I was beaten by my housemaster in spite of my plea of justified non-exposure. But our Peeping Tomasina was cured and was replaced next term.

My second term a red-haired boy called Hammond died of blood poisoning. He had cut himself on some glass in the lab and the wound had become infected. He was not in my house and I hardly knew him, but I was impressed by the accident and took extra care with my experiments. The only other boy's death I had known was that of a scout, one of the two hundred or so Sir Francis Vane had brought over to camp at Hardelot in a field near the château. He was drowned while bathing in the sea. I happened to be riding on the beach at the time and galloped back with the news. Both these were, as it were, theoretical deaths. I had so far never seen a body.

I do not remember any tremendous emotional upheaval with the onset of puberty among any of us. I do not think we were even fully aware of what had taken place. We now had erections, wet dreams and some boys masturbated secretly, terrified of being caught, beaten and possibly expelled. Masturbation, we were told, led to lunacy and blindness. This we doubted. My father had told me not to touch myself and I didn't. Not till the war. Nor did I smoke.

Romain Rolland in *Journey's End* summed things up very well when he wrote: 'If a man told children that there is an age in adolescence when the soul, not yet having found its balance, is capable of crimes and suicide and the worst sort of physical and moral depravity and were to excuse these things, at once these offences would spring into being.' And this is what has now happened. Romain Rolland saw the possibility in 1910.

My erotic interests, like those of most of my friends, were concerned with seeing how high we could pee in the urinal, and looking up sexy bits in the Bible where 'carnal knowledge' and 'lying with' occurred. Reading the Song of Solomon and the story of Susannah and the Elders in the Apocrypha, which was included in some of the chapel Bibles. There were three or four very pretty boys, always very neatly dressed, who were said to be the friends of bigger, older boys. But I never paid much attention to the gossip. To be caught in someone else's bed led to being expelled, which in those days meant a ruined career. No university or Sandhurst, if they were going into the army, would accept them. No chance of any public service.

Fear, malnutrition, cold baths, compulsory games and a great deal of work, even if I learned very little, all kept the moral standard relatively high. The atmosphere as well as the architecture of Lancing was monastic. As far as I was concerned it was better for me than a co-educational school where my attraction to girls would certainly have led me astray at an early age. My criticism of those American high schools I visited was that they were too comfortable and the children too happy. You go to school to learn, not to enjoy yourself. And if it is unpleasant one leaves it much better able to face a world in which one has to fight one's way.

Every boy took a rug to school with him. And we needed them. There were never enough blankets in winter. Too few blankets could be a contributory cause of homosexuality, forcing boys to creep into each other's beds for warmth, snuggling together like puppies. In summer we used the blankets to lie on outside when we watched cricket matches or read under the trees.

Every night we knelt by our beds to say our prayers, and under every bed was a chamber-pot, emptied in the morning by the chamber maids. This was general everywhere. Under double beds, two chamber-pots. They generally matched the jug and basin on the washstand. These sets, which included a slop pail, were usually painted with flower designs and were often made of the best china – Crown Derby, Worcester, Spode and other ware. Later, when living in America, Raymond Massey, the actor, showed me his collection. They looked like giant tea cups in an enormous glass-fronted cabinet. To us at school, where we had plain white ones, they were jerries or piss-pots. And boys with sisters told jokes about how they had put Eno's Fruit Salts into their sisters' chambers, which fizzed and frightened them when put into use. There was also a toilet but this was only supposed to be used for major purposes. Boys were not allowed to wander round the dormitory. Lights were put out at 9.30 or 10 but some of us used to read with flashlights hidden under the bedclothes. I used to sleep in my socks and keep my vest and drawers in the bed so that they would be warm when I put them on. Many of us also dressed under the covers after the cold baths which were compulsory every morning, even in mid-winter. We had a hot bath once a week. There were hot showers in the changing room which we used after games.

Until they begin to be interested in girls, boys do not as a rule worry very much about dirt. I changed, however, and really began to like washing when we grew some loofahs in the garden. They are a kind of cucumber. When ripe, they are hung and allowed to dry out. The flesh then falls away and the fibres are left. I really enjoyed using my loofah. At home I bathed in the lake and the sea so much that I had to be forced to bath in hot water. It seemed such a waste of time.

I really do not remember any adolescent problems bar some horrified surprise at my first wet dream, because I thought I had wet my bed. We had a couple of bedwetters in the house who slept on rubber sheets and were ostracized for something they could not help. In those days there was no psychological understanding of these things and boys are particularly brutal to each other when faced by any unusual behaviour. Like all the others, I had fought for my rights since I was seven, punching and wrestling with boys who crossed me, pinched my pencils or used my books, or to solve arguments which could only be resolved by force. All this, till some kind of pecking order was established.

There were three Russian princes at Lancing, two of them – Michael and Constantine – in 'Olds', my house. Constantine was very fat and strong and a fine swimmer, with a placid disposition. Michael was my age and very strong. He and I fought in a semi-friendly manner at least once a week. But never decisively. We regarded our princes as exotic abnormalities. They had big estates in the Crimea and a special teacher came once a week to teach them Russian. Their guardian used to visit them, coming in a big chauffeur-driven car when cars were still almost a curiosity.

The swimming bath was indoors and heated. We swam more or less whenever we wanted to. Most of us were uncircumcized and were interested in each other's sexual organs. We bathed naked and I still remember one boy's eight-inch penis. I do not think we were particularly prurient-minded but such an organ was bound to cause comment and envy. The toilets we used in the daytime were really latrines, the seats, separated by doorless partitions, were placed over a concrete trough that was periodically flushed with water. But the smell of excrement and Jeyes Fluid was always strong, particularly in summer.

Since my time I understand that everything has been much improved, just as, before my time, things were very much worse at all the famous schools of England. One outstanding fact, from a boy's point of view, was that we did not get enough to eat. Each term we took a tuckbox with us. These boxes were made of deal with standard black enamel hinges and a lock or padlock. Our parents filled them with food of different kinds, a compromise between the boys' choice and the parents' nutritional views. I always took a big seven-pound jar of marmalade, several pots of assorted jams, a variety of potted meats, such as shrimp paste, chicken and ham, and bloater paste. One round flat white china jar of Gentleman's Relish, tins of sardines, corned beef, pilchards in tomato sauce, and a very big and rich fruit cake, the kind that will keep for months. These foods were used to supplement the meals we got – particularly in giving us something to spread on our bread. There was plenty of bread.

Then there was extra food. This our parents paid for. It consisted of a boiled egg with our tea and I suppose about one boy in six obtained this luxury. It was very embarrassing to eat it under the eyes of the eggless boys, but hunger is possibly the strongest motive force in the world and fortunately it is very difficult to share a boiled egg.

We did our preparation in our house common room which had benches and tables round three sides. On the fourth side there was a fireplace with two high-backed settles which were used only by the sixth form, who were also allowed cushions which we called very aptly soft arses. Behind the tables and benches were the lockers where we kept our books, papers and treasures. They had no locks but nothing was ever stolen. On the doors we pinned our pin-ups. Very respectable photographs of actresses, race horses and yachts. I had pictures of Gertie Millar, Lily Elsie and Gladys Cooper on mine.

One of the practical jokes we played on each other was to put itching powder in a boy's underclothes when he was asleep. I got a very superior kind called *poil à gratter* in France. It tickled so much that it sent you crazy. We had a good library. We were allowed to read reference books there and take out other books such as selected novels and short stories for which we signed and were responsible.

At quite an early age I showed signs of not being respectable or, as Louise, my mother's French maid, always put it, not being at all *comme il faut*. One of the first sayings of my father's that I remember was that there were more ways of killing a cat than by choking it with butter. My interpretation of the phrase was that there was usually a way out of, or round, any forbidden situation. So when I was made to play soccer, a game I despised, like my Boer ancestors, I made a plan. First I ran about hard getting very hot and receiving great praise for my activity. Then I ceased to be active. I merely stood still in the cold east wind till I was thoroughly chilled. The next day I was in the Sanatorium.

I never liked being forbidden to do things and so, as we were not allowed to eat in class, I made a plan to eat in class. I made no effort to disguise what I was doing.

'What are you eating, Graham?'

'Vaseline, sir.'

'Show it to me.' I showed him the pot.

'Now eat some.' I scooped up a big fingerful and let it melt on my tongue and then swallowed it. It was not unpleasant. It didn't taste of anything.

'Why do you do that?'

'A sore throat, sir. My mother said it was good for a sore throat.' My mother had never said anything of the kind. It was a piece of original thinking. But it worked, and the masters became conditioned to my eating Vaseline. 'He eats Vaseline,' they said. But I didn't, not all the time, though I always carried a pot in my pocket.

Then French. The French lessons bored me. I knew French very well. I refused to learn the rules of grammar. I knew the exceptions by ear, so why should I learn that bedbugs, cabbages and pebbles were exceptions of some kind? They could not catch me as I knew them all. A chair to me was as female as a cow. How could anyone imagine a cup to be male? So I said I wanted to read French books and improve my mind in prep. I obtained permission, tore the yellow backs off some of my mother's novels inserted them in the hard cover of a copy of a French classic like the *Lettres de Mon Moulin* or *Tartarin de Tarascon*, which I had disembowelled, and proceeded to regale myself with romances so highly sexed that I only understood a word here and there, and what I did understand bored me to distraction because I could not see why people wanted to do such things. Why did they keep going to bed in the afternoon? Still, I knew that I was committing a sin, that I was flouting authority, that I was enjoying a secret triumph.

Then there was fagging. Our fagging was not individual. Every boy in the lower school was a fag and their business was to attend to the wants of the prefects who, when they wanted anything, shouted 'Boy!' and all the boys got up and ran like a pack of little hounds. Down passages, up stairs, they rushed towards the voice, in an agony of fear, for any dilatoriness was liable to end in corporal punishment administered by an artist. Some prefects marked the victim's trousers with a chalk line and tried to hit it with every blow. The blows were limited to six but six cuts in one place with a cane as thick as the little finger given bv a powerful young athlete of eighteen will break the skin and draw blood. Naturally no one ever cried out. Some ended in tears but they were silent ones. This punishment took place in the prefects' common room at the end of the passage where the sixth form had their studies, and the victim was always met by a welcoming committee of his curious peers. How hard was it? Who did it? (Some were known to be worse than others.) Show me! When can we see? There is no doubt that this system served, on the whole, a useful purpose. It was legal. It functioned under a rigid code controlled by the head of the house and captain of the school. It was separate from but answerable to the higher authority of the house and head masters and was designed to deal with breaches of manners, taste, good sportsmanship and the like. A boy who funked his cold bath in the morning when there was ice on the water was disciplined. It never made him like cold water. At least it never made me like it, but it made me do a lot of things I didn't like doing.

Another beating I certainly deserved was due to raiding a kingfisher's nest in a bank by the river which we all knew about and had been warned not to touch. But I could not resist it and cut my way into the nest. Kingfishers build at the end of a tunnel in the earth where they construct a little room which they line with fishbones. And here, as I enlarged the hole, I saw the round smooth white eggs gleaming. I had done it now and there was no going back. Even if I left the nest the birds would desert and everyone would know someone had been at it because the excavation could not be hidden. So I took the eggs. What followed I should have foreseen. At roll-call it was given out that the nest had been robbed and would the boy who had done it report to the head of the school. I owned up and got what I well deserved. But it taught me to think about the price one must pay for sins which could not be concealed.

Being beaten or caned was part of the cultural pattern of my time and class. Why should I have resented it when everyone who had been to a public school had had the same treatment? Cabinet ministers, peers, parsons, generals, had all been treated in the same way. Being beaten served a number of purposes: it was a deterrent, it taught you to bear pain stoically, it taught you discipline and the cost of failure. As far as I was concerned it was much better than being reasoned with. It was no use explaining that I had done wrong, been lazy or stupid. I knew it. I resented what we called a 'pie-jaw' much more than a caning. I was never thrashed. This I would never have forgiven and I understand boys killing fathers who have brutalized them, or knocked their mothers about.

But there was much that was lovely at school. The long walks over the downs on Sunday afternoons with a couple of friends, the views of the sea, the Channel that separated me from home. It cannot have been more than fifty miles away. The sea gulls, the scent of the wild thyme, dwarfed in the poor soil and crushed beneath our feet. The chalk blue butterflies that rose in clouds. The skylarks that flung themselves singing into the sky, the grazing sheep, the shepherds standing leaning on their crooks, their dogs at their side. Putting up a hare from its form in a tussock of grass, watching rabbits play at the edge of a spinney. We knew fox earths and badger bolts, and some that were shared by both animals. We collected moorhens' eggs from the ponds and ate them.

It was all very big, very wide, a fine open part of England that was old and had history. There were traces of Roman earthworks. Hastings, where King Harold had fallen, was not far away. There were neolithic flints to be found and bits of ancient pottery and Roman glass, prismatic with exposure. There were lizards and grass snakes to be caught. The downs had an everlasting quality, they seemed like great green waves, rolling on for ever. It was strange to think that they had once been forested and that it was here that the early iron works of England had had their birth. That was where the Sussex forests had gone, up in smoke, to smelt that ancient iron for swords, for helms, for armour. To a boy the downs had much romance.

Then below the chapel there was an elm wood with a rookery. Several hundred rooks nested there and the ground beneath the trees was white with droppings and scattered with the building twigs that had been discarded, broken egg shells and sometimes a baby rook that had fallen out of the nest. These trees had seldom been climbed. It was forbidden, partly to preserve as a sanctuary for the birds, and partly because elms are dangerous trees, the branches being unreliable and breaking easily. Beyond these trees came the playing fields. I loathed cricket because I was no good at it. I was always bowled in the first over and I never learnt the places in the field. Slips, cover point and the rest remained a mere jargon to me. Longstop was the only position I knew and coveted as it was comparatively safe. The ball, if it passed the gloved hands of the wicket-keeper – and he was the only one who wore gloves – usually came low and could be stopped by the foot with relative ease. Another thing I didn't like about cricket was the fact that everyone changed position each over. By the time I was in a nice daydream I had to move. But I found a way out of cricket and that was to volunteer to mark on the rifle range – you got paid for it too. I liked sitting in a pit below the targets and pointing to each hole with a marker.

At last I was excused from all games because one of the masters, Allan Haig Brown, who shot a lot, put me in charge of his ferrets. I used to go rabbiting with him and work them. The ferrets, which are domesticated polecats, yellowish-white in colour, are put down a hole in a rabbit warren and the rabbits bolt when they scent their approach. As they come out they are shot. It is good sport as they come out fast and there is no knowing from which hole they will emerge. I also used the ferrets to poach a bit on my own with cabbage nets. These nets are pegged round the exits and when the rabbit bolts it rushes into the net which closes round it. It is then easily caught. Sometimes the ferrets would kill a rabbit and lie up. Then we would try a line ferret. We had one big polecat ferret, a different variety, dark brown and white in colour, that was put into the burrow with a collar and a long whipcord lead. With luck he would start eating the dead rabbit and, since he would not let go, he could be pulled out with the rabbit in his jaws. As ferrets hold on, there is a certain amount of trouble if they bite your finger. The only thing to do is to take the ferret's foot in your teeth and bite him back. He will then let go, but you have to be careful that he doesn't transfer his grip to your nose.

Sometimes a ferret will stay underground for a few days or even a week. But I always got them back in the end by going to the warren in the evening and picking them up as they wandered about in the twilight, which they generally do when they have had their fill of killing. A ferret is picked up between thumb and fore-finger just behind the head. Some become very tame. I had one I used to carry about with me all day. She once got out of my trouser pocket in chapel, but fortunately I spotted her before anything was noticed. Ferrets have to be kept very clean and the floors of their hutches are generally made of small mesh wire as they are subject to foot rot. I fed them mainly on bread and milk with bits of rabbit for a treat.

When a ferret is lost down a hole it can often be attracted by paunching a rabbit. To do this, the belly is opened and the hot guts pulled a little way out. The rabbit is then put into the mouth of a likely hole, well into it, and you lie down and blow the smell, which is very strong, down into the darkness. As a rule the ferret will come out at once unless it has killed. We also used ferrets for ratting in the neighbouring farmers' buildings at their request. There they flushed the rats which were killed with sticks and dogs. It takes a good ferret to face a rat and they often get badly bitten.

The other sport we had was beating the downs for partridges and hares. Twenty or so of us boys would walk over the hills, the roots and crops in the fertile bottoms, and drive the game up to the guns.

And so for a few years I climbed and fought my way slowly upwards, finally ending in the lower fifth form. My parents were determined that I should be a mining engineer, specializing in oil, because a friend of my father's had big oil interests in the Near East. I could imagine nothing less suitable. I was no good at mathematics. I hated all forms of engineering and engines and it seemed to me highly improbable that I should ever matriculate, much less get into a university. Should I succeed, however, it was my intention to tell my parents that I was going in for zoology and not engineering. I had put the idea of soldiering or being a painter out of my head as impracticable, and was prepared to accept natural history as a second or third best.

As I did not expect to pass any exam of any kind and thus get into a university, I thought I should go to Africa or the East and become a planter of tea, coffee or rubber, or go to Australia and work on a cattle station. Canada had no attraction for me as I did not like the cold and snow had no appeal.

During these years there was a lot of talk about Home Rule for Ireland, and suffragettes. Mrs Pankhurst, her daughter Christabel, and many others were sent to prison for breaking windows and chaining themselves to railings. They went on hunger strikes and were forcibly fed. England was split with pros and cons as the vote for women movement was discussed. It was in some ways like the American civil rights question of today. Women wanted to be first-class citizens. They were tired of being chattels – either servants or playthings. None of this affected me as a schoolboy except through what I read in the papers, which left me un-emotionally involved till in the 1913 Derby Emily Davidson threw herself under Anmer, the King's horse, as it came round Tattenham Corner. She was badly hurt and died shortly after-wards in hospital. This struck me as an act of mad bravery and I began to take the women's cause more seriously. Like many others, I suddenly realized that women were people, and that half the people in the world were women. Just as today we are realizing that most of the people in the world are not white.

During these years I commuted between school and my home in France. At school I wasted time, trickling it through my fingers like sand, just waiting for it to pass. At home I squandered it, throwing it away with both hands. At school a three months' term took a year to pass. I used to cross off the days and say, after half term, only forty, only thirty days. But at home even the six weeks' summer holiday went in a flash. I had hardly unpacked before I was packing up again.

CHAPTER 13

THE KING'S COMMISSION

IT must be as difficult for those who did not know the pre-First World War world to visualize it as it would have been for us, in those days, to visualize the Jules Verne–George Orwell world of today. The science fiction of Verne has come to pass, and been surpassed, as the dreams of the next lot of science-fiction writers, with their space ships and trips to the moon, are actually taking place.

The story of my life and that of my contemporaries is that of men and women who lived through this extraordinary period of unprecedented progress. If, in the end, it turns out to be progress.

There is another possibility: that of having created a Frankenstein in which not only human liberty but human character is lost in a computerized syndrome in which facts and figures take the place of human judgments and affections. Even now men are selected for jobs by machines, and wives, half in fun, are sometimes chosen by computers. We may also destroy ourselves by an atomic holocaust, a population explosion, or, less dramatically, by pollution of the air and water.

More and more people are living in cities which resemble giant antheaps – the only possible analogy – and the people themselves become more and more antlike in their behaviour patterns. There is less place for original thought or an original character. It is interesting to imagine what a great novelist like Dickens would make of people today. Mankind is no longer divided into classes, scarcely into sexes, nor into people who are good or bad. The evil are regarded as sick men. The anti-social elements blame the society that gave them birth for their failure. Personal responsibility is a thing of the past. Education has become a method of training the young to fit into a slot in the industrial or commercial machine rather than a means of developing an independent intellect. One of the results of this trend is the unbelievable boredom of Western man, who appears to welcome even war as a break in the monotony of his life. Violence, drugs, alcohol, sex are used as escape mechanisms. Boredom is a new disease, the product of an affluent society on the one hand and crippling taxation, which removes the excitement of success, on the other.

The present emphasis on sex may be due not merely to such contraceptive devices as the pill, which makes it safe, but to an attempt to escape from the mechanized computerized inhuman world into the most primitive and unchanging of all activities.

The giants of the past, from Cecil John Rhodes to John D. Rockefeller and Jacob Astor, are regarded as monsters. Respect for the law, good manners, morality, hard work, frugality, honesty, and chastity are now considered, if not actually laughable, at least unimportant.

The abandonment of the gold standard was much more than an economic measure. Gold had other, more mystic values. The phrases golden rule, a golden wedding, golden girl, golden fleece, heart of gold – all exemplify them. Life had, as it were, a golden frame, whereas today it has no frame at all. The very fact that there is a world currency crisis based on the value of gold, and that gold is being bought and hoarded, is of great psychological significance. Gold is a reality, indestructible, while paper remains paper – something which can become valueless overnight. Hoarded notes can be eaten by rats or white ants. I well remember the feel of a golden sovereign when I was tipped by a relative. Even as a boy I felt it. It might only be worth eight half-crowns but it had much more significance in those pre-war days.

Money itself is of no value, not even gold, if there is nothing to buy. A millionaire can starve on a desert island. Money is only worth what it can buy and it can buy very little today, which is why it is absurd to compare the earnings of today with those of yesterday, when a custom-made suit in the West End cost about seven guineas and a dinner jacket fourteen.

I have lived on what I made since I left school. Even in the army I managed to live on my pay. I have always had a very old-fashioned economic theory: that what I made in a year was what I had left over at the end of it. To spend all I made, whether it was £500 or £5000, meant I had only made a living. I also tried to have sufficient savings to live for a year without working, which gave me a great sense of independence and freedom. Money has several uses: the first is to live on, the second to act as a cushion against disaster.

But this was all to come. I was still at school with my dreams, hopes and fears of the real world that would, within a few years, lie before me.

I learned little at school which served any useful purpose when I left except simple arithmetic, which I was badly taught. Since then I have thought a great deal about education and feel that history and geography should be combined. National products, trade routes and wars are inextricably bound together. Practical commercial arithmetic and some understanding of the stock market are for most boys more important than algebra. If five hundred to a thousand nouns and the present tense of five verbs were taught in French, German, Spanish and Italian, anyone could make himself understood in those languages and, should he so desire, perfect his knowledge on his own. 'The pen of my aunt' is no aid to communication.

Most wars have been fought for gold, diamonds, coal, ivory, oil, rubber and timber; for lands that produced grain, silk or furs; for seas that produced fish. History did not begin with the Battle of Hastings. It began with the growing of crops and the invention of the wheel. It developed along the trade routes by sea and by land, along the rivers which were used as roads by riverine communities. Trade and religion are history; anthropology is prehistory.

But all this we have to learn on our own after we leave school. My chief memories of school are of boredom. I was not good at anything. The only subjects I liked were English as taught by W. B. (Dick) Harris and I did well at it. I was usually top of my form with essays, so much so that my father kept some that I sent him. I even won a prize – a leather-bound copy of Carlyle's *French Revolution* – for English; the only prize I ever won in my life except a book on sports and pastimes that I won when I was seven for winning a race at the racing club in Paris. I don't think I ever looked at it. Sports and pastimes did not interest me. I only cared for dogs, horses, guns and the natural history which is usually a by-product of these interests.

At school I remember eating suet pudding, roly-poly with jam in it, plum duff, rice pudding and tapioca, which we called frog spawn. All of them only acceptable because we were so hungry. During the Easter term there was a five-mile cross-country race. This meant jumping thorn hedges and swimming through dykes full of icy water. I never raced, I just jogged along and came in with the last batch. Another memory was the changing-room that smelled of boys' sweat, steam from the showers, and blacking, because the old men who cleaned boots did them in this dungeon.

Lancing gave singing scholarships and some small boys sang solo anthems in chapel. Their voices were beautiful and, as I found out later, it was to preserve this quality that until about 1880 certain choir boys in Rome were castrated to enable them to sing in St Peter's. The *castrati*. A curious custom to the glory of God. Chapel twice a day and three times on Sunday was a bore. Boys fainted in the winter from cold and hunger since morning chapel took place before breakfast. I got my life-saving certificate which meant I could have a badge sewn on the chest of the bathing dress I wore in the holidays. We learnt Rudyard Kipling's 'If' – 'If you can keep your head when all about you are losing theirs . . .' and other poems. Macaulay's *Lays of Ancient Rome*; all calculated, or perhaps not calculated, to inculcate the idea of a stiff upper lip, a relatively new idea which began in Dr Arnold's time at Rugby. Before that brave men cried with great facility at the loss of a friend, a dog or a horse. General Sir Harry Smith, in his autobiography, continually mentions bursting into tears on such occasions and he was one of England's great fighting soldiers.

Boys seldom called each other by their Christian names – surnames were used with major, minor or minimus to distinguish brothers of different ages.

But the memories are confused. They bleed into each other. Some of the boys had nicknames. One was known as Cow Pat – I never knew why – perhaps he had slipped in one. Another boy had a matchbox full of pubic hair he said he had got from several women – which did not seem very romantic to me. There was the school sweetshop, or Grubber, as we called it. My favourite things were Jello, which I ate as it came out of the box, a bit like Turkish Delight only much tougher. Another was Nestlé's condensed milk. I used to make two holes in the can and suck it. This had the advantage, like boiled eggs, of not being shareable.

In lessons I disliked Maths which confused me most. I never saw why x plus y should equal anything. And Latin. On the whole my memories are of boredom, hunger, cold, chilblains and general discomfort. But school may have been fine for boys who were good at games and did not have a horse and dogs waiting for them at home.

There was one incident of vandalism in which I participated. After a field day in which we fought mock battles with the OTC's of other schools (including Eton, whose boys were dressed in a kind of crushed-strawberry coloured uniform instead of khaki), which seemed to me a futile and inexplicable exercise, we entrained to go back to Shoreham, our railhead. In our carriage and most of the others, the boys suddenly went mad, stabbing the upholstery with bayonets and cutting the window straps. It was almost the last week of term and there were no repercussions, but I still wonder why we did it.

At the end of the summer term most of the boys in the corps went to camp for ten days but I always succeeded in getting out of it on one excuse or another.

We had a good gymnasium but I disliked gym. The only thing I was good at was climbing the ropes, which struck me as a useful accomplishment.

I had now reached the upper fifth and was out of the lower school. Promotion from one class to another did not go by age. There were some quite young boys in the upper fifth and one big boy never succeeded in getting out of the third, the lowest form.

I do not think I was much concerned with the future, though I doubted my ability to get into a university. But I was still sure I should, as the French say *débrouiller* myself. As a last resort I could enlist in the cavalry or join the police. I was big, strong, relatively good-looking and not really stupid, though academically a failure. All it took to succeed was drive, guts, will-power, and a certain ruthlessness. There were also the colonies. There were endless possibilities. All I had to do was to stick this out, wait a year or two and the world was my oyster. This was simply a preparation, a waiting period while I matured. The main point is, I think, that I and my friends were eager to get on with it. To start our real lives, to make our own money, to pick our friends, to find our women. I was ignorant of them but I knew that, too, would come. Women were still a mystery and I was glad of it. I was not ready yet. Puberty, I felt, was the least part of it. Any fool can load a gun and fire it. Even then, as a boy, I knew there was more to it than the placing of organ A into organ B, and my opinion has never changed. Biologically speaking, I knew all about it, having lived with animals and bred them since childhood. Man was an animal but he was also something more. And sometimes something less. I had the idealism of boyhood but it was diluted with cynicism from what I had observed. My friends and I seldom discussed sex. We talked very little smut, which I always found embarrassing. We felt, I think, that when the train came in it came in, and that was that. After all, it was simple enough. It was not, however, till many years later that I realized that girls were quite as interested in the subject as boys and that if anything happened it was only because the girl had created a situation where it could take place. I also – and this is much later too – did not take advantage of many opportunities because I felt they had no spiritual content. I was just being used at stud. The danger here is that the so-called act of love can be performed with hate, or a sense of being exploited.

My relationship to women has always been a combination of affection, respect and sensuality, that is to say, I have slept only with my friends and never without emotional involvement. Love. How many songs there are about it and how few people want it. Women want adulation, flattery, petting like cats, gifts; but never the responsibility of a man's love, God forbid. Children can accept love and give it till they are betrayed. And animals. But not adult human beings, or only very few of them. Most women, without even knowing it, see men as fathers to their children and providers. So the man is lost in the child and the woman lost to the man. Maternity brings both biological and psychological changes. Companionship has gone with the diapers. There are men who like this, born fathers of families. There are others, like myself, who don't, who would be jealous of their children. I think I always knew this unconsciously, even as a boy. I have never changed.

When I got back from school in July 1914 I found my mother

busy with her jam and marmalade making. We made all our own jams: plum, greengage, vegetable marrow and ginger, tomato, orange and lemon marmalade. Green tomato chutney. Mother also had a delicious way of putting up fresh herrings in white wine and cloves. She made *pâté* of duck, chicken and ham. The meat was first put through the mincer and then pounded in our big white marble mortar and pestle. I saw one exactly like it in George Washington's house at Mount Vernon. These pastes were sealed with hot salted molten butter, the jars covered with green pig bladders and tied with string. They contracted like drum heads as they dried. We made sausages by forcing the meat into freshly washed pig entrails which were tied with string at suitable sausage-length intervals. Today people would be shocked at the use of these unsterilized natural products. Eggs were preserved by the hundred in great earthenware crocks filled with waterglass. They kept quite well for a year but were chiefly used for cooking. There were usually enough fresh eggs for breakfast purposes. In those days the farmyard hens were not highly bred for laying and we only got eggs in profusion during the spring and early summer months. We had mostly heavy breeds: crossbred Plymouth Rocks, Buff Orpingtons, Rhode Islands and Faverolles which went broody and were set on their own eggs. We usually raised two hundred chicks a year as replacements and for the table. We set the hens in boxes on twelve eggs and they generally raised seven or eight chicks. The best mothers – some were much better than others – were never killed and we had hens that must have been at least twelve years old. They would attack any dog or cat that came near their brood. The game hens – we had a few crossbreds – would even stand up to a hawk. There were chickens then outside every cottage and on every road; with only horse-drawn traffic they were in little danger of being run over. Not for that matter were people. I hardly ever remember hearing of a traffic accident. Even as a child I would walk through traffic and if a horse came too close get hold of his bit and slow him up. The only accidents were caused by runaways, which were infrequent.

The garden at Hardelot was in full flower when I got home, the house filled with the perfume from the vases of roses and sweet peas my mother had everywhere. Bowls of pot-pourri she

made perfumed the drawing-room. The blue spikes of delphin-
iums stood out against the pink and sulphur-coloured hollyhocks.
The geraniums in front of the house were redder than blood.
This was the beautiful world of July 1914, the summer calm of
flowers, humming bees and bird song.

But there was again talk of war. And more than talk. France
was mobilized when I had my seventeenth birthday on July 23rd.
On August 1st Germany violated Belgium's neutrality and
crossed the frontier. For some days, till August 4th, when
England declared war, the English were very unpopular. *Sales
Anglais*, perfidious Albion, and what after all had the *Entente
cordiale* been but another scrap of paper? The English were as bad,
or almost as bad, as the *Boches*. For us in the country things were
not dangerous but English people living in the towns of France
were warned to stay in their houses.

There were suddenly no men left in the village of Condette.
They had been called up, old and young. An order was brought
round that all horses were to be taken to the *Mairie* for inspection
by the army veterinary service. I took Gypsy – fortunately she
was rejected. But there must have been four hundred horses in the
place, some magnificent Boulonnais mares, this being to my mind
one of the finest draught horses in the world, even superior to the
Percheron. Many of the boys and women who had brought them
were in tears when they were passed for service.

Then, as soon as the British came in, everything changed. We
were brave comrades, splendid, and our men, when they saw
them, of a *physique magnifique*. So magnificent that the first Highland
regiments of the British Expeditionary Force had to be incarcerated, protected by the iron bars of a school, from the curiosity
of the ladies of the town who wanted to know what they wore
under their kilts and became much excited when they found they
wore nothing.

We naturally went to see our troops arriving, driving to
Boulogne in the trap. A battalion of rifles was commanded by a
connection of ours – Colonel Northey, later General Sir Edward
Northey and Governor of Kenya – a small, dapper man.

The Belgians in retreat. That was the first time I saw beaten
soldiers. They looked beaten. I remember their packs made of
white and red oxhide, like the shields of the Zulus. The Belgian

forts had fallen. All in that direction was lost. The Channel ports were open to the enemy. A single German staff officer could have occupied them. But more British were pouring in. Regulars – long-service men whose accurate, rapid fire made it impossible for the Germans to believe that the British only had two machine guns to a battalion.

And the cavalry. My dream horsemen – long columns of hussars, of dragoons, of lancers, their steel points pricking the sky. And I nearly went with them. It was almost arranged that I should go as an interpreter. My father had seen the Divisional General, it was all unofficial, but they were short of interpreters. I could talk French and ride. The red tape they would see to later. But it was too much for Mother. So I did not ride with the British cavalry and I saw no Uhlans till four years later when I fought them dismounted. But still it was war. The British Army was in action; I must get into it. I revived my old childhood dreams again. No one would stop me even if they tried. I would enlist under a false name and give my age as eighteen.

My parents decided to go to England. The place and stock were left in charge of the gardener and his wife. The night before we sailed we heard the guns. There was continuous fire. It was a background to the singing of the nightingales. It has often seemed to me that gunfire makes birds sing, or is it just that the paradox is so great that one never forgets it and always associates the two?

I was sent to Jimmy's. His establishment was in Lexham Gardens and he was supposed to be the best army crammer in England, having succeeded in getting boys through the Sandhurst exam who were all but mentally defective. Well, I thought, he'd have to be good to get me in. The other boys there whom I remember were Dashwood, a big, dark, powerful boy; Courtenay Evans, a very good-looking, slim, fair boy, and a boy called Gates who was medium-sized and rather dark complexioned. The others – and there must have been forty of us – I cannot remember at all. One of them, however, was able to fart 'God Save the King', which seemed to us a great and patriotic achievement.

A crammer does not teach. He crams young men with facts which they need only remember till the exam is over, the way geese are crammed to make *pâté* in Strasbourg. It has no effect on the brain or personality of the victim. The process is devised by a study of the last ten years' examinations – in this case for Sandhurst. The crammer works out a hit or miss, by guess or by God, schedule of what is likely to be asked and you learn it. I have no doubt today they use computers.

A couple of interesting events occurred at this time. I met a Lancing boy much older than I whom I had hardly known at school in the street one day and he took me to a basement in the City, where he was working, and introduced me to a curious and apparently legal neo-brothel-cum-tea-room where the waitresses – all pretty young women – permitted what were to me unheard of familiarities. Although nothing more went on on the premises, I gathered the girls were available and assignations were made for later meetings. This was the boy who had shown us a matchbox full of pubic hair he had collected in the holidays while I was collecting butterflies and stamps. I was frightened out of my life by the whole affair and escaped as soon as I could, but he was evidently an habitué as all the girls seemed to know him. The place was half dark and arranged with cubicles in which tea – to conform with the law, I suppose – was served but seldom drunk.

My mother, who had been at school with the Duchess of Rutland, took me to call on her at Arlington House. I think she felt a connection of this kind might be useful to me, and so it might have been if I had ever followed it up. I do not remember the Duchess but while having tea in the drawing-room overlooking Green Park I met her daughter, Lady Diana Manners, later Lady Duff Cooper. She must have been three or four years older than I – about twenty or twenty-one – and dressed in a grey nurse's uniform with grey suède shoes and grey silk stockings. With her pale blonde hair enhanced by her white nurse's cap, she made an indelible impression on me. She epitomized the fair-haired English-rose type of beauty that is beyond compare. Gladys Cooper and one or two other women I have seen or met resembled her, bringing back the old story of the English child slaves on the Roman market of whom the priest said: '*Non Angli sed Angeli.*'

One thing, though, I do remember about the Duchess: she wrote her letters on half sheets, on the backs of other people's lettets, and on scraps. My mother often showed them to me. An endearing eccentricity, I thought.

I now started to smoke and to shave with a cut-throat razor, then in general use. My face was quite smooth but I thought shaving would stimulate the growth of hair and thus give an impression of greater maturity. I was very clothes- and still more girl-conscious. My favourite suit was a black and white herring-bone tweed. I wore heavily brogued shoes and cloth spats that I had bought from a friend. At Selfridge's I got myself two pairs of lisle socks, one green and one blue. I wore my hair long and slicked down with Anzora or Lime Cream, or both. My brother Lovel had given me six pairs of maroon silk socks, of which I was very proud. Maroon has remained my favourite colour for socks. I also bought a beautiful grey suede waistcoat, grey reindeer skin gloves, yellow chamois gloves, brown gloves and a walking stick. A Homburg hat. I liked to be well dressed or else to wear quite old clothes. Nothing in between. I did not yet own a dinner-jacket.

At Jimmy's I crammed, I learned, I memorized. But the exam was in September and, being convinced of failure, I thought I would try for a temporary commission. These were now being offered to public school boys if suitably recommended by two officers. Here Captain Harvey, a retired naval officer, a great friend of my mother's, helped me. He took me to the barracks at Hounslow – a scene of indescribable confusion – and the colonel of the Regiment, who was a friend of his, signed my papers almost without looking at me. The Army Council instruction was to commission public school boys between the ages of seventeen and thirty for Kitchener's Army – the first 100,000. In addition to this Colonel's recommendation, Allan Haig Brown, who commanded the Lancing OTC and whose ferrets I had looked after, had given me a letter saying I had served under him, as was required, but in a letter to me he expressed surprise that I should be trying for a commission when I had not even been in the army class. He was killed commanding a battalion of the Middlesex a couple of years later.

The examination for Sandhurst took place at Burlington House. We drove there, the five of us, in Gates's tiny three-wheeled Morgan. Two in front, two in the dickey and I rode on the bonnet. When we told the police where we were going, nobody bothered us. Now I was faced with those abominable printed questions. I was surprised that I could answer any of them. And then before the Maths paper, which was the one I most feared, I received a large envelope marked OHMS. It contained a large stiff piece of paper, almost like cardboard, which read:

Temporary

GEORGE by the Grace of God, of the United Kingdom of Great Britain and Ireland and of the British Dominions beyond the Seas. King. Defender of the Faith. Emperor of India, etc. To our Trusty and well beloved Edward Fairley Stuart Graham. Greetings.

We, reposing especial Trust and Confidence in your Loyalty. Courage and good Conduct, do by these Presents Constitute and Appoint you to be an Officer in Our Land Forces from the twenty-second day of September 1914. You are therefore carefully and diligently to discharge your Duty as such in the Rank of 2nd Lieutenant or in such higher rank as We may from time to time hereafter be pleased to promote or appoint you to, of which a notification will be made in the London Gazette, and you are at all times to exercise and well discipline in Arms both the inferior Officers and Men serving under you and use your best endeavours to keep them in good Order and Discipline. And We do hereby Command them to Obey you as their superior Officer and you to observe and to follow such Orders and Directions as from time to time you shall receive from Us, or your superior Officer, according to the Rules and Discipline of War, in pursuance of the Trust hereby reposed in you.

Given at Our Court at Saint James's the Twenty-first day of September 1914 in the Fifth Year of our Reign.

By His Majesty's Command

Edward Fairley Stuart Graham
2nd Lieutenant
Land Forces

I now had my commission as a temporary second-lieutenant of His Majesty's Land Forces. I had achieved my ambition. I was an officer in the British Army. Probably the youngest officer in it. I was seventeen and two months old. Anyway I was in and the exam was out. I later realized I had made a great mistake in not going through with it – because no one failed, so great was the need for officers in the new armies now being formed. So I lost two years' seniority, the training I should have had at Sandhurst and the friends I should have made. As it was, I got my regular commission in the field, recommended by my colonel and brigadier, when I was nineteen, in the middle of the Somme Battle, for although I was an acting captain commanding a company at the time, and had been in action for several months, no one was eligible for a regular commission till he was nineteen unless he had been to Sandhurst. So it was not till 1916 that I became a regular second-lieutenant and a temporary captain. Had I gone to Sandhurst, so great were the casualties, I might have been a regular major. I might also have been dead.

But now to offset all this, as if things could not be allowed to go too well, an incident occurred which cut the very foundations of my life from beneath me.

My father, taking me by the arm, said: 'There is something I must tell you. You are going out into the world, and I should not want you to hear it from anyone else.'

'Yes,' I said. We were in my brother Ronald's study at No. 8, Bolton Gardens. The window looked out on the old Cromwell Road, and I watched the traffic, wondering what he was going to say.

'I don't know how to begin,' he said. There were tears in his eyes. Then he burst out: 'I have been in jail. In prison. I did six months in Wormwood Scrubs. I changed my name to Graham when I came out and we went to live in Antwerp.' He broke down completely. It was a terrible thing to see. A terrible thing to hear.

I remember feeling stunned, and at the same time exercising the self-control I had learned at school – the so-called *sang froid anglais* with which one was supposed to face disaster.

'And our real name is what?' I asked.

'Cloete,' he said. 'Christ,' he said, 'it was such a near thing. It was safe enough, but it was not legal, and there was a man who did not like me . . .'

I never got the rights of it, but as far as I could see, he, being a director of a number of companies, had used the assets of several in his control to cover another deal. A big oil deal in Persia which would have made him a millionaire. There was a great deal of publicity. Our name was in the public eye, because his brother, my uncle Broderick, was one of the best-known racing men in England.

Dad recovered and went on: 'I'll say this for your mother. She stuck to me. But she could have saved me, boy. If she'd just been nice to the man. If . . .'

My impression was that this enemy of my father's wanted to sleep with her and she turned him down. That had been the price of his silence.

It was a novelist's plot and there I was in the middle of it.

I never looked the case up in the back numbers of the papers. I never spoke of it again. But it was a great shock to me. As great, or greater, than being told I was illegitimate, or an adopted child. There is no doubt that this extraordinary news had a profound effect on my character and life. It made me wildly ambitious. It drove me like a whip. It gave me a terrible secret to keep that I only told to two women before I married them. That this should happen on the very day I got my commission made it doubly important, a real break with all that I had ever known or felt before.

I knew I must regain my own name and did later, changing it to Cloete by deed poll, published in *The Times* and *Daily Telegraph* on June 12, 1925.

Part Three

THE MAN

CHAPTER 14

THE LIEUTENANT

I HAD been deeply shaken by what my father had told me, but felt even then that he should have faced the music rather than changing his name to Graham and bolting to the Continent. Antwerp first, and then Paris. Some of his friends would probably have stood by him. Instead he lost the lot and had to start again from scratch on every level.

I have known four men who have been jailed. One for illicit diamond buying; one for being caught in bed with a coloured girl – a crime according to the rather curious South African laws on miscegenation; and two for business misdemeanours, one of whom at least is again completely rehabilitated and now a millionaire race-horse owner. The other two resumed their place in society as soon as they came out, though the one condemned under the Immorality Act went to live in England.

Apart from men who have been in jail I have known two men and one woman who have been murdered, more than twenty suicides, and certainly half the people we know in America (and this includes ourselves) have been divorced at least once. We even had one friend who has had six wives. Any of this would, of course, have been inconceivable in the 'eighties of the last century. I doubt if my parents knew anyone who had been murdered or even committed suicide, and certainly very few divorcées. This incident, so tragic to my father, so serious in its effect on me, underlines the immense social changes that have taken place in the last hundred years.

This news certainly took some of the gilt off my gingerbread – commission, new uniform and all. But I determined then and there to regain my real name and if possible make something of myself. So that in a curious way any success I may have had has been due to this tremendous setback for which I had to overcompensate.

Almost overnight, through the assassination of the Archduke Franz Ferdinand at Sarajevo – a place no one had ever heard of – the world picture altered. As the wheels of history gained their destructive momentum the lives of millions of people were changed, and through the British declaration of war I had achieved what had always been my first ambition – to be a soldier. I was free. With a job, pay, a cheque-book and an account at Cox's. The umbilical cord was finally severed. That it had been replaced by an iron chain of army discipline meant nothing to me. I could accept that much more easily; indeed I embraced it. It was, as the Americans say, 'for real'.

Inevitably some of the episodes that follow have appeared in my novel *How Young They Died* since it was, to some extent, auto-biographical as any war novel must be if written by a soldier. Though the approach is now different, being more direct and analytical: the characters unmanipulated to fit the plot since there is no plot. Just the simple story of an individual's survival in a holocaust in which so many died. It is obviously the greatest event in my life, my adult starting-point. It is impossible for me to say I hated the war. I did not. I was continually frightened, but the fear was compensated for by the comradeship of the men I served with; by a curious sense of brotherhood; by a feeling that I was participating in a great event; by the greatest relief a man can know – the cessation of fear; by the feeling that each day might be the last, which led to an immense appreciation of every-thing. A lark singing. A rose in flower. A gallop on a good horse. All assumed a new importance. One might never see or do their like again.

I liked soldiering – had I been mounted I should have liked it even better. I should have liked to have been an officer in the Light Cavalry of the Napoleonic era. I was not particularly anti-German. I was a soldier and ready to fight. This I assume was the spirit of professional mercenaries of the Renaissance. Much later in the 'thirties, when I heard that the Chinese were trying to recruit ex-officers to train troops, I should have had a go at it if I had not been married. It was a job I knew and liked. What an extraordinary confession! But after all I had gone to war straight from school and knew nothing else. I had no moral scruples about

taking life after what I had seen and been through. I have a feeling
that, as Robert Ardrey suggests, men are born killers. Savages
that are tamed only by the disciplines of ordinary life; when
those are removed and they are given military training many of
them revert with great facility.

The hero is out today. In books and plays we find a new cult –
that of the non-hero, of the drug addict, the alcoholic, the
criminal. This is the day of the failure. And it is never his fault.
He fails because he is underprivileged, comes from a broken
home, or is a Negro. His excuses are endless – his parents, his
teachers, society in general. The only person he never blames is
himself. It is the *reductio ad absurdum* of democracy. Taken to its
logical conclusion, everyone would be on relief and all equally
idle.

The beatnik-hippie philosophy is an example of this principle.
The beatnik simply gives up, life does not concern him, though
that he continues to live is only due to the energy and charity of
others.

It is unbelievable but true that both in the USA and England
crowds of people have not protected women they have seen
attacked, or even tried to save a drowning child. They were playing it cool. It was none of their business. 'Let George do it. I'm
OK, Jack . . .' These are the slogans. Patriotism, honour, courage,
truth, honesty, chastity and politeness are all considered old-
fashioned today. Yet only by the acceptance of these standards can
a stable society be built.

I believe that mankind demands heroes. But it is interesting to
see the efforts that are being made to destroy them. To debunk
them in history and deny them in fiction and drama: to prove that
George Washington, Nelson, Wellington, Cecil Rhodes, Paul
Kruger, Napoleon and Churchill all had feet of clay. Perhaps they
had, but this does not cancel out their achievements. Our culture,
from the knight errant of chivalry rescuing maidens from
ravenous dragons to boy scouts helping old ladies across a street,
is based on this unstated code. The code of the strong protecting
the weak. Of women and children first in disaster, of heroism and
sacrifice.

I was brought up on this code. My aims were heroic, as were
those of most young men in 1914, when on every billboard and

hoarding there were great pictures of Kitchener, blue-eyed and moustached, pointing his finger at the passers-by over the caption: 'Your King and Country Need You.' You. Me. We were the first hundred thousand. Kitchener's Army.

This was the Poor Little Belgium period. Everyone was sorry for Belgium, in spite of the fact that the Belgians put up a very poor show of resistance, their famous fortresses going down like ninepins in a bowling alley. Nurse Edith Cavell's execution by a firing squad excited intense anger, though she knew the penalty for helping British soldiers to escape from behind the German lines.

There were stories of German atrocities. Civilians shot, women with their breasts cut off, babies tossed about on bayonets. Some true, perhaps, but all vastly exaggerated to generate the hatred necessary for war. The term 'propaganda' was not known then but that is what it was, and its necessity was proved when the British and German soldiers fraternized in no-man's-land at Christmas in 1915. The Establishment soon put a stop to that but it went to prove that ordinary fighting men, unless continually prodded, are somewhat loth to kill each other. This was particularly true of the British and Germans in the First World War, and possibly in such cases as Rommel's Afrika Korps and Montgomery's Desert Rats in the Second. The SS and Japanese never came into this category as their peculiar psychology was too alien to our own.

My fears were those of John Luard, a cornet of Light Dragoons, who in Napoleonic times, wrote to his father saying: 'I wish they would send me over there' [to Portugal]. Like him, we were afraid the war would be over before we got into it. The psychological force behind this idea seems to be of a dual nature. First something was going on that was too big to be missed – adventure on an heroic scale; secondly, the eagerness of a young man to test himself, to try out, as it were, his own guts. I do not think I was particularly patriotic. Soldiers went to war; it was as simple as that.

In *How Young They Died* I used many of my own experiences, blew them up and added the extra love interests, as the truth – a young man going through four years of war, reaching the age of twenty-one, and being married a virgin to a virgin girl – would seem incredible to the readers of today. With that apology for any repetition in the two books – the true and the fictional – I begin this section of the book.

A few days after receiving my commission I was gazetted to the Ninth King's Own Yorkshire Light Infantry. This was the first time my name had appeared in print since the notification of my birth. Normally, without the war, without my having become a writer, it would probably have appeared three times more – once when engaged, once in the marriage column, and finally in the deaths. This is assuming I was not divorced, murdered, or concerned in some crime, misdemeanour or accident. These are what might be called the normal press notices of a lifetime.

I was much excited to see my name in the paper. How grand it was to be a temporary second-lieutenant, gazetted to the KOYLI, to have a cheque-book and an account at Cox's Bank. My father took me to get my uniform. No tailor could make it. They were too busy with their regular customers and I was too young to have a tailor. So we went to Moss Bros., as they are still called, who sold misfits of various kinds and hired out clothes for weddings, coronations, and other social events to those members of society who had not the means to live up to their positions sartorially. It was not unlike those curious shops on Sixth and Eighth Avenues in New York where you can hire a tuxedo or tails for the night; it was, as it were, their titled uncle.

Anyway, I got it. The badge, like all Light Infantry badges, was a French horn, and ours had in its centre a little silver rose. We were differentiated from other regiments, too, by wearing a heavy green whistle lanyard round our necks instead of over the shoulder.

The KOYLI (the old 51st Foot) were a famous regiment, one of the six which had, on August 1, 1759, performed an exploit never equalled, much less surpassed, in the history of warfare. Advancing in two lines, they attacked and defeated ten thousand magnificently equipped French cavalry (75 squadrons).

This action was commemorated every year by Minden Day, August 1, when all ranks were issued with white roses to be worn in our caps, as our predecessors had done on that famous day, when on the way to battle they advanced through rose gardens

and plucked them to decorate their tricorne and grenadier ·ps
with this emblem of England.

It is these regimental traditions that give (or gave) the British
a unique quality and had a profound effect on morale. Every
regiment had lectures about the battle honours on its standard.

The sword knot on our swords was black, as was that of the
officers of the 43rd, in memory of Sir John Moore who commanded these regiments which, among others in the Peninsular
War, formed his famous Light Division. Sir John had served in
the 51st as an ensign and field officer.

I got my Sam Browne belt and a .45 pistol. This was a Webley
Fosberry that reloaded itself by the cylinder recoiling over a stud
that engaged in diagonal grooves which ran round it. I bought a
sword. Imagine it! A sword like a knight in ancient times. A
paladin. A sword was synonymous with glory. Only one thing
would have been better – a lance. All officers carried swords in
those days. We even did sword drill.

When the Expeditionary Force left England the officers were
armed with swords. They chucked them away after the retreat.
But we had not retreated yet. The cavalry kept them of course, the
arme blanc, the white weapon, and they were very proud of the
long straight sword that was employed at the charge by holding
it straight out over the horse's neck as they leant forward, the
impetus of the horse giving it its power. This weapon was said to
be much better than the old cut and thrust curved sabre of the
Crimea, and its reach longer than that of a British lance (which
was too short). It was also suited to British cavalry action, which
was supposed to culminate in a charge at full gallop, like a fox
hunter's, and bore no relation to the charge of heavy Continental
cuirassiers and dragoons, which attacked in close formation at an
earth-shaking canter. In those days we still believed in cavalry.
We were taught to form squares to meet cavalry – the British
Infantry square that no Frenchman or anyone else had ever
broken. The outside men kneeling, the ranks behind them stand
ing, the whole formation a bristling hedgehog of bayonet points
– the scarlet rock against which the waves of foreign onslaught
could dash themselves in vain. The officers stood in the second
rank with their swords. The space in the centre of the hollow

square was reserved for spare ammunition and the wounded. We wore khaki, but the old scarlet uniform of 'The Thin Red Line' and other war pictures was always in my mind.

At first there was no uniform for the men. Then every sort of ancient garb was dug out of the army store houses – old scarlet tunics, white pipe-clayed belts, ancient muskets for drill purposes, and wooden ones, issued by the thousand like wooden guns manufactured for a giant's children – which we were; our Empire was a giant. We were the first hundred thousand – the pick of England, the first of the volunteers. I do not think there has ever been a finer or more interesting body of men assembled at any time in the history of the world.

When I joined my regiment, among the officers were men from all professions and all parts of the world. Barristers, solicitors, undergraduates, stockbrokers, surveyors, authors, naturalists, chartered accountants, professors, businessmen, stockmen from Australia, rancheros from the Argentine, planters. Many had served in other campaigns in the Colonies, some wore both the King's and Queen's Boer War medals. The Boer War had ended only twelve years before. There was the black and yellow ribbon of the Matabele War, the purple and green of the North-West Frontier. If you knew the medals you could read a man's service on his breast as you read a book. This was the book of glory. It was the book I wanted to read. Our Brigadier, a lancer, had been at Omdurman in the fuzzy-wuzzy campaign. That ribbon was dark blue and white stripes. He was a tall lean man with a cavalry stoop that came from hundreds of hours of stooping exhausted in the saddle. We had one officer who wore a beard. There are no beards in the British Army; they were abolished because it was found that they were a convenient handle for an enemy to hold while he slit your throat. But this officer had a special dispensation from the King himself. His face had been so scarred with shrapnel in the Boer War that it was impossible for him to shave.

We had men of all ages. Boys who had falsified their date of birth, and old sweats with twenty-one years of service who had dyed their hair to join up again. The sergeant-major's hair was black as a crow's wing, and so was his waxed moustache, but he had two rows of medal ribbons sewn into his waistcoat that proved him well over age. He wore a navy blue suit, a bowler hat, carried a swagger stick under his arm, and began at once to knock the battalion into shape.

The man who taught me most about soldiering, especially old soldiering, was an Australian called Tommy Cook. He had been in the Queensland Bush Rangers in the Boer War. They had a reputation for toughness even among their own people. With Tommy I was always warm and well fed. We found things, and sometimes our neighbours complained of the things they had lost. Tommy even pinched a horse once and faked the numbers burnt into its hoof. He looked for men who had been poachers or burglars in the ranks and re-employed them at their own trades. What he taught me was worth knowing – something that it generally takes a long campaign to pick up.

Tommy Cook was, I suppose, a man of thirty-five, a real Aussie from the bush, who did not give a damn for God or man. A splendid specimen of the now extinct 'bloody Colonial' who had come from all over the Empire to fight for the mother country. This characteristic showed up in the mess. Dinner was relatively formal ending with a toast in port to 'The King, God bless him'. Well, Tommy didn't mind that but he did insist on having a pot of tea with his meal – tea at 8 p.m., a heresy! The Colonel said: No tea. Tommy said he'd have his tea, or else. He said he would go to the Brigadier, or the Divisional General if he was not allowed to have it. He said he'd left a good job and come twelve thousand miles to fight for this bloody country, but if he could not have tea with his dinner he'd resign and go home. He got his tea.

He had one interesting story about the Boer War. The men of his squadron were complaining at one time at having no milk for their tea. They were used to drinking it black from their billies but still they complained. And then suddenly one of them appeared with a bucket of milk. He collected money from the men who wanted milk as he said it was expensive. Day after day it came and at last Tommy became curious as there was not a cow around for miles. The country had been swept clean of beef by both Boers and British. With this in mind Tommy proceeded to stalk the milk salesman. He followed him to a native *kraal* and hiding behind the reed fence of one of the huts he watched the native women milking themselves into gourds which they then decanted into a pail. Money changed hands and everyone was happy. Tommy never told anyone and continued to have milk in his tea.

He was a mining engineer by profession and told me a story about an upcountry mine he was told to take over. When he got there – it was deep in the bush – he asked for the boss. The mine manager appeared out of a tent and said: 'I'm the boss, I'm the man who's fucking the monkey here.'

'Oh,' said Tommy, presenting him with a letter from the Sydney office. 'Well, I'm the man who's fucking the man who's fucking the monkey here.'

The men swore a great deal. Everything was qualified with bloody or effing. The butter, the bread, the Colonel. It meant nothing but it upset some people.

When our transport animals came we had nearly seventy horses and mules. Chargers for the Colonel, Adjutant, company commanders and doctor, and draught animals for the limbers – mess cart, water carts and field kitchens. We found that they were almost all from the Argentine and understood only Spanish. No one could do anything with them till Spender, who had been a rancher in the Argentine, took over and by teaching the drivers some Spanish and the mules some English, restored the equilibrium so that we could at least harness them up.

Some of the horses I remember. The bearded officer had a liver chestnut mare that he sometimes lent me. She was about three-quarter bred, a bit long in the body, but fast, with a lovely mouth and a sweet nature. The Adjutant's cob I remember, too, a very showy, fast little bright chestnut. The Adjutant's name was Butler. He was a regular and had been at home on leave from Burma when the war broke out. He was a splendid officer with a bright red face, which gave him his nickname of Ruby. His jaw was shot away at Loos but he went on fighting till he died.

That battle was more than a disaster; it was a scandal when the 21st Division – ours – was flung into action. The men were green. They had never heard a shot fired but still behaved magnificently, being mown down like corn as they tried to get through the uncut wire. The 21st and 24th Division had only been in France a few weeks when they found themselves making a forced march of three days to the battle which was going on at Loos. It was raining and their transport, including camp cookers and water carts, had been destroyed by shellfire so they had no hot food. They were told the Germans had broken and that they were simply going to follow them up, whereas in fact they had to attack over the open in daylight against uncut wire that was too strong for the cutters they had been issued with. The wire was six feet wide and four feet high and as they tried to penetrate this barrier they were torn to pieces. In three hours the 10,000 men who had attacked the German position were reduced to some 2,000 effectives and nothing had been gained.

That I did not sail with the regiment and thus avoided the battle was due to a curious incident. When I joined the regiment they were in billets in Aylesbury. I reported to the Adjutant and then I drew from the Quartermaster's stores three blankets marked with the Government broad arrow, a mess tin, a razor and brush – both of the poorest quality and no use to me anyway as I had nothing to shave – a hussif, or housewife – a sewing kit in a little case – and a big jack-knife. I already had my Wolsey valise and sleeping-bag, my green folding canvas bath and basin, and camp bed. I was quartered at the Rose and Crown and shared a room with a senior officer who, although he was killed, shall remain nameless. He was a homosexual and made a pass at me. I opened my new jack-knife, put it under my pillow and said: 'If you try to get into my bed again I'll stick it into you.' He did not try again but had no love for me after that and, owing to his influence, I was left behind as being too young and incompetent to go with the battalion. He may even have been right. He certainly saved my life.

From the billets we moved into camp at Halton Park near Tring, the property of one of the Rothschilds. The one who collected fleas, I believe, or so we were told. I never knew till then that there were more than four hundred kinds of flea.

This was winter in England – very cold and wet. The camp was a sea of mud and men died of cold. The junior officers were sleeping two to a bell tent. The captains and field officers had a tent each. But the men were sleeping seventeen to a tent, this was one to a seam, and owing to this overcrowding cerebrospinal meningitis broke out and we lost several men. We lost more in the forced marches that our divisional general insisted on. We were a light division (Light Infantry and Riflemen) like Sir John Moore's historic division in the Peninsular Campaign. We marched at great speed, with short steps, carrying our rifles at the trail when marching past. These route marches were performed in full marching order with full packs and dummy ammunition made of chunks of iron. Our record was twenty-six miles, over snowy roads, in six hours, twenty-six minutes' marching time. To that had to be added sixty minutes for the halts of ten minutes every hour, and an hour's rest at lunch. We lost six men, dead from heart failure, on that trek. It served no purpose. Not one, at least, that warranted such expenditure of life. I ended that march carrying four men's rifles.

I saw, as everyone has seen in war, much useless sacrifice. One of my friends was killed by being sent out on patrol to get a prisoner with a harvest moon shining. He knew, and I knew, he was going to his death. It might have come off with artillery preparation, attacking under the shelter of a box barrage. But men are very alert in moonlight and impossible to approach. A raid can sometimes be carried out in the heat of midday, when no one is paying much attention. Both the Australians and Canadians specialized in this daring form of raid.

But that comes later. At the moment I was learning close order drill with matches arranged on a table as platoons. I was drilling a company and later, to pass out as a first lieutenant, I drilled a battalion and finally a brigade. This required a great range of voice. My dear friend Maurice Cambie, who was killed with the others at Loos, had the best barrack-square voice I have ever heard, which includes even warrant officers of the Brigade of Guards. It came from his stomach, as it has to, and had incredible power.

Our next move was to Maidenhead, out of canvas into billets again. And here I found myself in a house with a pretty girl. I think people who had daughters applied for young officers, but I thought it was luck. She was a big dark-haired girl who came from Devonshire, called Nancy Wright. We held hands, went walks and sometimes I kissed her. This I considered very daring. At Halton there had been a girl too, Joyce Wood, the daughter of a parson who lived in a neighbouring village. On Sundays I used to go and see her on my bicycle. We went for long walks together and then she gave me tea at the vicarage. She was a nice girl, fresh and clean though not very pretty. I was happy with her. All I wanted then was the society of a girl or woman. I used to spend a lot of time with the wives of some of the officers. With Leslie Head's wife and Ethel Gordon. They were about twenty-five years old, I suppose. They would give me tea and I would sit in their rooms, just glad to be with them.

When Nancy went back home – she had been on a visit – I applied for a new billet. I think I went to the chief of police, who was responsible for the billeting, and said I wanted a change and should like to go somewhere where there was a pretty girl. My direct approach must have amused him and he sent me to a billet where I at once became attached to a girl called Enid Hopkins. She had long dark hair and lived with her aunt, who bred Samoyeds. She had a sister, Leslie, and my half-section, Hewlett, became her friend. It was a very pleasant boy-and-girl relation-ship. I had a motor-cycle now, a Triumph with a sidecar, and took her out to various places in the country round about to lunch and tea, when I could get away.

While in Maidenhead I hired a grey mare from a job-master and went for a ride on the thicket – a kind of common. Galloping over a nice piece of turf, I came unexpectedly on to an asphalt road and the mare slipped and fell on her side. As I felt her go I raised my right knee a little and so did not damage it seriously. The mare was unhurt but there was a London sequel. When on leave I rode a big grey horse called Peter, belonging to Oswald Norman. He had said I could take him out whenever I wanted to. I used to go along to the mews and Oswald's coachman – John Leech, a very fine old man – would saddle Peter up and off I'd go for a ride in the Park. As a rule everything went very well, but this time after my fall I had no grip in my right knee and Peter put me down in Rotten Row in front of a crowd of people. I was very upset because I had felt pretty good on my big grey horse. It had been raining and so I remounted and rode back plastered with mud. Probably a very salutary experience but most embarrassing at the time.

I used to ride up to London on my motor-cycle, which made me independent of trains and taxis and I enjoyed riding it.

I was sent on a signal course about this time but found it too much for me. I never even learnt the Morse code, much less semaphore. I have never been able to learn anything that bored me, so I gave it up and spent my time with a Canadian battery, helping them break in some remounts. I got into quite a bit of trouble when I got back because they had wanted me to be signal officer and now they had to get someone else. Here again, if I hadn't failed, I should have gone to France with the regiment and been killed, as my replacement was, while repairing a telephone line under fire.

But I was always in trouble over horses. Within a month of joining the regiment I had taken out the Colonel's charger – a roan – without leave, and had been caught riding him. Colonel Holland was a dugout from the Indian Army who sometimes, in a fit of absent-mindedness, addressed his Yorkshiremen in Hindustani.

Among the most interesting officers we had were two Australians, Nott and Sligh. Sligh had a Sunbeam car. Cars were very rare then. There was only one other – a Ford – in the regiment. Nott was the finest horseman I have ever seen. The Australians are probably the best riders in the world. I have seen American and Canadian cowboys, South Africans, Cossacks, British cavalrymen and fox-hunters, but never anyone to touch an Aussie. To see Nott on a horse was to watch a ballet. He would be up with one jump on to an unrideable horse and sit there, his reins slack, a cigarette in the corner of his mouth. The horse could do what it liked. He never moved, just sat balanced in the saddle till the horse had done. Then he rode him. Years later, I met another rider, also an Australian, called Beck, who was his equal.

Among other interesting men were Douglas Jones, a coffee planter from Uganda, Prendergast, a rubber planter from Borneo who had a Japanese mistress, and Radcliff Dugmore, the famous animal photographer and naturalist. I can remember the names of some others: Leslie Head, Bradford Gordon, Gordon Haswell, Hewlett, two Telfer brothers, Jacobs, Yeo, Lambert, Johnson, Lynch.

By now the men had khaki uniforms and modern rifles. They had graduated from civilian clothes to blue uniforms and forage caps, piped with red, and from them to khaki, and from the wooden rifles through the long Lee Enfield Mark II to the short modern Mark III. We had a Lewis gun and a trench mortar section and, fully armed, we moved by road to Aldershot. This was the last move; we were to finish our training in these famous camps and barracks before joining the BEF. We were there a couple of months and then the division sailed, leaving me with the sick, the sorry and the misfits. I was returned to store – to the reserve battalion at Rugeley in Staffordshire. And I began to agitate for foreign service on my own. I got leave, went to the War Office and found that the officer in charge of replacements to the KOYLI in France was a Captain in the Seaforths who had been rendered unfit for further active service by wounds received early on in the war.

He said: 'So you want to go to France?'

I said: 'Yes.'

He said: 'How old are you?'

'Eighteen.'

'There's plenty of time then; it's going to be a long war.'

'My battalion was destroyed at Loos,' I said.

'A bad show that. Green troops. The men had no rest. Forced marches. No hot food.'

'The wire wasn't cut,' I said. I went on worrying him. Every time I could get leave I popped into the War House. And at last he put me on his list.

The regiment had left England in August 1915, was cut to pieces almost at once, and I was in France by April 1916. I often thought of my dead friends, particularly Maurice Cambie with whom I had shared quarters. We had become very close. And the men I had served with; most of them were coal miners, rather short, magnificently developed down to the waist from their work, but with poor legs. Almost all of them had blue scars on their faces or bodies from accidents in the mine in which coal dust had become embedded.

While I was waiting I got some grouse-shooting and a few days hunting on a big bay horse borrowed from a senior officer. Apart from him, and I forget his name, I took a dislike to the whole staff at the reserve battalion. They were safe with home service jobs, and very smug about it. They had sorted themselves out with the local squires and were dining and spending weekends in the big houses, hunting, shooting and fishing, making love to the girls and treating the officers who were not on the permanent establishment as cannon fodder. I found I had the greatest objection, even at the age of eighteen, to being regarded as expendable, even if I was doing my best to achieve this end. But these gentlemen acted as if we, and the men who were with us – the other ranks – were malingerers and cowards whom they, these pudding-faced toy soldiers, would ferret out and send back to do their duty. Later, when I came back from the war, things were even worse. Some of these officers who had been junior to me and had never seen a shot fired except on the rifle-range had been promoted over me and could give me orders. By that time all but half a dozen officers of the old type had been killed and it was time to get out. This was in the future, but I should have guessed it then. It was all there for anyone to see.

Meanwhile there was the waiting, and while we waited there was drilling, musketry, digging practice trenches, route marches, lectures, time spent reading and writing, talking and leave, most of which I spent worrying my Seaforth friend and wandering about London by myself. By this time I had a decent uniform made by Humphrey and Crook in the Haymarket, who oddly enough was also my Uncle Montrose's tailor.

I had been invited to join the Junior Naval and Military Club. All the Service clubs were opening their doors to the young officers of the new armies. We had no members over field rank and it was a nice place to drop in for a drink, watch the traffic in Piccadilly or read the paper and current periodicals. The Club entrance was on White Horse Street leading to Shepherd's Market and is now the site of the Penthouse Club with bunny-girl type waitresses. We should have liked them.

My tailor was bombed in the Blitz and the American Express building has risen on the ruins. My Uncle Montrose's house on the corner of Berkeley Square and Charles Street is now a bank. These changes in fifty years are just glimpses into a future that none of us could foresee and relatively few of us lived to enjoy. Changes of this kind were inconceivable. Our world was still almost that of Queen Victoria. We were too young to see the cracks in the social, moral and financial façade of society. We were fighting for the Empire, the *status quo*.

Christmas 1915 I spent alone, or started alone, with a single table at the Elysee in Piccadilly, a favourite place of mine, with a half-bottle of champagne. I knew quite well what would happen. No one could see a young officer dining alone at Christmas. I was asked to join a party, which I did. I had no home in London. My father was doing something with Belgian refugees. He had the job because the South African *patois*, the *taal*, that he spoke, could be understood by peasants from the Low Countries. My mother was doing something else and the atmosphere of No. 8, with my religious aunt, I found intolerable, so I spent as much time as I could alone, eating out, talking to other officers, going to the Club to write letters, and to Maxim's, Hatchett's, the Criterion and such places for meals. I used to go to shows by myself at the Alhambra and the old Empire, where I would watch the tarts parading and wonder if I would ever get up enough courage to go home with one again.

Some of these women were very beautiful. Their age must have varied from seventeen to forty, and they were the pick of their profession and could be watched in comfort as they pea-cocked along, smiling their way through the scarlet and gold decorations of the promenade.

I had been drunk a couple of times. Once had been an accident – I had mixed my drinks by mistake – and once had been a bet. I bet someone five pounds I would drink a tumbler of *crème de menthe*. I did it and have seldom been so sick. I got my fiver and haven't touched a peppermint since.

I knew that to grow up one must get drunk and sleep with women. But it wasn't as easy as that. At least not for me. Maurice had always told me how wonderful it was. He and a few other officers between them kept a girl called Mona in a flat in Maida Vale. They had some system of apportioning out her time. An arrangement – a roster – I imagine, of whose night it was, which appeared to work to everyone's satisfaction. He said it was a kind of club and offered to include me, but I was too shy.

Several factors had always kept me free from women. Fear of venereal disease, which in those days was not just like catching a cold. The anti-Syphilis vaccine 606 had been discovered but the venereal hospitals did not treat their patients in such a way as to encourage them to take chances that would bring them back. So that wrote off the bad girls. The good girls I was afraid of putting in the family way. Contraceptive knowledge was not in the hands of every teenager then. Next came my shyness, and finally my taste, which was so highly developed that the only girls who attracted me were the million-dollar babies I was not able to afford. In fact, I have only paid one lady. The one I finally chose for the great experiment. She was a big blonde of at least thirty, dressed in pink, with a large pink hat, that I had so often seen on the promenade that she almost seemed a friend. Besides, it seemed to me that at her age she would know what she was about, and be more patient than a girl. I'm afraid I picked her rather like a horse. This was strange new country to me and I wanted something safe. Later on I'd go for the pretty, fast ones, the difficult ones that took some handling, but obviously this business, like everything else, had to be learnt.

Of course, had I still been in Paris, my father would have arranged something, or some young married woman would have taken me on. But this was London and so I went home with my blonde. She had a nice apartment. I slept very comfortably with her and did absolutely nothing except eat a splendid breakfast of bacon and three eggs that she cooked for me on a gas-stove. I gave her five pounds.

Shortly after this the promenade was closed and the women thrown out on to the streets. I do not think that this reduced prostitution, it simply made it more uncomfortable for all concerned. Today it really has been swept under the carpet and the girls forced into houses where they can be exploited by the underworld.

Later in France I went to brothels with my friends but never had a woman. It always seemed to me rather like eating off someone else's dirty plate. In the men's brothels they queued up and no man got more than five minutes with a girl. For officers things were not so bad but the difference was only one of degree. So I bought sweet champagne for semi-nude ladies who got a commission from the madam, and watched them flop their breasts as they danced to the music of the gramophone. I was shown dirty postcards and filthy books printed in Portugal and Spain.

I remained a virgin but began to masturbate. I had never touched myself till this period, but still consider the procedure an improvement on promiscuous copulation, and even found that its practice by young diplomats was advised by Talleyrand as a protection against the power of women. Just as he advised these same gentlemen to empty their bladders on all possible occasions because, in an argument, a gentleman with an empty bladder had a great advantage over one whose bladder was full.

CHAPTER 15

ORDERS

At last I got my orders. I saw my name on the notice-board in the ante-room. I was given ten days' final leave which I spent in London, and then returned to Rugeley to pick up the draft I was to take overseas. I do not remember my goodbyes. They were not important. Goodbyes are only important when they are said to a woman, and in this sense, mothers are not women. However poignant the parting is for her, it is less so to her son. For him it is just another severing of the apron strings, the final cutting of the umbilical cord. Any sadness, and this was reflected sadness from the tears in her eyes, was offset by the excitement of the soldier boy marching off to war.

Goodbye was London. London is associated in my mind with goodbyes, so is New York. Later there were some bad ones. It is assumed that as you grow older you suffer less. This may be so but perhaps you simply have less to suffer with, or have had more practice and have learnt something of the technique of it – some cynicism which informs you that half a bottle of champagne and a Luminal or two is a great help. And that the best way of getting over one girl is another girl. These are great truths but unfortunately they are not the whole truth. Or I may be at fault; perhaps I never grew older, never even grew up at all. But this goodbye was nothing to me. I said it and went back to Rugeley. Next day I marched my draft to the station behind a sulky fife and drum band – they did not like getting up so early.

Here I do not have to rely on my memory; I have my diary. I left Charing Cross station at 9.10 a.m. on Wednesday, January 12th, 1916 for Folkestone. Crossed the Channel and arrived in Boulogne at 3 p.m. I went to Caveng, the cake shop, where I had coffee, cream cakes and chocolate with a big dollop of cream on it. If I had left England a fortnight sooner, I should have qualified for a '15 Star.

I saw some friends, officers I had known in England, and met an Army Service Corps captain who gave me a lift to the base at Etaples where I was due to report. I had handed my draft over in Boulogne. I got leave to go home next day. Hardelot was only fifteen miles away. I got a lift in a car. My father was away so I missed him, but Rusty the fox-terrier was pleased to see me. I walked over the place and then went and had lunch and tea with the Danfords. The car that should have picked me up did not turn up so I walked back. I left at 11 p.m. and arrived at 3 a.m. In the morning my father appeared in camp and got leave for me to go home with him. I slept in my mother's room. Next day I was back in camp and my father spent the night at the Hôtel des Voyageurs. I dined with him.

My address was 32nd Infantry Base Depot. S.17. c/o. APO, BEF. France. I was very proud of this. I was with the British Expeditionary Force at last.

I now said goodbye to my father and settled down to life at the base. We were there – thousands of us officers and men – simply waiting till people were killed or wounded and we were needed to replace them. This was, as it were, the stockroom of the army. We had lectures, drills, physical training, bayonet fighting and the rest of the time-fillers. Nothing was co-ordinated because we were all on call. On the 21st mine came. I took a draft up the line and handed it over to an officer of the Manchesters at Mericourt. I returned to Abbeville and slept at a café which turned out to be a brothel. Sunday the 23rd I left Abbeville and joined an en-trenching battalion. These battalions did fatigues, digging trenches and putting up wire for the front-line troops, and were a sort of hardening-off phase for green troops, preparing them slowly for the sights and sounds of war. They were gradually drawn into the fighting units as they were needed.

The battalion was commanded by a Major Radford who had a very nice honey-gold gelding with black points. Sometimes he let me ride him.

On the 25th I saw my first dog-fight – and archie fire – called flak now. It was very pretty to watch – little puffs of white cottonwool-like smoke bursting in the blue of the sky with a faintly audible pop. On the 28th I was under shellfire for the first time. I made no comment on it in my diary. I got a poisoned heel and was sick a few days with a big lump on the groin. There are various notes. I picked wild flowers. I saw two kestrels courting. I was shown an aluminium ring by a corporal in the RAMC which, when you held it to the light, had the picture of a naked lady set in a hole in its face. Later on I got one for myself. They were supposed to be made out of German shell fuses. It was very cold with much snow.

I seem to have had trouble with my poisoned heel. I did a lot of shooting on the range and improved a great deal. I could fire as many rounds as I wanted to and was hitting a halfpenny (five-centime piece) set in a cleft stick at thirty yards three times out of five with rapid fire before long. In April I heard a cuckoo and saw the first swallows. That is where I seem to have left the entrenching battalion and joined the 6th KOYLI. They were resting behind the lines after a tour of duty in the Ypres salient.

Though the front line was still some miles away, the noise of firing was intense. A rumour spread. A battle. The Third Battle of Ypres. The Germans had broken through and were using gas. We were sent up as reinforcements. Suddenly there was a shout: 'Stand clear!' and the guns came. Battery after battery. Six horse teams at full gallop, the drivers leaning over their horses' necks using their whips. Canadians going into action, galloping *ventre à terre* – belly to the ground – the guns and limbers leaping like tops, sometimes on one wheel sometimes on the other behind their sweating teams. Team after team went up the line, it went on for half an hour. The horses' iron shoes struck sparks from the *pavé*. The whole horizon was salmon pink with exploding gunfire. Flares and signals were going up like fireworks on Guy Fawkes night. Three red balls, three green. Showers of golden rain. Rockets, each with a meaning, each a call for artillery retaliation, for reinforcements. Desperate cries for help. Men were dying up there. Being blown to bits, buried alive, left limbless, an arm or a leg neatly amputated by flying steel. Machine-guns chattered, spitting nickel-coated lead in streams like horizontal rain. Very lights. Magnesium flares. Rifle shots.

And if normal terror was not enough, gas – the unknown quantity – was added to it. This invisible miasma with a faint garlic-onion smell that sent men coughing to their deaths. This was what we were going into.

This was the first time I saw gas used. It was a terrible thing to see a man gasp his life away. It was chlorine. Mustard and tear gas had not yet been invented. We carried gas-masks – grey-coloured flannel bags soaked in some chemical that we pulled over our heads and tucked into our tunics. There was a band of celluloid over the eyes to give us some visibility and we breathed through a big rubber dummy teat, sucking in the air the way a baby sucks milk.

We were clear of Ypres now, which was just as well as the Germans were plastering it. The word was passed back to fix bayonets and prepare gas-masks – loosen them in their little yellow canvas bags so that they would be ready to use. There was a rattle of equipment; a series of rasps as the bayonets were drawn from their scabbards. Sharp clicks as they were snapped into place. Load. The magazines came out, were filled and slammed home. Now we were ready. We might go straight into action at any moment. We were marching fast towards the inferno in front of us. In my mind I saw the Canadian guns unlimbering, unhitching their teams of sweating, trembling horses. The guns would be in action. Loading, firing, the guns leaping to the lanyards' pull, recoiling as if they were alive. Insects withdrawing their stings to strike again, spitting fire, firing low trajectory shells with the gunners sweating and cursing the masks that cramped them. How many horses were gassed? The lot, probably. And still we marched on unbelievingly into the uncertainty of battle. Into the confusion of it. Orders came to put on masks. We became strangers to each other. The horrible sticky treated flannel stuck to our faces. The end of the mask was tucked into our tunics. The bloody tit, like a baby's comforter, in our mouths. The clip on our noses. Fight? How the hell did you fight in these things? The goggles fogged.

We passed some howitzers with the field guns only a few yards ahead of them belching fire – dragons, almost wheel to wheel. Wounded men, gassed and hit, came staggering by in bloody bandages. The Germans had reached the support line. It was the front. An officer, masked, muzzled and gagged into silence, stopped us with his raised hand and pointed to the parapet behind where his men were stood-to, waiting to counter-attack. There was something frightful about all these masked khaki figures vaguely illuminated by the lights of battle – Very lights, gun flashes, flares. They stood in silhouette. In spite of the fact that there were no trenches, only breastworks, we were standing in a foot of icy mud where there were no duckboards.

Then it came, though how the hell it came since no one could give verbal orders in a mask – an order to advance and the line climbed out, rifles at the high port, the bayonets black spear points. Out into the churned mushy clay that clung to our boots and sucked them into it as if loath to let us go, as if it wanted us to stand there and be killed. We were advancing with an interval of about a yard between each man. More wounded on their way back passed through us. The British guns were pounding the front. I stepped over a body. We were near the old front line now. The German machine-guns had opened up on us under the light of the flares. Men went down but the line continued to advance. Headless men with eyes set in their flannel necks. The pace had changed to a slow trot, the rifles had come down a bit from the high port into an attack position. A regiment of ghosts, of men from Mars, we charged into the German trench, silent because we could not shout, and fought silent, mute as bulldogs, and took it.

It was amazing how much shelling you could walk through on soft ground. The shells bury themselves before exploding and then send up spectacular geysers of black dirt or mud but do relatively little harm unless you get a direct hit. On a road, particularly if it is stone-paved, the shell bursts on contact sending out a spray of shrapnel and shell-casing and broken stones only a few feet above ground level that may knock out twenty or thirty men, which is why, when moving along roads subject to shellfire, we always moved in very small parties with a wide interval between us.

I remember very little of the action. I remember jumping into the trench and firing my revolver. I remember bombs going off but both sight and sound were mixed, muffled by the masks. When in Christ's name would we be able to take them off? If the wind changed. If the wind changed it would blow the gas away, back towards the German lines.

Then our Lewis guns were on the parapet sweeping no-man's-land. The Very lights soared hissing upwards and sank slowly, lighting the dead and dying. The Germans who had broken through had not been able to push the attack home.

I wondered if I'd had anybody hit. There was no way of finding out in these bloody things. My mouth was sore from sucking air through the rubber nipple. I was tired and cold. My feet were wet. I was wet to the knees. We'd had a long march. But I'd been in action, in a battle, and all I was supposed to have done was to bring up some reinforcements to the battalion. To march them up, hand them over and report for duty. There was much confusion now. Christ, I did not even know what division I was with. From their badges most of the men round me, other than my own, were Lincolns. They wore a sphinx.

Next day we were back in the rest camp again. But here are some more extracts from the diary when we returned to the line after a series of tours a month or so later.

May 1st. Lovely day. Breach in my parapet by whizzbang. One bay rendered untenable. Dead men, both Boche and Scots Guards. Stink like hell. There is a man buried in the parapet of my dugout. Put out wire with Broadbent. Have never been so terrified in my life. Could hear German working party hammering in stakes. I had not had time to be frightened in the battle. This was different, putting up wire was like a peacetime job.

May 2nd. Not much doing. Sleep all day. Think Fritz was relieved last night for he has been very quiet, has done quite a lot of sniping. Has got a machine-gun sweeping our parapet. Fires it whenever a Very light goes up. Bond goes out on patrol with Captain Bell Acton, who is killed.

That gives something of a picture of trench warfare. Patrols, sniping, wiring parties. Stand-to an hour before dawn. Rations. Rum issues. An endless routine of boredom punctuated by casualties and fear.

I slowly learned to control my nervousness. One thing I noticed repeatedly was that those men who were fearless at first cracked suddenly, and were never any good again. I think they simply did not realize the danger and when they did they were finished.

After every march there was a foot inspection. The men sat with bare feet, after washing them, and the platoon officers and NCOs examined them for blisters and other damage – an Army marches on its feet, not its stomach. Old soldiers rubbed their feet with wet soap and often wore two pairs of socks to absorb friction. Boots had to be checked – for fit, for repairs and general condition. We had one penis inspection, 'short arm inspection', the men called it. An embarrassing performance for all concerned, but it was a divisional order. So the men stood with open flies holding their cocks – long ones, short ones, thick ones, thin ones. Circumcised and uncircumcised, and the officers were supposed to check them for venereal infection, which none of us, unless it was in its last stages, could have recognized.

There were inspections of clothes to be replaced or repaired, arrangements to be made for bathing at the divisional baths whenever there was an opportunity – seldom as often as once a month. When they did get the use of the baths the men marched in by companies and washed, a platoon at a time, with hot water in big wooden laundry tubs, leaving their clothes to be fumigated and de-loused. The cholera belts that looked rather like the lower half of a woollen vest had long ago been discarded. Their issue was a hangover from service in India and South Africa and they served no purpose except as a breeding-ground for lice.

There was a daily rum ration in the line.

But all those things were routine, the housekeeping chores, as it were, that were supervised by the company officers and NCOs.

Food was cooked in the company mobile cookers and brought up in big dixies by carrying parties when in the trenches, two men to a dixie. It was emptied into individual mess tins. The food was usually a kind of stew. There were tins of bully beef and maconochie, bacon, biscuits like big square dog biscuits. Bread, butter and jam (usually Tickler's plum and apple) in tins. Tea, sugar, condensed milk already mixed.

But this was if we were in the line or resting. In action we lived on bully beef, biscuits and black tea if we had the opportunity to brew it up.

At times the mud was so bad that wheeled transport could not be used and everything, including bombs, SAA and even 18 lb shells for the gunners, was brought up on pack animals, which suffered terribly, sometimes sinking up to their bellies in this glutinous muck that had once been soil. Great shell-holes filled with poisonous water impinged on each other, and everything, men and transport animals, had to wind their way round these miniature craters, lakes in which it was possible to drown. And this went on and on, from horizon to horizon. Hundreds of square miles of it, with the remains of shattered woods standing up like broken matchsticks. Farms and villages disappeared. Only if a shell hit their foundations and sent up a cloud of red brick dust could one suspect their existence.

The diary now stops as action increased. The tempo of war was being speeded up. There was Hill 60. There was a battalion of the Rifle Brigade next to us who were mined. We had held that section before them in another tour of duty, and had heard the sound of picks beneath us. They may have been Germans or they may have been our own sappers counter-mining. There was always a sort of race between the two tunnelling parties. But it was not a comfortable feeling to have them under you. I knew the entrance to our people's tunnel and saw them sometimes carrying canaries in cages. They were used to test the air underground.

We had forward listening-posts only a few yards from the German line. We had encounters in the night with bombs. No-man's-land here in the Ypres salient was just a narrow strip of ground, sometimes only twenty yards wide, sometimes a hundred or more. On both sides, owing to the clay soil and the height of the water table, trenches were in many places replaced by parapets built of sandbags. But in general the Germans held the higher ground and the water they pumped out drained into our lines. We were never dry and many men suffered from trench feet, a sort of scurvy due to the feet being immersed in icy water for days at a time. We naturally had no dugouts, merely shelters built into the sandbagged parapets which leaked like sieves. Later, we got some sort of thick oil for dressing our feet and legs which almost eliminated trench feet.

We made bombs out of jam tins. I forget what we filled them with but the explosive was gelignite. It came in little, almost sausage-like rolls and was perfectly safe to handle. It tasted rather sweet and some men ate it in the hope of its affecting their hearts. This had been an old soldier's malingering trick in the

Boer War, a pre-gelignite era in which they had taken the cordite out of their cartridges to chew. To arm a jam-tin bomb we pushed a copper detonator down the middle of the sausage, then we pushed a length – a foot or so – of fuse into the detonator, clamped it tight with our teeth and rammed it home. When the opportunity occurred and the Germans were near enough, or in an attack, we lit the fuse with a match and threw the bomb. The match had to be a fuzzie which would not go out in the wind, and the whole business, from arming the bomb to throwing it, was quite tricky.

It was in this Hill 60 area I made my first acquaintance with trench mortars – *Minenwerfers* or flying pigs. After the mine had gone up we took over the defence of the crater from the Rifles and we could see the mines coming, wobbling through the air, and we tried to avoid them by moving to the right or left.

One Belgian spy in this area was caught and shot after a divisional court martial. He was giving information to the Germans by the manner in which he harnessed his horses when he ploughed his fields. The peasants were working quite near the line and often had their houses damaged by shellfire. This farmer's method was to change the position of his two horses according to the billet situation in his rear. One horse was grey and the other brown. Someone found this curious and reported it to the Intelligence Section.

The two sectors we held turn and turn about were Potije Château, a ruined country house, and the village of Wiltje – or what was left of it. The Germans were straight up the road, two hundred yards away from Company Headquarters. Both sides had fixed rifles that were fired up or down the road whenever anyone thought of it. A fixed rifle is a sighted rifle bolted on to a frame so that the action of re-loading and firing will not affect the sights. Anyone passing near it is supposed to fire a round. This just has nuisance value. It is annoying to have a bullet whizz past you as you cross a road. I suppose sometimes someone was hit.

The weather warmed up; it was spring, early summer, and the Flanders poppies were very bright on the sides of the communication trenches. Red as blood, and the corn flowers very blue. And there was a kind of big yellow daisy. In the air the larks sang and there were other birds – jays, magpies and smaller birds that did not seem to mind the war at all. They had been hatched into this world of shellfire and regarded it as normal.

Steel helmets or tin hats, as we called them, were now issued. They saved many men's lives but were uncomfortable till we got used to them. The men hated them and we received one Army Instruction to be read to the troops on parade, informing them that steel helmets 'were not to be used for culinary or other purposes'. The other purposes were varied; anything from a saucepan to a washbasin or chamber-pot.

We almost always had cats in the line. They had survived the devastation of the villages or were the descendants of the survivors. The troops fed them and they killed the mice and rats that swarmed in the dugouts. If a war went on long enough no doubt everything, including children who had been born into it, would regard it as normal – as a perpetual state of rather dangerous thunderstorm. This is what must have happened in such countries as China, Poland, the Ukraine and Vietnam. To such children and young people peace must seem like a wonderful dream, an abnormality. They are as conditioned to danger as our Stone Age ancestors were. If it was not too bad, a war might be easier to live through than some of the anxieties suffered in so-called normality. Many people would probably exchange a small physical risk for the security of permanent employment. A state of continuous quiet war, such as we had in some sectors, though I was never in them for very long, might be better than the furious drive of competitive city life, over which hangs the perpetual threat of atomic avalanche. Something that is not generally understood is that though there is danger in the army, there is also security. There are no worries. You obey orders. You issue orders according to an established pattern. If you are sick or wounded you are taken care of and pensioned. If you are killed your dependants become a charge on the state. You are a member of a great brotherhood of men and, like a monk in a curious monastery, lead a very sheltered if dangerous life. As the monk has his cloth, so you have your uniform which insulates you from the rest of mankind and protects you as a servant of the Crown.

There is no question but that the quiet times at the front were very pleasant. If the weather was fine and there was not much shelling, nothing could have been nicer. It was a boy's dream of an endless picnic on an unprecedented scale. The dugouts were often very comfortable and well furnished with the loot of abandoned houses. At Potije we had armchairs, draperies on the walls, pictures, mirrors and carpets. And we lived well. We drew our army rations and our friends and relations sent us parcels from home. We also imported luxuries from shops like Fortnum and Mason's, Harrod's and Selfridge's. We bought our wine from local wine-merchants behind the lines. We generally had porridge and bacon and egg, toast and marmalade for breakfast. Soup, stew, or curry – meat in some form – followed by blancmange and tinned peaches for dessert, with coffee and a glass of port for lunch. Tea was bread and jam, with a piece of cake from home sometimes. Dinner was like lunch, only more elaborate, with wine to drink or whisky and soda, and it ended with liqueurs. This, of course, only applied behind the lines when we were resting, or if things were quiet. If it was wet and things were bad, there was only bully beef and biscuits – a bit of hot tea with rum if you were lucky. The water came up in petrol tins which had never been properly cleaned and was strongly flavoured with chloride of lime put into it by the medical officer to purify it. Pure it may have been but the taste was very odd.

It was very pleasant to sit in the sunshine with the birds singing round you while the company barber cut your hair outside the dugout. It was nice to have your meals outside on a table that your predecessors had built in the shade of a tree. I was enjoying my tea one lovely afternoon, sitting with my tin cup resting on the table. I was holding it and about to pick it up when a shell burst above my head, a piece of shrapnel went through my cup into the table, and all my tea ran out over the book I had been reading.

But I had some variety in life. I got scabies – a skin disease due to dirt and very prevalent among the troops. It usually showed up between the fingers. As it was contagious I was sent to hospital at divisional headquarters. The old-fashioned cure was unpleasant but not painful. The body was rubbed from head to foot with a mixture of fat and sulphur. This was done daily for about a week and then one was cured. But it showed me how a dog with mange must feel. Then I got trench fever. This is a louse-borne disease and the first thing I knew about it was finding myself in the hospital train. I remembered having felt ill for some days but had not reported sick as we were short of officers. I heard afterwards that I was picked up on the duckboards of the trench and that the stretcher-bearers were sent for as my sergeant, who found me, thought I had been killed. The hospital was the Hôtel Splendide at Wimerieux, near Boulogne, a place I knew very well. My mother and father came to see me and I became much attached to a charming nurse called Theodora. Trench fever comes in bouts, spells of alternate feverishness and shivering, rather like malaria, which pass and one seems to be well till suddenly one goes down again.

I went on a tactics course at Berk Plage and here came into contact with the 22nd (Vandoos) Canadians. They were a French-speaking regiment and as tough as they come. I travelled with one of them, a full lieutenant, and got on well with him as I spoke French. We carried rations, bully and biscuits, as there were no cooking facilities, but our servants, who accompanied us some-times, managed when the train stopped to get a little hot water from the engine's boiler and brew up a cup of tea. At one of these meals the Canadian, who was opening a tin of bully, cut himself badly. The train had given a lurch at a critical moment and the can, with an edge like a razor, had cut off about half his finger. He never turned a hair. He just went on eating his biscuits and bully with a sauce of his own blood. At the course he went to bed because he was tired and said he knew more about scouting, tracking, tactics and shooting than anyone there, instructors included, as he was a trapper and guide by profession, that he had been sent on the course by his CO for a rest and that he had his pistol by his bed and would shoot anyone who disturbed him. So there he lay, resting and sleeping for fourteen days while his servant brought him food.

Later I had a bit of luck getting chosen for a sniping course. The instructional centre was the Trappist monastery at the Mont des Cat in Belgium. It was strange to see the white-robed monks, dedicated to silence, going about their affairs. This order had seen other wars, for this was the cockpit of Europe – the Flanders plain – and they were unmoved. No doubt they prayed for us as we learnt new and very precise ways of killing. We learnt camou-flage, which was new then, the use of telescopic sights, indirect

fire, the construction of snipers' posts and loopholes. I passed out
very high as I was interested in the subject, and when I rejoined
found myself as sniping officer living at battalion headquarters.
This was a great improvement as far as comfort was concerned. I
lived with the Colonel, the second-in-command, the Adjutant,
the doctor and the trench-mortar officer. I no longer slept in the
line. When it was wet I slept dry. Battalion headquarters was
usually half a mile or so behind the front line. It had to be, so as
to be equally accessible to all the companies spread out along a
front of a thousand yards or more.

I spent most of the day in the trenches, checking snipers'
reports, sniping myself and watching the German line from
behind a heavy iron loophole plate with a high-powered telescope.
We often saw Germans moving about a mile or more away. It
gave me a curious feeling to watch them. Watching and reporting
all movement was part of the sniper's job. I sent a report of what
we had seen to Divisional Intelligence by runner every night.
We looked for their snipers' posts and when we found them we
tried to destroy them. There were no armour-piercing bullets
then. So we used a heavy sporting rifle – a 600 Express. These
heavy rifles had been donated to the army by British big-game
hunters and when we hit a plate we stove it right in, into the
German sniper's face. But it had to be fired from a standing or
kneeling position to take up the recoil. The first man who fired it
in the prone position had his collar-bone broken. I hit two
Germans at long range – about four hundred yards – with
telescopic sights, and fired at a good many others. My best sniper
turned out, when his parents at last traced him, to be only fourteen
years old. He was discharged as under age. He was the finest shot
and the best little soldier I had. A very nice boy, always happy.
I got him a military medal and when he went back to Blighty and,
I suppose, to school, he had a credit of six Germans hit. He was
big for his age and had lied about it when he enlisted under a false
name, and then had had sufficient self-restraint to write to no one.
I had noticed that he received no mail and wrote no letters but
had never spoken to him about it. The snipers worked in pairs,
one observer with a telescope and one with the rifle. They
changed over every half hour as it is very tiring to use a telescope
for a long period. In action the sniper's job was to work in-

dependently and try to pick off any enemy leaders he could see. That was what the Germans did to us and they had no difficulty as we wore officers' uniforms with long tunics, riding breeches, trench boots and Sam Browne belts. This was one reason why the officers' casualties were so high. The Germans had a further advantage in their sniping. With them it was done by their Jaeger battalions, picked sharpshooters who in peacetime had been gamekeepers and guides. They wore green uniforms instead of grey and were permanently stationed in one sector, so that they knew every blade of grass in front of them and spotted the slightest change; this gave them a big edge on us because we were moved quite often.

I enjoyed sniping. I was on my own, which I have always liked, responsible only to the Colonel and Brigadier. I got on well with the CO. His name was Robinson and he often let me exercise his chargers. One was a Waler, a dark brown, almost black thoroughbred that would never walk or trot, called Rajah. He always went sideways, which infuriated the Colonel but which I quite liked. At least he was full of life. He was killed under me later. The CO's second horse was an Argentine polo pony, a very clever little bay. I also rode the other HQ horses and won a divisional race on Ellen, the doctor's mare.

The Colonel had a great sense of humour and I remember that once I shared a dugout with him in a railway embankment behind which one of our big howitzers – ten- or twelve-inch – had an emplacement. It fired a single round about every thirty minutes with an explosion that shook the world to its foundations but which, after a few days, never even woke me. The first night, seeing what it did, the Colonel filled a mug with water on a shelf above my head after I was asleep and waited for it to upset on me. It only took about four rounds to move it to the edge of the shelf and over it. We both laughed a lot and had a drink. We became great friends. He and all Headquarters, except me, were killed a few months later by a direct hit on the shell crater in which they were sitting, having something to eat, during an attack.

Once when the transport officer was on leave I took over his job as I was the only officer who understood not only horses but harness, carts and waggons. The transport lines were about ten miles back, as they had to be. They were occupied by the Padre, the quartermaster, the transport officer and their staff of clerks, farriers, cooks and drivers. Further back still, say another ten or so miles, were the divisional dumps. These were in charge of the Army Service Corps. They brought the rations, ammunition and material that we had indented for to a forward dump about half way between their HQ and our transport lines. We sent for it there and then later conveyed it up the line to a point where carrying parties were waiting to take it into the trenches. Each night the limbers set out with the battalion's rations, small arms ammunition, stores of various kinds, water in petrol tins, rum and mail. These limbers were pulled by two pairs of horses or mules, with a driver mounted on each offside animal. The driver who rode the wheeler had a steel guard on his left leg to save it from being damaged by the pole. We could not move off until dark as there was only one road and it was under observation from the German sausage balloons. Of course they knew we were on it all night and shelled it at intervals, but at least in the dark they could not observe their fire. Incidentally there was a certain amount of reciprocity in this shelling of transport. They also only had one road up to their lines and if they shelled us too badly we gave them a pasting back, so the night shelling was desultory, which was just as well as the road was packed solid and we could seldom go faster than a walk as the whole division's transport was moving up the line at once. If we got a hit on our animals we cut them out of the traces, shot them if they were badly hit, and dragged them and the broken vehicles off the road. If the animals were not too badly hit we sent them back to our lines. I found mules much quieter under fire than horses, and much steadier when hit. I have had a mule standing quite still with one leg blown off below the knee, while I shot him, whereas a horse, if he's touched at all, goes half crazy. Other transport officers have disagreed with me, claiming the reverse to be true.

It would take us four to five hours to do the ten miles to the battalion rendezvous where the carrying party would be waiting for us. They took up everything by hand from there and left us with the dead and seriously wounded to take back. The dead were wrapped in blankets and buried by the Padre in the divisional cemetery with a burial party drawn as a fatigue from the transport lines. The most dangerous part of the trip was going through

Ypres itself since, if we got into trouble there, the transport was liable to block the streets for hours as nothing could be moved off the road because of the ruined houses.

Ypres was a strange and wonderful sight by night – the ruined buildings stood up like skeletons, jagged, fantastically shaped against the bright rosy glow of the gunfire which edged the whole horizon in a complete circle. This was due to its being a salient, a sort of peninsula pushed into the German sea. Our guns on its short base stood almost wheel to wheel, and the German guns surrounded us except for that base, and enfiladed all our positions. That is to say, they could fire not merely at our trenches but down them. In traffic terms it would be like a pedestrian trying to cross a road with traffic going not only down it but crossing it from both pavements as well. But the vehicles were shells – anything from seventeen-inchers to field guns that weighed several tons and made a crater thirty foot across.

There were still Canadians in this area and I got to know many of them. I liked them, but they were a bit rough when drunk and fond of throwing champagne bottles which burst like bombs against the walls of the *estaminets* where we spent our leisure drinking and singing songs that someone vamped on the piano. There were generally girls of a sort about and some officers went with them. These Canadian officers were armed with Ross rifles – fine sporting gun with a peepsight, but a poor weapon for war and one that cost many Canadian lives before it was replaced. It was equipped with a short bayonet not much longer than a dagger. By a curious coincidence I met Lady Ross, the widow of Sir Charles Ross, the inventor of the rifle, in New York about twenty years later, and later still when my friend Senator Ballinger came to stay on my farm in Africa I found that he had been Sir Charles's secretary at one time. This is merely another of those occasions when the cliché 'it's a small world' was proved true.

In June the order came to go south. Big things were brewing. We had heard rumours. Latrine rumours, flavoured with chloride of lime. Big things, boys, big things. And so we marched off with the band playing, 'Goodbye, Piccadilly, Farewell, Leicester Square.'

It was goodbye Ypres, the Asylum, Poperinghe, Potige, Wiltje and the rest. Goodbye, salient, the salient that was supposed to

be so bad but which later we looked back to with nostalgia and
spoke of as a rest home.

We were on our way to the Battle of the Somme. The big push
that would smash through the German lines and end the war.

CHAPTER 16

THE SOUND OF THE TRUMPET

WE did not march very fast, though we covered about fifteen miles a day, good for a division which, with its transport took up ten or more miles of road space. Because of my knowledge of French I did the billeting for the brigade and rode on ahead on Rajah, Colonel Robinson's brown Waler. Now that we could go fast, he no longer crab-stepped. This was a nice job. A good horse and on my own with time to see the countryside; able to get a good meal at an inn before the troops arrived to eat the place out of house and home. I used to go straight to the *mairie*, introduce myself to the mayor and, having arranged the billets for so many officers and men, have time to myself till the brigade arrived. I always had an advance party which came ahead of the battalion in light marching order and acted as guides to the billets when our people came in. I was very fond of Rajah and one of my pleasures before we moved and when things were quiet was to ride him down to listen to the divisional band playing in the evening, which it did whenever we were resting out of the line. The troops would assemble in hundreds to listen to the music and a good many officers would come too. But I liked to listen on horseback. Rajah would prance and dance and shake his head in time to the music. He would circle, buck and play up in a good-tempered way just to show how much he enjoyed it.

But at Bailleul, which should have been safe enough, I lost my friend. As I rode into the square a shell burst on the *pavé* just in front of us and wounded him so badly that I had to shoot him. I was quite untouched except for the bruises where I fell on the stones when he went down.

As far as my French was concerned, I had one adventure when, on returning from a course, I found myself in Amiens very late at night looking for somewhere to sleep. I woke up a hotel manager, who sent for the police, telling them he had a German spy at his place masquerading as a British soldier. How did he know? Name of a dog, how did he know! No British officer spoke French like that, like a Frenchman. Therefore he was a Boche. They must shoot him at once.

As we marched south the character of the country changed. We left the flat land and came to rolling ploughlands. We came to Doullens, which was the railhead for the Somme.

The show was on. This was the last of August. There had already been over two hundred thousand British casualties, with a very high proportion of officers dead. Division after division, corps after corps, army after army, had been flung against the German line. There were great victories according to the Press, where, at the cost of thousands of men, we won a few hundred yards of muddy ground. But there were still plenty of men. This was only the beginning. There were mountains of stores, great hills of ammunition, water, food, new hospital tents. Everything was active, only the dead in their thousands lay still. I had seen dead before but this was a new experience. There were more dead lying about than could be buried. It was new to have the mummified body of a German officer used as a landmark, a rendezvous for guides – a golden-haired young man who was sitting up, desiccated, in a beautiful state of preservation, a kind of mummy. Another landmark was a smashed horse-drawn ambulance. Then there were woods with every tree smashed: Bernifay Wood, Trones Wood, where the South Africans had fought so bravely and had been decimated – of the 7000 who were in action only 300 came out on their own feet. We were to fight there later. Happy Valley, Mondicourt – the names all come back.

It was at the dressing station at Mondicourt that I saw an ammunition limber drive at full gallop over four stretchers on which lay living men. They weren't alive when six horses and two limbers had gone over them. It was nobody's fault. The stretchers had been put on the track while some change was being made. Ammunition had been sent for urgently. It was not expected in the daylight and a shell had burst near the leaders, making them shy out of the driver's control. The stretchered men sat up as the wheels went over them and burst like grapes – a terrible bloody sight.

One day I was sent to reconnoitre a position at Guillemont. I saw white-painted noticeboards with the name Guillemont on them, but no village. It was behind the German lines. Even the glasses showed nothing. Then I watched the shells bursting and noticed that in one place they were sending up clouds of red brick dust. I had found my village.

We now saw German prisoners by the hundred. We saw them marching back. We saw them in cages in the rear as we came in. They were the first I had ever seen. As I saw these people I came to admire them – their discipline, their hardness – and to model myself on it. I had my hair cropped like them. I went without things just to teach myself discipline. They were real soldiers, something I wanted to be. This phase lasted for some time.

Our people were good, especially the men, but our staff work was terrible. There were fifty or sixty officers on the staff of a division and once when I rode back to Headquarters in a château with a message there was only one officer on duty – the others were all playing cricket – and he knew nothing. And this was in the middle of a battle! I could not imagine this happening in the German Army.

The message had been urgent. As far as I remember we were being shelled by our own heavies and all the telephone lines were cut. The Colonel had sent me to the transport lines, which were well forward, and told me to take any horse I wanted. I took his second horse, a bay Argentine pony, and then found this captain who could not even read a map.

Now we were really fighting. The next months are blurred. I see only major pictures. I know I was soon alone. All my friends were dead or wounded. I was leading strangers. If we lost fifty per cent in an attack we had done well. Often it was more. So everyone was a replacement. We had what is called a fighting brigadier. His brigade was always ready for action. He was much decorated and later knighted. At one time he put me under arrest and nearly had me court-martialled. He came up the line after an attack. We had fought hard and I had mounted my sentries, checked my wire and posted my Lewis guns, and he wanted me to turn out my men to inspect their rifles. I refused. He said I was under arrest. At that time I was so tired that I did not care. We had been in action for two days, had taken all our objectives and were waiting to be relieved when he turned up. The men were lying exhausted in all sorts of positions on the firestep and floor of the trench. Only the sentries were alert.

I said: 'The men are done, sir. There are none in dugouts. They can stand-to in a minute. I've inspected their rifles. Everything is in order, sir.'

'Do you refuse?' he said.

'No, sir. Not if you will give me the order in writing.' Every officer is entitled to ask for an order in writing if he does not like the sound of it. To wake the men after what they had already been through would impair their efficiency. We had had a lot of casualties and were pretty thin on the ground.

'Consider yourself under arrest,' he said.

I said: 'Yes, sir.'

'By God, I'll have you court-martialled,' he said. 'The men are filthy, unshaven – filthy.'

I said: 'We've lost a lot of men. We've been fighting two days, and if the men are dirty their rifles are loaded and clean. They are ready for action, sir.'

The men in the trenches generally kept an old sock over their rifle-bolts to keep them clean. He had even taken exception to this.

He said nothing more but went off. One thing about him was his guts. He was the only general I ever saw in the line. Nor did I ever see a staff officer. The front line was too dangerous and too dirty. Too full of rough, licentious, foul-mouthed men – common soldiers, in fact. They were also generally lousy.

By this time I was in a fine temper. I was exhausted, commanding a company of less than a hundred men, many of them not even in my regiment. This always happened in a show. Men got isolated, lost, and joined up with the nearest officer they could find.

When Colonel Robinson turned up I told him what had happened. He said: 'My God, you're a bloody young fool – but I see your point.'

I said: 'I've got to hold this bit of line. I may be counter-attacked at any moment and I'd like the men to be a bit rested. I can have them in action in a couple of minutes.'

'I'll talk to Division about it,' he said. 'I don't think anything will come of it.'

As a matter of fact he was right. In the end I heard that when the Brigadier got over his anger he said: 'We could do with a few more like that young chap.'

By this time I was sure my luck was running out. After all you can only count on Mr Luck so far. I felt by this time that Mr Death had his eye on me.

I had one more ride on the Colonel's pony that I remember. That was a night ride, again for the same reason. Communication had broken down and I galloped the pony down a railway line between the rails and over the ties. That was about the most dangerous ride I have ever taken as the line ran on a raised embankment which had been heavily shelled. But he was a wonderful pony; able to see in the dark, he'd jump and change feet whenever he had to. But I didn't care. By that time I was so tired that it didn't matter. Anyway it's not a bad end to break your neck off a horse.

This countryside which once had been the fairest fields of France was now so pitted with shell-holes that they cut into each other. There wasn't a blade of grass, nor a living thing, only earth and broken men and equipment for as far as the eye could see. And then it began to rain. Winter was on its way. The craters filled up with water in which bodies floated. We lost men drowned in the mud. A Lewis gunner fell into a crater on one march. The gun on his shoulder pushed him under and we never got him out.

We moved across vast empty fields that had been tilled by the exploding shells, straggling in single file, a few yards between each man, loaded with all that we could carry till we got to an assembly trench, or what was left of it, and took over from our exhausted predecessors and prepared to attack. Once, after a show and ten days in the line beating off counter-attacks, we had just got back to Carnoy for a few days' rest when we were stood-to again. We had got in after a march of five hours through mud up to our knees. We had just had supper. I had seen to the men and was getting ready to creep into my valise – we were lying in the open – when the order came. The trenches we had taken had been lost and we were to go back and re-take them. We marched back through the mud. I made the men fix bayonets and prod anyone in front of them who looked like falling asleep to keep him awake.

That made the best part of ten hours' marching in knee-deep mud. We got back just before dawn and attacked at once over the top with bombs and bayonets. The men lost their tiredness in their fury. These were the bastards who'd come between them and their rest. I ended up the only officer in the battalion, with the trench cleared of Germans, and then handed over to a major of another brigade who had come to reinforce us, but he gave us no credit.

This was my worst battle. I was so angry, so exhausted, so certain my number was up, that I didn't even care and had fought in the open, on top of the trenches, with a party of men who felt as I did, bombing and shooting our way along, killing Germans like fish in a barrel. They could not get at us. Our danger was from desultory gunfire and machine-guns.

We were now fairly deep in captured country and had the use of the German dugouts. They were deeper and better made than ours. The only trouble was that they faced the wrong way and there was always some danger of getting a shell down the spout, as it were. I was certainly tougher now than I had been. I remember after one show rolling a dead German off a bed in a dugout and going to sleep with him beside me on the floor.

It was growing cold and we were in fighting order, without blankets or coats. All I had was a trench coat and the men had groundsheets, so when in a dugout I found whole unopened crates of German overcoats that had not been issued, I took one myself and wore it. I was nearly killed that night by one of our men as I stood in the trench without my tin hat in my German overcoat and cropped head. So far I had been lucky about lice but now I got them and they sent me nearly mad. Going through the seams of our clothes for lice as we sat on the firestep became a pastime for all ranks. It was not so much the bite as their walking about which irritated me. A Frenchman put this very well when he said: '*Ce n'est pas la piqure, c'est la promenade.*' Once when they were particularly bad and I was near a gun emplacement, I gave an artillery sergeant a pound for his riding breeches and put them on, still warm from his legs. In war one loses daintiness.

After one attack we got no rations for seventy hours. The pack animals could not get through. We blamed no one, we knew our transport would kill themselves to get us our rations if it was possible, so we began to search the dead Germans who were lying all round us, and though they were in a very poor state of preservation the food in their packs was edible – the cans being naturally completely unaffected and some of the sausage excellent.

We had some interesting experiences at this time with German snipers. We were losing men shot in the back as we were moving forward and only after we had lost several did we tumble to the trick. Some of the Germans lying behind us were not dead. They had put snipers among the corpses. So I posted men to watch the dead. We caught one of them and killed him at once. There was talk of prisoners being killed and I think some were. Some men, rather than take a ten-mile march to the rear with a party of Germans, would just kill them, but I imagine this must occur in all countries and in every war. Had the men who did it been caught, they would have been court-martialled and shot.

It was now September and the big thing was coming. The battle that would end the war. All the rest, it appeared, had been no more than a prelude. We would know all about it soon. Meanwhile rest, a few days' fattening up, and then the day came. We paraded and loaded up for action. I cannot understand how we ever fought carrying all that impedimenta – picks, shovels, flares, rockets, sandbags, extra ammunition (a spare bandolier) and bombs. When we had gone about five miles we saw a sight that will never be seen again: three divisions of cavalry standing by their horses with slack girths. The horses all had bandoliers of ammunition round their necks. Forty thousand of the finest horses in the world and forty thousand regular cavalrymen. They were waiting for us to make a breach in the German line which they would sweep through and before fanning out, silencing the guns, cutting the communications in traditional cavalry style, blowing up bridges and railway lines and capturing generals surprised at their headquarters.

We were issued with maps and told that we would halt at Combles that night. Combles was six or seven miles behind the German lines, and then suddenly we saw the reason for all this optimism. Hidden in the little woods were great steel monsters from which their crews were pulling camouflage canvas covers. Tanks. The first that had ever been seen. They were going to smash the wire. We would follow them with bomb and bayonet, clearing up, then the cavalry would sweep through at full gallop and the war would be won. One more action and the war was over. These monsters which now began to creep forward, clanking and clattering, would do it for us.

And they might have if there had been two thousand of them instead of thirty, and if we had known how to fight with them. Knowing no better, we clustered near them like chicks near a mother hen. But this was, nevertheless, a famous day. It was September 25th, 1916, when tanks were used for the first time and cavalry for the last. To a soldier of today this must seem indescribably funny – as funny as the tactics of an Indian fighter or a Welsh archer would have been to us. But it wasn't funny then. It was terrible.

We attacked with the tanks and had very heavy casualties, as they drew all the fire which soon knocked most of them out. Others stuck, straddling trenches too wide for them. Others broke down. But a few got through and we went with them. It very nearly came off. A thousand tanks, a few hundred even, and it would have. This had been for once a well-kept secret. The surprise had been complete. The actual figures I found out later were: 39 tanks landed, 20 broke down before they reached the line and only five penetrated the German trenches. As it was, we went further than we ever had before, and I saw some Indian cavalry in action.

I saw the points of their lances shining in the sunlight as they rode up a sunken road. I saw them debouch and lower their lances and charge past us up the road where we were waiting to advance. There was a British officer leading them with one native officer and about twenty troopers – a cavalry patrol sent to feel out the enemy. I heard the German machine-guns open and within five minutes they were coming back with half the saddles empty. I caught one of the horses and, as I had a man wounded in the hand whom I wanted to send to the rear, I told him to lead the horse back to our transport lines. So I got something out of it: a nice little bay mare which I kept for a month or so.

But it was a great day, an historic day. Another to add in red figures to the calendar of my memories. Something that will never be seen again.

Tanks were an answer to the German wire as they flattened

paths through it. They came in two kinds: male and female. The females were armed only with machine-guns, the males had a Hotchkiss gun sticking out of the turret – like a cock out of its steel flies.

It must be remembered that this battle on the Somme was the greatest the world has ever seen. Completely undecisive, it was a war of men against high explosive. It was without mobility except in the periods of attack. There were no wild charges. We synchronized our watches, drove wooden pegs into the parapet in front of us and waited while the guns pounded the German line. The shells went over like a gale above us. Among them we could hear the big ones – howitzer projectiles – that sounded like passing trains. We went on looking at our watches. The attacks generally took place an hour before dawn, when the night was at its coldest. It was the hour before death for many of us. We joked obscenely to keep up our spirits; some men prayed. We tightened our belts and adjusted our equipment. We checked the immense burdens we had to carry. Two bandoliers of ammunition, digging implements (picks and shovels), Very pistols to light up the darkness. Hundreds of sandbags that we should need to consolidate the captured positions. Rockets and flares to signal when we needed artillery retaliation or reinforcement if we were being counter-attacked. We had our Lewis guns and spare drums and ammunition and parts for them, stretchers and first-aid material and bandages and iodine. We had our pistols, maps, compasses and field-glasses. We had Mills bombs in haversacks and gas-masks slung beneath our chins. We carried iron rations and water-bottles.

The men are very still. They are standing-to. They stare into the darkness in front of them and see the enemy's wire silhouetted against the red glow of the shells bursting behind it. We hope the wire is cut. We were told it had been cut yesterday before we moved in. We hope it's true. We are rested, fat for slaughter – shock troops.

I look at my watch again. How funny to live by a watch, minute by minute, as if I were going to catch a train. It is growing a little lighter. The sky begins to turn grey.

Fix bayonets. There is a clatter of metal against metal, the sharp sigh of steel withdrawn from the secrecy of its scabbard.

The hard irrevocable click as the bayonets go home in their sockets. Ten minutes. Five minutes.

'How much longer, sir?'

'Four minutes.'

He passes the word. A tremor goes through the few men I can see in my bay. What are they thinking of? Home? They have had their rum ration. I issued it an hour ago. One sixty-fourth part of a gallon, which is a small coffee cupful, per man. It came up the line in big brown stone jars. It was black fragrant West Indian rum – overproof.

Suddenly there is a roar. Our barrage has come down. The whole of our front is scarlet and yellow with bursting shells, black with the thrown-up soil of the German trenches. The soil grows like trees out of the ground. One minute to go. I watch the second hand of the watch. I put my whistle in my mouth and blow. No one can hear it, drop it so that it hangs from the lanyard round my neck. Pick up the pick handle I always carry and climb out of the comparative security of the trench into no-man's-land.

We are like men naked. The walls of the trench were our clothes. As far as I can see on both sides of me, men are climbing out and moving forward, their rifles at the port, ready, their bayonets glinting in the dawn.

We do not run. We walk. We stroll behind our barrage as if it was a curtain. It is a curtain, a curtain of fire and death. We must stay close to it but not close enough to be hit. If we are not close, the survivors of the bombardment who have been driven underground into the dugouts will have time to come up again.

It was a magnificent sight. On our right was the Guards Division. They might have been walking across the parade ground. Big, calm men who were there to kill. The excitement was there. The blood was up. The rum. The roar of the guns. The terrible fear before we started had turned to anger, and anger killed the fear. A hare got up in front of us. How long had it lived in no-man's-land? It ran down the line. As if they were beaters, the men lunged at it. A man caught it on the point of his bayonet and held up his rifle with one hand. The men cheered. It was blood, first blood – except, of course, that of the men we had lost as we strolled along. The Germans were dropping a lot of stuff on us. But when a man was hit the others just closed in to occupy the blank he had left.

We came to the first objective. The blue line, it was called on our maps. The wire had been cut; we had no difficulty. We jumped into the trench. There were a lot of dead men in it, grotesque as the dead always are. Some of them had been blown to pieces. A machine-gun opened on us and was attacked by the bombers, who were followed by a bayonet section. We threw bombs down all the dugouts. They went bumpety-bump down the steps. We heard screams. Some Germans bolted out with their hands up. Prisoners. They were herded together like sheep and sent back with a guard who had instructions to shoot them if they gave any trouble. Headquarters wanted prisoners as soon as possible for identification purposes.

I looked at my watch again. We had been quick. It had not taken as long as had been allowed. Another five minutes and we would go on to the second objective. And then to the third, where we were to dig in and consolidate. By that time there would not be so many of us.

In the next line – the support – we had more trouble. The trenches were deeper and they had made some slits that were safe except for a direct hit. The troops were better, too – Prussians. They got out of the trench to meet us and we fought hand to hand. Bayonet met bayonet while the machine-guns spat and bombs were lobbed like cricket balls. German stick bombs and our pineapple-like Mills bombs. This was the only time I saw a fight like this. It is very rare for bayonet to meet bayonet. Bayoneted men may go towards each other but as a rule one will break and run before the steel. I saw the results on another occasion where the Scots Guards had engaged the Prussian Guards and had fought till hardly any of either regiment were left alive. We found them later, some still erect, impaled on one another's steel.

The sun swelled up the dead with gas and often turned them blue, almost navy blue. Then, when the gas escaped from their bodies, they dried up like mummies and were frozen in their death positions. There was even a man bandaging himself who had been killed by a shell fragment as he unrolled the bandage. There were sitting bodies, kneeling bodies, bodies in almost every position, though naturally most of them lay on their bellies or their backs. The crows had pecked out the eyes of some and rats lived on bodies that lay in the abandoned dugouts or half buried in the crumbled trenches. These rats were very large and many of them were piebald, blotched with pink, where they had lost great patches of their hair. They were quite fearless, their familiarity with the dead having made them contemptuous of the living. One night one fell on my face in a dugout and bit me. It must have been running along a beam above me and the vibration of a shell exploding nearby had knocked it off.

Burial was impossible. In ordinary warfare the bodies went down with the limbers that brought up the rations. But then there were seldom more than three or four in a day. Now there were hundreds, thousands, not merely ours but German as well. And where we fought several times over the same ground bodies became incorporated in the material of the trenches themselves. In one place we had to dig through corpses of Frenchmen who had been killed and buried in 1915. These bodies were putrid, of the consistency of Camembert cheese. I once fell and put my hand right through the belly of a man. It was days before I got the smell out of my nails. I remember wondering if I could get blood poisoning and thinking it would be ironic to have survived so much and then be killed by a long-dead Frenchman.

The only previous experience I had had of rotting bodies had been at Serre, where, as a battalion, we dealt with the best part of a thousand dead who came to pieces in our hands. As you lifted a body by its arms and legs they detached themselves from the torso, and this was not the worst thing. Each body was covered inches deep with a black fur of flies which flew up into your face, into your mouth, eyes and nostrils, as you approached. The bodies crawled with maggots. There had been a disaster here. An attack by green, badly led troops who had had too big a rum ration – some of them had not even fixed their bayonets – against a strong position where the wire was still uncut. They hung like washing on the barbs. Like scarecrows which scared no crows since they were edible. The birds disputed the bodies with us. This was a job for all ranks. No one could expect the men to handle these bodies unless the officers did their share. We worked with sandbags on our hands, stopping every now and then to puke.

It was here that I first came into contact with the Guards, whom I was one day to join, and heard about their exploits. On one occasion when the Germans broke through the regiments on either flank fell back; the Guards wired in their flanks while they waited for orders and then, when ordered to retreat, cut their way through the Germans, who had by this time surrounded them. To see them marching up to the line brought even the peasants, bored with the war, to the roadside to watch. The division, fifteen thousand men, all six feet tall, all in step, marching in perfect alignment with long, rather slow strides which, because they were so tall, still took them along at four miles an hour, was something to see and a still greater thing to be a part of. For among these regiments – the Grenadiers, Coldstreamers, Scots, Irish and Welsh Guards – there was a great feeling of brotherhood and solidarity. They were without fear because each regiment had absolute confidence in the others. They could not fail. They could only be destroyed. The non-commissioned officers were superb and the officers led them well. Boys straight from school were pitched into battle and behaved with unbelievable courage. When I joined the Guards Division later on I was to some extent hardened. But some of these young men were not and I remember seeing a strange sight. We were held up by enemy shelling and were waiting for it to end, the way one waits for a shower of rain, when I saw a young officer bring out a little leather manicure set from his pocket and begin to trim his nails without even looking up. A sissy – but the kind men love and will follow.

For attacking troops, taking their objective was only the beginning. It had to be held until fresh troops could be brought up. Naturally the enemy put down a barrage between us and our reinforcements, cutting us off from the rear. Food and water parties had to go through a rain of shells to reach us and the stretcher-bearers had to go through it to dump their wounded and then come back. In the meantime the Germans plastered us. They had the exact range of their old trenches. They poured in high explosive and burst the heavy black shrapnel shells we called 'woolly bears' above us. As soon as they thought we were softened up they would launch their counter-attacks, sometimes one wave coming after another. We mowed them down at times till our rifles were almost too hot to hold.

We had no comforts with us. No blankets or coats. Our packs had been left before we attacked. We were in 'fighting order' with only a haversack on our shoulders. We had our iron rations – a tin or two of bully, some square hardtack biscuits, and in a little canvas bag a mixture of tea and sugar so that we could make tea if we had a chance of lighting a fire. If it rained we got wet. If it froze we froze. There were patrols to be sent out to get in touch with the enemy in front and the units on one's flanks so as to check any gaps in the line. It was strange to think of it running without a break from the Channel coast to the Swiss border.

The movement of troops followed a pattern. Leaving the billets or camps in the rear, the men marched up by battalions in columns of fours till they reached the danger zone. Then they broke up into small parties, platoons or even sections, so that should there be a direct hit on the road casualties would be reduced to a minimum and moved two deep or in single file on the verges, where they would not show up so conspicuously from the air.

When the support trenches were reached the battalion straggled through them till the new position was taken over from the troops that were being relieved. There was a strange predictable pattern about it all, even about the certainty that if one went on long enough one would be hit or killed.

In October when we took Le Transloi we suffered a lot of casualties. We were rather widely spaced and I was amazed to see a rifle pointing at me and realized that the enormous German who held it was going to pull the trigger. He had sprung from the ground at my feet like a bloody great Jack-in-the-box. A battle was different from the curious objectivity of trench warfare where you sat and were shelled for hours, even days, at a time. There you felt that it was all an act of God – a terrific storm of explosive hailstones. One of them would either hit you or it would not. One either had your name on it or it did not. You knew men had come through without being touched. You knew others who were killed in their first hour in the line. Naturally after a while, as you learnt something about the tricks of war, you were a little safer than you were in the beginning. But only a little.

This situation, too, was different from trench raids and fighting in the restricted area of the trench itself where you were in close contact with the enemy, with pistol, knife, club and bomb, and surrounded by your men. This was neither hand to hand nor being sniped at from a distance. We were in the open. The nearest other Yorkshiremen were themselves engaged ten or fifteen yards away. We had lost a lot of our people and were scattered pretty widely along the front. So to all intents and purposes the German and I were alone in a green field that had been only partially ploughed by recent shellfire. It all took a very long time, like a picture in slow motion. I thought: I've only had my regular commission three days and now I'm going to be killed.

Shortly before we went into action the Colonel had sent me a chit to say my regular commission had just come through. I had applied for it some months earlier, recommended by the Colonel and Brigadier-General, but regular commissions were not given to officers under nineteen although at the time of my application I was commanding a company, it did not affect the regulation.

The German's cheek lay along the butt of his rifle. I could see the black hole of the muzzle. I could see the point of the bayonet. That was the focus of everything. The man, the rifle ending in a steel point. The whole weight of it ending in something little bigger or sharper than my mother's embroidery scissors that were shaped like two gilded cranes. A point was a point.

I moved towards him with my pistol in my hand. My feet dragged. As I advanced the rifle barrel continued to move, following me. Why didn't he shoot? Why didn't he? Why did he hold his fire? Suddenly I ran to close in. As I ran, he fired. I spun round and sat down. I felt no pain. I felt as if someone had hit me in the shoulder with a great wooden mallet with such force as to knock me over. Now he was coming for me. The bayonet was lowered. I got the full perspective – the point, the blade, the rifle and the big man leaning forward as he ran. He became enormous, a giant. The rifle was a battering ram, the bayonet a lance. When he was almost on me I fired. As he fell, I fired again and he fell on me. Now I began to think about myself. The war had got away from me. I could see the men very small against the horizon as I sat on the ground. I had not tried to get up yet.

We had been in the second wave, mopping up, throwing bombs into dugouts and taking prisoners. Soon the Huns would drop a barrage behind our advance. Meanwhile there was a very pleasant sound of our shells going like the rush of birds' wings over my head. I stood up. I did not feel too bad. Now I had to make the big decision. I could go on fighting and be a hero. But I had been a hero about a fortnight before and got nothing out of it. Someone else, the Major in the 2nd Downshires, had taken the credit for what we had done and was getting a DSO. I was pretty certain from the way we had been knocked about and the dead I had seen that if I did go on and manage to survive I might find myself in command of the battalion, if not the brigade. Last time we had gone over the brigade had been reduced from a nominal strength of four thousand to three hundred men. Whatever happened, I should be in a very responsible position. I should have to prepare for the counter-attack that would come that night. I should have to get out new wire, convert the German trenches by cutting firesteps in the parados, arrange about evacuating the wounded, about getting rations and reinforcements, and might have to fight for two or three more days before we were relieved. On the other hand I had ample excuse to walk off and leave the war. I wanted a medal. Medals are very valuable to a regular soldier. But one does not get medals unless one is seen being brave. Besides I was very tired and already a survivor. I felt this 'blighty' was the last present I should get from Mr Luck. We had been over the top six times in four weeks and had never lost less than fifty per cent in casualties. I was the last officer but one who had come through. I had always felt luck to be expendable and I had had about my share. Now I had my blighty and was off. I bent down and took the dead German's belt. I wiped the blood off it on his trousers, removed the bayonet scabbard and fastened the belt with its *Gott mit Uns* buckle round my own waist. Souvenir, I thought, and a good one. I felt somewhat elated. I had been in close fighting before but that was always such a muck-up, so confused that you never quite knew what you had done. And I had sniped a couple of Germans with telescopic sights but they had not seemed real – just little mannikins who stood in the circle of my telescope doubly bisected by the crossed hairs that centred it. But this was real. This one I had killed. I think it would not have been difficult for me to have scalped him, as some of the Indians among the French Canadians were said to have done. But I couldn't do it.

I began to laugh. It was against the King's regulations and the Geneva Convention. But it was a pity. It is easy to understand how atrocities are committed as men revert to savagery under pressure. He had tried to kill me. The bastard. I left my German with regret and turned my back on the war.

Here was another new sensation – being alone on a battlefield, strolling through it as if it was a garden. I remember thinking how untidy it was. There were hundreds of bodies– our own and Germans. There were torn and bloody bandages, burst haversacks, equipment, abandoned rifles driven muzzle first into the churned-up soil to mark a body, a wounded man perhaps who had died before he got help. And paper – there was masses of torn paper, letters, postcards, wrapping from parcels. Pictures of girls, women with children. A piece of shaving mirror winked in the sun like a heliograph. There were dead horses and mules, broken waggons, limbers, discarded harness, heaps of ammunition. By now I was through the area we had fought over this morning, still green between the new shell-holes, and back in the trenches that we had attacked from.

There was no grass here, only mud and duckboard tracks winding their way between the craters, many of them ten feet deep and filled with mud and water. If I slipped I should drown. I still felt no pain but I was tired. At this point I became two men. My mind left my body, went ahead and stood on a hill. From there I watched, quite objectively and with some amusement, the struggles of this body of mine staggering over the duckboards and wading through the mud where the duckboards were smashed. I watched it duck when a salvo of German shells came over. I saw it fall flat on its face when a concealed battery of our own whizzbangs opened up within a few yards of it. I saw it converse with the gunners who, stripped to the waist, loaded, pulled the lanyards of their guns and jumped away from the leaping recoil. The gunners were too busy to talk but a corporal gave my body some rum which seemed to strengthen it. I was most interested in the process.

I then rejoined my body. The rum may have done it. And after another mile or so we came to the heavies. Six- or eight-inch. I forget, but they were more dilatory than the eighteen-pounders. They didn't bark like terriers, they roared like lions at sixty-second intervals. With this battery there was a staff captain who asked for news of the war. I gave it to him. He took me down into a dugout and I showed him where we had got to on the map. I was given tea laced with whisky and he dressed my shoulder. I was not bleeding much but my shoulder-blade was smashed up and I was spitting a little blood. I was feeling cold so he lent me his trench coat. He said he'd come and get it later at the casualty clearing station. His name was Geoffrey Gilbey. Later we became great friends. There were more wounded converging on the first-aid station. Walking wounded and parties of prisoners carrying stretchers accompanied by guards with fixed bayonets. I saw the medical officer. He said: 'Are you all right?'

I said: 'Yes.'

Then he said: 'Well, sit there and get into an ambulance when they come.' They came before long. A string of Fords marked with red crosses on a white circle. The walking wounded who did not need immediate attention and the stretcher cases were loaded up. It was a rough ride and dark when we reached the casualty clearing station.

It was a large tent and, coming in from the dark, the glare was dazzling. It was lit by a number of acetylene flares like those used by costers to illuminate their wares in the London slums. Under each flare was a doctor dressed in white. The white was scarlet with blood from waist to neck. Their hands and forearms dripped with blood. Their faces were streaked where they had wiped the sweat from their eyes and foreheads. They were attended by male orderlies also dressed in bloody white. In a corner of the great marquee there was a heap of severed legs and arms as tall as I.

There was nothing for me here but I had been fed into the assembly line that led to the meat-grinder. An orderly extracted me from it.

'Tetanus,' he said as he led me away to a curtained-off section where an intern injected me. I do not know how they do it now but in those days they pushed about thirty cubic centimetres into you, using a syringe like a grease gun with a needle the size of a two-inch nail and just about as blunt, so that the intern who did the job had to shove to get the needle through the skin above my left breast. I then had a label tied round my neck and was marked on the forehead with a purple indelible pencil which the orderly moistened in his mouth before using. By that time I didn't care. Let him spit in my eye.

Another wait. Another ambulance, and then the hospital train. It was white with red crosses painted on it. Women. English women again. The sound of their starched skirts and women's voices was like the sound of running water to a man dying of thirst. Pyjamas, sheets, warm, properly cooked food. I had died. I was in heaven. I had, for the second time in my life, achieved my heart's desire. I had my regular commission. I was wounded, not sufficiently to damage me seriously, only enough to make me interesting. I was nineteen years old. A nice-looking boy. A war hero with a gold wound stripe. Now I could relax. It was wonderful. I don't think I had been so relaxed since I was a baby in a pram. Well, now I was a baby again, someone else could look after me and, by God, I was tired of taking care of myself and a lot of men, many of them old enough to be my father.

They dressed my wound. I was still in no pain; my nerve centres were too bruised. I had been hit in the left breast. The bullet had touched my lung and come out, smashing my shoulder-blade.

This period was extraordinary. A terrible nightmare of fear, hardship, exhaustion and unbelievable loneliness. I had lived with two gods – Mr Luck and Mr Death. I was not particularly afraid of being killed. I think what most of us feared was being crippled, blinded or hit in the genitals. There seems to be a natural instinct when fighting to lean forward, bending to protect them. Freud's castration complex is a reality in action. I had become very sensitive to atmosphere, to the three zones of war: the line where there were only fighting men; the next zone that was semi-immune to shellfire, where there were the ancillary services, Army Service Corps, casualty clearing stations, horse lines, and possibly some heavy guns. There were also some civilians and one could buy food, wine and women – women whose cupidity was stronger than their fear; and finally the back areas peopled by old men, cripples, children and virtuous women. This arrangement must have applied equally to the German side. Between us lay no-man's-land, most aptly named. Uninhabited, filled with flowers and long grass, unshelled except by accident, but the scene of small fortuitous encounters between patrols.

When resting out of the line we had regimental and brigade sports. Football matches, races, concerts, wrestling and boxing. We had no heavyweight boxers, our men being on the small side, but some good middle-weights, one in particular, Sergeant Little, whom I never saw beaten. A curious feature of our boxing was the way the handlers would refresh their men as they sat in their corners between rounds. They would dip a tumbler into a pail, fill their mouths with water and spray it out over the boxer's face.

Exhaustion and hardship do curious things to the brain, to the imagination. The Somme Battle was a period of fantastic contrasts. One day while the battalion was being rested and fattened up with food and new drafts of men I could be galloping Rajah over untouched fields, riding down partridges – if you marked them, they generally only made three flights, you could catch them if you could find them – and the next we were back in it. It was a period of summer hayfields, singing birds and flowers on the one hand, and of mud, blood and the stink of dead bodies on the other, with nothing to separate these two worlds, the summer idyll and the inferno, but a few hours of marching time.

Action bled into action, march into march. When I could I wrote post-dated field service postcards to my mother, ten days or so ahead, one for each day and left them with the transport to be posted. I crossed out everything except 'I am well.' One of them might easily arrive after I had been hit or killed.

Other things of psychological importance took place in this period. I had read some serious books belonging to other officers. The one that made the greatest impression on me was Otto Weiniger's *Sex and Character*, with his sexual theory that a well-mated married couple formed between them a unit that was 100 per cent male and 100 per cent female. This accounted for some marriages I had seen where a very feminine man married to a very masculine woman made a success of it because they balanced out. I had taken to smoking heavily. I lived on cigarettes and tea. I never drank much. Sex was pressing me hard and I began to masturbate regularly. I was not going to touch the kind of whores who were available and even refused Paris leave because I was afraid – shy of the better-class prostitutes – and also because I felt that if once I broke the rhythm of war life I should have great difficulty in getting back into it. Forty-eight-hours Paris leave was simply not worth it to me.

Then there was the strange effect of living in German dugouts sixty feet below ground in absolute silence while the war was going on above one's head. I knew I was not what I had been when I came to France. I was someone else. The I, the me, had changed.

Next day I was at Rouen in the base hospital. I wrote letters. Telegrams were sent. I would be on the casualty list. I would wear a gold wound stripe on my left cuff. But I was in pain now. Dressing my wound consisted of plugging it with medicated tape which the sister pushed through me with a sort of knitting-needle as an orderly fed it to her out of a bottle of disinfectant. It was a very unpleasant procedure.

The nurses here were regulars. They were beribboned with service medals and wore grey uniforms with scarlet-lined capes. Any milk of kindness they may have had as young women had long since evaporated under the heat of tropic suns. Their handling of wounded men was rough; the male orderlies were more gentle.

The man next to me died the second day I was there. He was a good-looking, hard-bitten Australian of thirty or so. There could be no illusion about his manhood. He was dying and he knew it, twelve thousand miles away from home. And he was dying angry, grandly, like a wounded lion. A padre approached his bed. This, too, was part of the routine of death. A padre to issue the necessary visa into the next world. C of E, RC . . . other religions. But the Australian would have none of it. 'I've lived without God and I'll die without Him,' he said.

The Matron ignored him and said: 'The padre's come to see you.'

'I don't want a bloody parson,' he said.

But the parson was there beside his bed, a captain in khaki with black Maltese cross badges. He had a little black book in his hand.

'I've come to help you,' he said. 'Help you to meet your Maker.'

'Maker?' the Aussie said. 'My maker was me dad, a drunken bastard who broke his neck when a buckjumper fell on him.

Die!' he said. 'That's right. I've had my chips. Turn up my toes, kick the bloody bucket, but I'll do it by myself, cobber. I'll die alone like a dog in a ditch.'

'You must think,' the padre said. 'Repent . . . forgiveness . . .'

'Think? Christ, what the hell do you think I'm doing? I'm thinking I'll never see down under again. I'll never smell the blue gums hot in the sun. Never throw a leg over another horse, drink a bottle of whisky or have a woman. That's what I'm thinking, Padre.'

The parson talked of repentance and remission of sins. The Australian said: 'I don't want to creep in by the back door. I'll stand by what I've done. A death-bed repentance, that's too easy, Padre. A man must pay for his sins and his pleasures.'

'Jesus paid for them on the cross.'

'No one pays my debts,' the Australian said.

The parson said something about comfort.

'Comfort?' he said. 'Like hell you can. What does a bloody sky-pilot know about life? Think of it, cobber.' He laughed.

'Aren't you afraid to meet your Maker?' the parson said.

'I ain't afraid of nothing. I've lived like a man, I'll die like one. When I die you'll bury me because I can't stop you. Neat as a whistle with my cobbers. Lined up. On parade. Numbered . . . named . . .'

'But . . . but . . .' the parson said. 'You should be thinking . . .'

'I am. Christ, am I thinking! I'm thinking of good horses and bad women. The feel of 'em, the sound of 'em, the smell of 'em. Now leave me to die in peace.'

The parson left. His lips were moving; he was praying silently.

This was the first time I had seen a man die in bed. Many men died in that war who would have been saved today. The symptoms of death were an extra visit or two from the doctor, a consultation with the nurses and sisters, and a red screen put round the bed.

In the morning the screen was gone and there was another man in his bed.

'Funny, isn't it,' the man on my other side said, 'the way they put a red screen round the chaps that are going to die. Must encourage them.'

'Seen it before?' I asked.

'Oh yes. This is the third one. Red screen, change the sheets and another chap is in the bed before the mattress cools. I was awake,' he said, 'and saw the orderlies come and wheel him out on rubber wheels, like a bicycle. Then they brought in the other chap.'

I thought. Dead men's shoes. Dead men's beds.

I had heard some of this going on behind the screen. Though I was asleep when they fetched him, I had heard him die in the night. He breathed very hard for a while and then he didn't breathe at all. He was dead. He died silent, game, without a whimper. I couldn't believe that God – if there was a God – would be angry with such a man, for it was God who had made him bold, who had made him a man. But his death made a great impression on me. I thought: that is the way to die – silent and game. But the man, with all that the word implied, was no longer with us. It seemed worse to die here in bed with white sheets and a red screen than under the open sky.

I was out of it in the best possible way for a while. But thinking it over I was amazed at the courage I had seen. I had not had time to think of it before. Of all the men I had seen hit. Of the badly wounded men lying on stretchers by the aid posts and casualty clearing stations. I had hardly heard one cry out. When they were hit they would gasp and say, 'I'm hit,' and someone would shout for stretcher-bearers. Word would be passed on, echoing down the line. I have heard boys on their stretchers crying with weakness, but all they ever asked for was water or a cigarette. The exception was a man hit through the palm of the hand. This I believe to be the most painful wound there is, as the sinews of the arm contract, tearing as if on a rack. Men with stomach wounds moaned. Otherwise there was silence.

A week later I was evacuated to England. I remember thinking that the Germans would be quite entitled to sink us, as I and most of the others with me would be fighting again in three months or so. That was part of my tough phase. I could easily have been trained, conditioned, to be merciless. I could, had I been a German in Hitler's time, have become a Nazi. That was what shocked me so much in the Second World War – that I could so easily have gone that way. There indeed but for the Grace of God, of luck, of circumstance, went I. It is now apparent that anyone can be conditioned into almost anything. A man can be forced to confess crimes he has never committed, a woman beaten into becoming a prostitute. Only a few, a very few, can resist a combination of psychological pressure and torture. These are the real heroes. Those of the Resistance Movements who died silent when tortured. I am not of that metal.

CHAPTER 17

THE LOVER

THE hospital I was sent to was in Reading. It was the old work-house and was remarkable for its inefficiency. The dressings were kept in a cupboard with such light refreshments as biscuits, potted meat and jugs of milk.

My wound was not particularly serious. The bullet had gone into my chest on the left side touching the lung and smashing quite a big hole in the shoulder-blade as it came out. My left arm was put in a sling and the wound plugged with medical tape, as had been done in Rouen. Even at best, dressing it was painful as the top end of the tape had to be pushed right through to the shoulder-blade. Done roughly, it was very painful. It is obviously impossible for doctors or nurses to get upset about patients. Too much sympathy would interfere with efficiency. But a certain amount of gentleness would seem possible as I was to find out later. But these women treated fighting men with less consideration than I employed with an injured animal when I was ranching.

I never had time to think about what we had gone through in terms of hardship quite apart from danger. When it rained I looked out of the window and thought of how we had spent days and nights in rain, sleet and snow marching, fighting or just standing like animals and taking it, I thought of the mud up to our knees, the bitter winds of the Flanders plain and wondered how we had stood it, why we had not all died of exposure. It was extraordinary the punishment the young human body could take. Marching heavily laden with pack and rifle, to the point of exhaustion and then going into battle. What upheld us? Pride in our regiments, and stubborn refusal to acknowledge we were beat. Youth, though many of us were not so young. Days, weeks and months of it, living almost in the open, hunting and hunted with only vestigial shelter unless we were deep underground like

animals – moles, foxes, badgers in our earths and burrows. I felt
an enormous pride in my body for having stood up to the strain.
I was in a state of shocked wonder at my luck in survival, for it
was luck pure and simple, it was without merit. I, those about me
in the ward, had come through it thanks to Mr Luck, to chance.
At night I heard some moans and screams as we fought again.
Soldiers' nightmares. We peeped through periscopes, we lay
sweating under a barrage waiting to advance. We shouted orders.
At night there was no escape from the war. Not yet. It was still
too near us.

I did not pay much attention to the other officers in the ward.
I was too preoccupied with my change of environment. The
silence. The feeling that for the next few weeks I need no longer
feel afraid or act with courage. Again, in Reading the sisters were
the same regulars who prided themselves on being tough.
Women without love. It seems essential that a woman should
love and be loved if she is to retain the characteristics of her
sex.

While in hospital I thought about the miles I had marched.
Hundreds. Thousands, perhaps. The ring of boots on the road.
Left, right, left, right. Left . . . the rhythm. The smell of sweat
and men's clothes. The metallic clink of weapons – rifles, side-
arms, entrenching tools. The battalion, a long segmented khaki
insect crawling along the roads while over it, like a garment, was
spread the sound of song. Soldiers had always sung as they
marched. On route marches. Into battle. Roman legions. British
archers. Men-at-arms. But not when they came out. Coming
away from it, with the dead and the noise behind them, they
were too tired. They had too much on their minds and in their
hearts.

Singing as we marched up the line was a kind of whistling in
the dark – the darkness of fear – like boys in a graveyard. All over
Europe these savage insects were crawling along the roads. In
England, France, Belgium, Germany, Russia. Insects, of khaki,
of horizon blue, of field grey . . . Marching towards each other to
meet and mate in a dance of death on this new frontier that
stretched like a long thin stage from the Alps of Switzerland to
the Belgian dunes. The training, the drills had all been dance
movements, a preparation for this terrible mass ballet, orches-

trated by explosions, illuminated by flares, by gun flashes, perfumed by poison gas, by lyddite and the rotting dead.

These were the clean-bed thoughts that came to me as I lay
with these others in the wings. How exclusively masculine it all
was. Virile, and at the same time sterile, since the virility could not
be spent. Only now in hospital were we on the periphery of
women. First the harpies of the base with hard fingers and dried-
out dugs. Then this place where among the harpies were girls as
eager for life as we were to give it. And outside the laughter of
children. For the moment at least, as long as we remained awake,
the nightmare was over.

My mind was on girls as I watched the VADs in the ward. On
the mystery of them. Of their bodies under the rustling starch of
their uniforms. I still knew nothing. The only woman I had seen
naked was Gwen, the Empire prostitute, and that had done
nothing to me. But I had changed a lot since then. I was a different
man, a soldier home from the wars. A boy in search of the Holy
Grail, the Golden Fleece, that would be the consummation of
desire.

What romantic rubbish that sounds in the world of today. But
that is the way many of us thought then. I had given up God –
not that I had ever had Him – but I knew my god would be a
woman. Venus Aphrodite . . . That would be my search when I
got out.

There was, I think, looking back, a certain tenderness for each
other among fighting troops. We looked at each other wondering
how long we should be together. Rough, often foul-mouthed
and blasphemous, we were tied by the string of our experiences
past, present and future. The men usually had a mate or buddy, or
sometimes three men banded together and managed to mess,
march and fight side by side. Though we would risk our lives for
a wounded man, the dead, even our friends, were not unduly
mourned. There was, in our unconscious minds, the feeling 'better
him than me'. There was in the early days before conscription
very little malingering and few SIWs (self-inflicted wounds).
New drafts were helped to become battlewise by old soldiers as
much for their own benefit as that of the strangers. It was
essential to have everyone steady in action. I had been in a curious
position, being so young, and until I was hit, so lucky I was

regarded by the men as a kind of mascot. When on duty in the line I was always being offered bits of bread fried in bacon fat, mugs of tea, and shown pictures of girls, wives and babies, of pet dogs and cats. My three gods were Mr Luck and Mr Death, with Mr Blighty somewhere in the middle. I had learnt to take care of myself as far as it is possible to do so, but was at the same time something of a fatalist, as I think were most of us, other than those who still pinned their faith on God and on the efficacy of prayer. Among other things I had picked up was the wearing of my pistol low down, strapped to my thigh like a cowboy. Tiny Nelthorpe, who had been ranching in the Argentine, taught me this. For active service in mud a Webley revolver was a much better weapon than an automatic pistol which jammed easily if dirty. I once picked up a rusted Webley from a body in no-man's-land and fired it. I was, however, astonished that this weapon with a .45 uncoated lead bullet ever passed the Geneva Convention. Any wound from it was almost certain to be fatal. But it had immense stopping power, which lighter nickel-plated bullets that would go right through a man did not have.

We had had men with some curious wounds. One man who was hit by a spent bullet in the buttock during an advance never knew anything about it till a week later he came out in boils from the infection. Another man had sixty-two gramophone needles in him from the explosion of a German potato-masher bomb with which some musical humorist had filled it.

About this time my brother Lovel turned up in London. He had been serving as a driver with the French Ambulance Corps but now had a commission in the Cambridgeshire regiment. He was my favourite brother.

Lovel was very fond of girls. I remember my mother telling me how she had arranged an abortion for one of his girl-friends, bought off another, and taken him to the doctor when he got VD. He and I were her favourite sons. She loved us, I think, because of our looks and faults. I have an idea that many mothers are half in love with their sons. Lovel was a very dashing young man. He dressed very well. He had the first really thin watch I had ever seen and a very thin watch-chain of platinum bars joined with little gold chains. Both from Tiffany's where he worked, and probably presents from women.

Ronald, who had been conscripted under the Derby scheme, said Lovel could use his flat when he was on leave, but later made a scene because he found he had taken a girl there. Ronald was not a woman's man. He was what the French call *sérieux* – serious. A solicitor now and engaged to the daughter of Sir Herbert Bartlett, a millionaire contractor who had a yacht at Cowes. After this quarrel I had very little time for Ronald as I could not see anything very wrong in taking a girl to his flat. That was what flats were for. She was Lovel's current girl-friend, not a tart or a pick-up. Her name was Bobby and I had a picture of them both with her sitting behind him on his motor-bike. Lovel and I visited our aunt, Broderick Cloete's widow, at her flat in Pont Street. My uncle, whom I never knew as he had broken with my father, went down on the *Lusitania* when she was torpedoed in 1915. He had a famous stud of race horses at Hare Park. He won some classic races, including a *Grand Prix*, with Paradox, who also ran second in the Derby with Fred Archer up, won the St Leger. Broderick won The Oaks in 1911 with Cherry-moya by Paradox out of Cherry – a chestnut mare. He had enormous interests in Mexico. A ranch bigger, I believe, than the King Ranch on the Sabinas River – four or five hundred square miles in size. He had other interests. He was a director of Vickers-Armstrong. His widow, Violet, later married Admiral Sir Bertram Thesiger, the brother of the actor. The Derby in which Paradox was declared second was a dead heat and would have been declared one except that there had been a dead heat the previous year (1884) with St Gatien and Harvester and the judges said they could not have one every year. Paradox also won the Thousand Guineas. My uncle's colours were cherry red with black and white sleeves. His horses were trained by Charlie, later Sir Richard, Marsh.

Broderick Cloete must have been a peculiar man, a great snob, who denied his South African colonial origin, claiming to be English and producing an enormous pedigree on parchment proving that he was descended from Henry VII of England and Robert III of Scotland. This genealogical *tour de force* was based on his grandmother's descent. She was a Graham of Fintry. Her husband, the Hon. Henry Cloete, was judge of the Supreme Court in the Cape Colony and later first High Commissioner of

Natal. His brother, General Sir Josias Cloete, fought as a Cornet of Horse in the Battle of Waterloo when he was fifteen and was the last Knight of Hanover to be created.

At Reading the discipline was very lax and though we were allowed to go out into the town by day we were not supposed to be out at night. But Bowles, a tea planter from Ceylon, who was hit in the leg, and I used to manage to climb the wall and get out whenever we wanted to. Between us we had three legs and three arms and the wall presented no insuperable difficulty to us although we had one or two falls. As wounded officers we did not have to wear uniform and I bought a navy blue suit off the peg at some cheap shop. I wanted to be able to drift about. It was much easier to do this if you were not well dressed – you could go anywhere and do anything. Not that I proposed to commit any great sins, but I wanted to eat things off barrows and spit on the pavement just for the hell of it, if I felt like it. I wanted to mix, to eavesdrop and be part of a crowd – not to be saluted and only be able to travel first class. This seems to be one of the first occasions that my ambivalence showed up. On the one hand I was a very class-conscious officer, modelling myself on the Prussians I had seen, and on the other I was anonymous, just an invisible part of the crowd, so much so that later on when my arm was well again I was once given a small white feather by a patriotic lady when I was sitting in the tube. This was a practice with some ladies. She must have thought I was evading service and was amazed when I laughed at her.

There was an RFC Observers School at Reading and again I thought of trying for the Flying Corps when I got well. But I abandoned the idea as I did not have the mathematical qualifications.

In Reading I ran across Gerald Sinclair again. He had a house at Twyford and was now a Captain in the 42nd Highlanders, the Black Watch. I had not seen him since we were children in Paris and we talked of how we had taken his Boston bull to the rata-drome with Flirt, my wire-haired bitch. He introduced me to some very nice girls and we got around quite a bit – in uniform then, naturally. The two girls I remember best were Dulcie and Mamie Clowes. Mamie was dark, keen on horses, and engaged to an Australian. She died later, having a baby out there. Looking back, it is odd how many girls I knew died having babies. Her sister, Dulcie, was quite lovely. So much so that she made me nervous. She was completely feminine – shape, perfume, *frou-frou*, and the rest of it, with charm to match. But she was the kind of girl I have always avoided. The kind I always felt could practically become pregnant if you kissed them – born mothers.

My wound gave no great trouble except that my left arm was paralysed and I continued to wear it in a sling. And after a month or so I was given my discharge and told to go on leave. The arm was still bad but the wound had healed and every available bed in England was needed for the never-ending stream of casualties that still poured over the Channel from France and Flanders.

In this sick-leave period after leaving hospital, eager as I was, I had no great success with women. There was a ballet dancer to whom I had been introduced by a friend. I took her out a couple of times to supper after the show. She was willing enough but I felt her to be too old – thirty at least – and her legs were bunchy with muscles. There was a Belgian girl who was being kept by a colonel. She said she was an actress and gave me a shiny postcard picture of herself in tights and spangles. Her stage experience, I decided, was as a conjuror's assistant, or doing tricks on a fat resin back horse in a circus. She liked me because I talked French to her and she was homesick. We got no further than talking.

The third, equally abortive, experience was with a beautiful, tall, dark, blue-eyed show girl called Phyllis, who had a room in Gower Street. She wanted too many presents and was unbelievably stupid. Later I heard through the grapevine that she had put her head in a gas oven.

I do not remember anything further till I found myself in a mental hospital at 10 Palace Green. I had apparently been picked up by the Military Police in a state of amnesia. It must have been delayed battle fatigue or, as we called it then, shell-shock. My left arm was now quite useless and I could feel nothing. It could be pricked with a needle without my knowing it.

When I came to myself there was a nurse framed in the doorway – a VAD – with several thermometers in the usual potted-meat jar. She was tall. Five foot eight and a half in flat hospital shoes.

Her uniform was pale blue with a white starched apron, belt, collar, cuffs and cap. I stared at her – or so she said afterwards – and instantly fell in love. Two years later, on October 30th, 1918, just before the Armistice and when I was recovering from other wounds, I married her.

She had a good figure and carried herself very well. Her hair was a very dark brown, almost black, and she had large blue-grey eyes with long lashes. They were pools in which a man could drown. And she had a beautiful speaking voice. She had nice ankles. Her face was beautiful. I was sunk. Finished. In an instant she had become my life.

I asked her name.

'I'm Nurse Horsman,' she said. 'Eileen Horsman.'

For me it was a lightning stroke, what the French call a *coup de foudre*. She became the focus, the central core of my life; nothing else mattered. There is something both pathetic and beautiful about young love based on that first fantastic rush of sex. Though animated by a furious atavistic necessity for reproduction, it can still remain an affair of tenderness and dreams. An idyll.

I came into contact with other nurses. I called Eileen DG for dark girl, and a very pretty blonde nurse who sometimes took her place FG for fair girl. There were a couple of nurses who, I gathered, were fast. They did not interest me. But there was something very sexy about the clean rustling starchiness of a nurse's uniform.

My nurse-wounded-soldier pattern was one with a thousand precedents. Gratitude on the part of the man, a reversion to infancy and a desire to be taken care of by a woman. On the woman's part, her sympathy for pain, an effort to make up to the soldier for what he had gone through, and a kind of almost incestuous maternal feeling for this man-baby. A whole galaxy of instincts, feelings, thoughts and passions on both sides. All in an atmosphere of war urgency.

These girls were not army nurses; they were volunteers. VADs. Young nubile women unhardened by years of experience.

When a boy has been forced into manhood by special circumstances such as war, then because there has been so much destruction of life, nature (which we usually try to deny as if we stood above it) increases sexual pressure. There is always talk of increased immorality, loss of virtue and the lowering of standards in war. But it is not that morals get worse, merely that the pressure against the restraints of what we describe as morals increases in a direct ratio to the losses in the field, in a fantastic race to replace the dead. It is the same force that makes desert plants flower, fruit and seed in such a frantic rush after a single shower of rain. If they are to survive, they must.

My love was an effect of this cause. As far as nature was concerned I was not a boy or a man. I was an organ of reproduction to be used before it was destroyed. This force was operating all round me as it has round every soldier in every war.

When I got better I used to meet Eileen in the street. Nurses were not allowed to go out with officers who were patients, but we could not help meeting them by accident. For the duration of the war her parents were living in Lancaster Gate off the Bayswater Road. To see them she turned left when her time off came. If she wanted to shop in Kensington High Street she turned right. I found a tea-room on the second floor in Kensington High Street that commanded a view of the Palace Green gates and I spent hours, day after day, watching for her. After all, I had spent hours watching Germans when I was sniping and I had my heredity – the patient blood of Boer hunters – in my veins. When I saw her I would run down the stairs and we would meet accidentally. On her half-days off she was not in uniform, which made things simple.

I knew by now that her fiancé – boy-friend in today's parlance though she had not actually slept with him – was killed in the early days of the Somme Battle. I had been hit almost at the end of it. This may have created some emotional pattern in her mind: some bond of blood between the dead lover and the living one.

I do not know what she saw in me. I was too young for her. I had no money. I was a regular soldier who could not, even in a line regiment, hope to keep a wife till I became a captain and that was ten years away at least in terms of peace-time soldiering. But I had drive. I never left her alone. Once when I found out she was out with an artillery major at the Marble Arch cinema I had her name thrown on to the screen saying she was wanted in an emergency by her father. I swept her off in a taxi. There was no emergency. I had not even met her father. I was, I suppose, from the photographs of those days a rather good-looking young chap. I was in a way a hero – we all were. I was sincere. Madly sincere. Madly in love, but I made no real pass at her. I didn't know how to. Nineteen, and a virgin. She was twenty-one and a virgin, or nearly. How queer that sounds today! But we both got something out of it. Romance. An emotional storm which is probably impossible today.

I was getting better every day and after about two months was discharged. I only had to report to another hospital for massage and electrical treatment, but life without Eileen was impossible. I had to see her every day and that could not be managed now. So I made a plan. My nerves were cured but they could easily be uncured, I was sure of that. So I set about producing another breakdown. For four days I did not go to bed. I lived on whisky and aspirin. I did not get drunk, I just kept myself going and when I had the real jitters I reported back to Palace Green.

What were we when I was discharged from hospital? Friends, with on my part overtones of passionate love, and on hers a curious interest in this strange young soldier. But I knew I could not leave it like this. I realized that I had to finish what I had begun. So I presented myself at the hospital and demanded to see Major Wood, the Commandant.

I saw him. I said: 'Sir, I've come back. I am worse than I was. I have lost the use of my left arm again and I feel terrible. You must take me back. And I want my old room; it was a private ward.' This meant Eileen.

She could not get over seeing me back in bed again. As soon as I saw her I burst into tears. She held my hand – it was supposed to be my pulse – while she took my temperature. It took two months of electric therapy to fix my arm. They gave me shocks. They shoved needles into me. But I felt nothing. Meanwhile Eileen helped me to eat, cut up my food, peeled grapes for me and took out the pips. I never told her I usually just swallowed grapes whole after giving them a single crunch to get the juice.

While my arm was paralysed I had taught myself to tie my tie with one hand and do up my shoe-laces by holding one end in my teeth.

I was allowed no visitors so I demanded to see a padre, a

request which I knew could not be refused. He came every day and we had some interesting conversations, which bore no fruit but which I think we both enjoyed.

It was no use him talking about Hell, I had just come out of it. Nor to say God was the God of love. A funny sort of love, I said. Nor death. I was not afraid of death, only pain. I had seen too many men die. They died calling on God, asking for their mothers, cursing God, or grimly silent. And why a judgment on these young men, almost boys, too young to have really sinned? Perhaps they had masturbated, had fornicated, some had committed adultery. But the whole concept of a God so concerned with bedrooms and sex seemed to me slightly blasphemous, even rather ridiculous, assuming the existence of this God. And what about the commandment, 'Thou shalt not kill'? When 'over there' we were killing with the blessing of the Church. The Germans, equally blessed, were doing the same. Two Christian nations at each other's throats.

I admitted to the padre a certain envy of those who had faith and found comfort in their beliefs. But I went no further than being certain there was a power that governed and ordered nature, of which we were a part. I was quite prepared to call this force God. But I could not believe, after my experiences, that he cared for individuals or that he could be placated by prayers and hymns. I said I believed in the sermon on the Mount, the Christian ethic and the golden rule, which I supposed made me an agnostic Unitarian.

If all this was true, if people really believed in Christ, surely they would behave like Christians?

In the end, what does it all add up to? I believe in no dogma, no revelation. There is obviously a force which governs the natural order. There was no chaos in the universe till man presumed to interfere with its processes. Perhaps what I think is best stated in the words of Gladstone Robertson in his book, *Gorbals Doctor*. He writes: 'I have long thought it vanity, if not indeed an affront, that man should identify himself with the Creator of the Universe, of whom he is utterly uninformed, while rating all other forms of planetary life on the lowest level. I can see no logical argument to justify the assumption that man is not the subject of the same laws as obtain throughout the animal and vegetable kingdom.'

This may explain why I feel as I do about animals, both domestic and wild. The wonder I have is in the actual quality of life, respecting it in the Albert Schweitzer sense.

This Life Force, this complex order of nature of which we are a part can well be called God, and good is that which is in tune with the design. It could be called love. Evil is anything destructive to good and beauty.

At my age I think a great deal about death, since I cannot have long to wait. I do not fear extinction. I fear a painful death, I fear leaving my wife and my dog and cats without the protection of my love, in a world that daily becomes more confused and less secure. These may just be the views of an old man, but except for the wild ambition which possessed me in my youth, I have changed very little.

It is perhaps a strange confession that looking back today, I think more of animals I have loved than people. Horses, dogs, cats, cows, donkeys. People can look after themselves. They have relatives, other friends, whereas my animals really only had me because I have always had a special relationship with them. This may be due to some personal inadequacy, though I doubt this as I have never been short of friends. So it may have something to do with a different dimension, a special empathy.

By now the situation with Eileen had changed. We had become more than friends but less than lovers. I do not know what I was to her. A kind of nearly incestuous brother, a link through the Somme Battle with the dead, a man who filled some kind of blank space in her life. It was a strange courtship in terms of today. Kisses in taxicabs and little more than that. Some trips to the country if the weather was fine and when she had her day off. I took her to Lancing. The school was empty; it was the Easter holiday. We lay on the Sussex downs fragrant with wild thyme and mint, watching chalk blue butterflies, listening to the singing of the larks and the distant sound of gunfire 'over there'.

In a little rabbit-shaved lawn surrounded by flowering gorse, things progressed further. But not much. Love continued to grow on my part, and affection on hers.

The courtship went according to plan for another couple of months, when it was decided to send me to a convalescent home at Lennel in Scotland. This was a lovely country house belonging to Major and Lady Clementine Waring. He was in the Life Guards and Lady Clementine ran the house as if we were guests staying with her for the shooting and fishing.

Lennel was a large property of four or five thousand acres with three miles of fishing on the Tweed, which was one boundary of the estate, with farms, moors, gardens, lakes and all the amenities that go with a place of this kind. If I could have had Eileen with me it would have been heaven – as it was, it was very pleasant. The life was home-like and the food was wonderful.

Looking back, I find love to be a very curious thing. I have fallen in love with other women, and seen houses and farms that I had to have. Seen horses and dogs. There is suddenly something between you and this love-object. Woman, horse, dog or place. An empathy. One year in New York at a poultry show I was deeply impressed with a Chinese goose; at a pet shop with a cockatoo that was stuck in the moult. Why should our hearts go out in a flash to meet this other personality of which – or of whom – we know nothing? Always with me it has been at first sight. A meeting of the eyes, whose power has never been properly examined. My father once told me never to look deeply into the eyes of a woman if I was not ready to make love to her, or into those of a man if I was not ready to fight him. Certainly we know, in a theatre for instance, if someone behind us is staring at us. Hunting – once one has marked a buck it is wiser not to look at him again or he will feel it and slip away. A drunk will seldom accost a man who does not meet his eyes.

Of the ten or a dozen officers from various regiments recovering from shell-shock at Lennel I remember the names of only two, Captain Alastair Lochnell Campbell of the Argyll and Sutherland Highlanders, and Major E. Harvey Jarvis, a Dublin Fusilier. There were also an Australian captain of Light Horse, a Scots Guardsman, a Marine lieutenant, two field gunners, one heavy gunner, and a chap from the Naval Brigade who entered every weekly competition in such papers as *John Bull*, *Tit-Bits* and *Home Chat*. He had the trick of it and nearly always won something. He said in peacetime he made a living this way. I often wondered if he really could and did. Lochnell Campbell was the finest fisherman I ever saw. He never came back without a creelful of trout or a salmon. Sometimes two. He knew just where the fish were and what fly they would take. He thought like a fish. He even looked like one – a salmon. He wrote articles and, I think, a book about game fish. He taught me to tie a fly and to fish, but I was no good at it. I lacked the patience. I am not a fisherman. But I did like fishing perch and jack on a big loch about ten miles away. The perch were quite big, well over half a pound, and some of the jack were enormous, though a five-pounder was the biggest that I caught. They are the most savage fresh waterfish and will take young duck and moorhens as they swim. The American equivalent is the muskelong. They are excellent cooked if stuffed with herbs and baked. Any muddy flavour can be removed by soaking them overnight in vinegar and water. This also applies to carp, bream, roach and perch.

The village of Coldstream was about two miles from the house on the Scottish side of the Tweed, and was famous for the runaway matches it had seen in the old days. It was amusing to think of eloping couples driving a postchaise at a gallop over the stone bridge pursued by the irate father of the abducted girl. The marriages were performed, I believe, by the local blacksmith. All that was required by Scottish law was an affirmation by both parties that they were man and wife in the presence of witnesses. I believe that this is still the law though it may have been modified. So a man who goes off with a young lady for a weekend and signs the register as Mr and Mrs may find himself married, much to his surprise.

We visited famous houses in the vicinity. I saw a holly hedge trimmed like a wall, over twenty feet high. We saw castles. We went to Edinburgh for medical boards and had one memorable expedition to the Farne Islands, a wild bird sanctuary. Here the terns' nests were so thick on the pebble beach that it was almost impossible to avoid treading on the eggs which looked exactly like the stones. The puffins nested in rabbit burrows and attacked you if you put your hand down to get an egg. We were not allowed to take eggs, but I got a few. There were guillemots nesting on the cliffs. They lay on tiny ledges. The egg is very pointed at one end and thick at the other. Because of its shape it cannot blow off. When the wind hits it it simply spins on the light end. These eggs are very handsome. Thick-shelled, as large as a goose's egg, pale blue in colour splotched with black.

Kittiwakes nested on the cliffs in hundreds and in sheltered places there were eider ducks sitting in nests of their own down. Their eggs are roundish and olive-green in colour. They sat so close that it was possible to stroke them. The females were marked like wild ducks, the feathers plain brown with black tips. But the drakes were spectacular – white, black and apple-green. There were thousands of lesser black-backed gulls who attacked anyone who went into their nesting ground, swooping down at their heads. I had my hat knocked off by one. It was amusing to see the puffins march like little men in black and white suits to the edge of a cliff and cast themselves off into the water. They have only vestigial wings and are nearly related to penguins. The birds rose in clouds when we moved in their nesting grounds, the terns particularly almost darkening the sky. They were of three varieties – common, arctic and roseate.

The Islands lie about twenty miles off the Northumberland coast near Berwick, and were once inhabited. There are the ruins of a monastery and what is left of a village – all stone-built and very old. It was said to be one of the first Christian outposts in the north. At this time the only inhabitants were the men in charge of the birds, and their wives. Two families, I think. The birds require protection as there is always a market for gulls' eggs. The big eggs, those of the black-back and herring gulls, were eaten locally and the terns' eggs, neatly arranged in little nests of green moss, were sold as plovers' eggs and are, as far as I am concerned, indistinguishable from them in both appearance and taste. We cooked some of the gulls' eggs we stole and they were excellent. Later, in South Africa, I ate penguin eggs, another delicacy, remarkable for the fact that the white remains transparent when cooked.

I used to like to take a gun and with Mousie, the black cocker, for company, potter about and pick up a rabbit or two. Jarvis and his wife and little daughter lived in a cottage. Joan, the little girl, was about seven and I used to go long walks with her and take her out in a boat on the Tweed. She was one of the few children I have ever loved. I suppose in these days in America the continued association of a young man of twenty with a girl of seven would have been looked upon with some suspicion. But we got on well. She was very obedient – a real soldier's daughter – so I was never afraid of her getting into trouble. If I said 'Stop! Don't move!' she stopped. She was good company. I met her once years later after she had married a man in the Tank Corps.

The Jarvises' cottage was a little way from the main house and as they had no maid (they were impossible to get) I often helped with the housework. They had a cairn terrier called Minx. I forget the dogs at Lennel except for Mousie and a fox-terrier, Tiger. The other animals of interest were a big bay thoroughbred that had once run in the Derby, and a pair of Iceland ponies – smaller than Shetlands – that pulled the children's trap. There were two children, Clematis – she was about ten – and a younger girl, Kitty. There was a French chef whom I met again later when I was poultry-farming in France at a house where I was selling broilers.

The visit to the bird sanctuary on the Farne Islands was the highlight of my convalescence. To pass the time we read, did jigsaw puzzles and some of the chaps played bridge or poker. We hardly spoke about the war. We were all shell-shock cases, which we felt to be rather embarrassing. Some of us had not even been wounded. Besides, we had nothing to say. We had all been there and knew about it: the noise, the wounded, the stinking dead. We had nothing in common except the King's commission. We were all of different ages. I was the youngest by some years. All from different regiments or branches of the services except for the two field gunners.

Lennel was very comfortable, but we were quiescent, in a kind of spiritual coma, licking war wounds. We all knew that when we left here we would go back into it. The war news in the papers we felt to be lies. Only the casualty lists could be relied on and those we watched carefully, looking for the names of our friends. During the height of the Somme Battle they had occupied several pages of close print. As far as I remember, cavalry was listed first, then foot guards, followed by infantry of the line. Then there were Royal Flying Corps, engineers, garrison artillery, field artillery, Army Service Corps and Royal Medical Corps. It was all very neat: just names and numbers that were men, each with women of their own: a wife, mother, sister, girl to worry about him or mourn him.

There was one rather interesting thing about a place like Lennel where a lot of salmon were killed: the servants refused to eat the fish, just as, in the deer forests, they refused to eat venison. I soon found out the reason. We got very tired of salmon ourselves. It is a rich, oily fish. It can only be boiled, served as salmon steaks, presented cold with mayonnaise or made into fish cakes.

While I was here my brother Lovel was killed at Passchendaele in a battle which equalled in horror, though not in duration, the engagement on the Somme. I got a few days' leave and went to see my mother. She was heartbroken.

A medical board now declared me fit for light duty and thus ended the Lennel episode. I do not think I got into any trouble except that Lady Clementine said I cut her towels when I dried my razor. But I do not think I was the culprit. After all, we all shaved. I still used a cut-throat, which I thought more virile – it was certainly more dangerous – but since I had practically no hair on my face it was rather like using a cavalry sabre to cut flowers for the house. But I was very keen on virility. I wanted to grow up. I was doing it, too. This year I should be twenty. The only other thing I remember was having an abscess in my ear that nearly sent me mad. We had to weigh ourselves each day and in three days I lost seven pounds.

I was given a week's leave that I spent in London, saw Eileen, and then joined a special service battalion of the Lincoln Regiment. All the officers and men were crocks. It was not an outfit to be proud of – the blind, the halt, the lame and the stupid. I served with them for some months in Halifax, a gloomy mill town. From the window of my quarters I could see thirty-two factory chimneys. And then I found we were going to be sent to India. This was no good to me, so I applied for another board and demanded to be sent back to my regiment. The Reserve Battalion at Rugeley on Cannock Chase.

Things here were really bad. There was not an officer I knew. I found none of my friends – most were dead by now. Officers who had seen no active service were, with one or two exceptions, running the show. Many of them came from the lower middle-class and had no manners, including table manners, of any kind. I was profoundly shocked by what I saw and heard. Officers in public places with shopgirls on their knees. The way they talked. We were of course much more class-conscious then than people are now. Still, when my room mate, a captain, said, 'I always wash me before I shave me,' I felt the bottom of the barrel had been scraped for officer material. The full tragedy of the Somme Battle was now beginning to show up: thousands of public schoolboys who should have been leading troops had been killed in the ranks of such regiments as the London Scottish, the HAC and Queen Victoria Rifles. This great loss of the cream of our country was to show up in the political situations which followed the war. This occurred not only in England but also in France and Russia, where the Bolsheviks eliminated the whole officer class, thus changing the structure of their society for good, as China is doing today. But all that was also in the future, the future we thought would be so bright when we had won the war, made England a home for heroes and democracy safe forever.

The only mitigating factor in this abominable place where I now found myself was the fact that few of the officers could ride and the horses needed exercise. So I rode every day and got in a bit of hunting. I started planning again. In the ante-room of the mess there were always notices asking officers to put their names down for this or that. The War Office was asking for officers who could train African natives. I could. And then there came a reasonable demand. The Household Battalion stationed at Windsor was short of officers and would anyone interested please apply? I sent in my name and qualifications, months of war service, date of gazette as temporary lieutenant, date of regular commission, actions I had been in, courses I had taken – tactics, musketry, sniping, and the rest of the rigmarole. I did not say that the real reason was that I could no longer stand my regiment and that I wanted to get into the London Command as I had a young woman there. A few days later I received orders to report for an interview and was given a railway warrant.

I spent the night in a hotel, had my hair cut, my uniform pressed and buttons cleaned by the valet and presented myself at the barracks. The Colonel – Colonel Hardy – a very smart, good-looking man with a DSO and the two South African ribbons, interviewed me. How old was I? Where had I been to school? How much war service had I had? Then, after a few minutes of general conversation, he said: 'All right, we'll take you. I'll give you a chit to your CO, and you'll report to Combermere Barracks at Windsor next week. You'd better have a few days' leave to get your buttons and badges changed.'

I saluted and turned about. I was now in the Household Cavalry – dismounted, unfortunately. But I was quit of the Reserve Battalion and would be stationed at Windsor in the London Command and only thirty miles or so away from Eileen at Palace Green.

CHAPTER 18

THE LONDON COMMAND

THE Household Battalion was a composite battalion whose officers and men came from the 1st and 2nd Life Guards and the Royal Horse Guards – The Blues – who wanted to see active service. They were a magnificent body of men and many of the non-commissioned officers had titles that were new to me. They had preserved the rank designations of the Household Cavalry and the old Regiments of Horse, from which they had evolved.

A sergeant-major was a corporal-major, and a sergeant was a corporal of horse, which seemed very romantic to me. In the London Command we got £60 a year extra pay, which was supposed to cover the increased expenses of living in this area, which of course it failed to do.

I was back in the army again and really began to learn something about the other side of soldiering. So far everything had been rough and ready, and though I was a regular I had never actually served with regulars. I was to now.

My first experience was that I was met at the station by Malcolm, the Adjutant. He was in flannels and had left a game of tennis to come and meet a very young junior officer joining the regiment. This was a lesson in manners that I never forgot. He was one of the finest soldiers I ever served under and one of the most charming men I ever associated with in a mess. Later, in command of the King's Company (Number One Company of the 1st Grenadier Guards – the 1st Foot Guards) he was killed and his body found later with thirty bayonet wounds in it, surrounded by German dead.

The other officers were of the same type, about half being either regular Household Cavalry officers or seconded from the Foot Guards, and half picked temporary officers or regulars like myself from line regiments. Among the Warrant Officers there were drill sergeants from the Foot Guards and I met them next day out on the square where I was put through it. We did close order drill for the best part of six hours a day, marching the long Guard stride in perfect alignment, with every rifle at exactly the same angle. Here I learnt the Guards way of giving orders, the stamp of feet, the step – almost a dance step – by which they change direction, the order being given while one foot is passing the other so that it can be slapped down, the weight taken on it, as the body's direction changed. A beautiful sight when well done. About all perfect drill there is something of the ballet and, much as I disliked it, I was later to learn its value. Only by it, only by close order drill of the highest quality, only by spit and polish of such perfection that I have yet to meet a housewife whom I would not confine to barracks for a filthy house and for being improperly dressed, can discipline such as ours be maintained in action. A man with a single button undone was described as being half naked on parade. But this is what makes Guard troops, not only British, all Guard troops, and there are none like them. It begins on the barrack square. It continues in the barracks, and in the lecture hall, where the history of the regiment is taught and the battles that had been fought by our predecessors are described. A famous regiment is a living family of officers and men who never die; they overlap from year to year for hundreds of years. The Coldstream, whom I was later to join, were founded by General Monk and were part of Cromwell's New Model Army. They were then known as the 2nd Foot Guards. The Household Cavalry dated from about the same time.

So we drilled. We marched and counter-marched. We did slow time – the parade step corresponding in its way to the German goose step. We did arms drill. Guards arms drill where you let go of the rifle as you change position and hit it with a bang. To see a battalion slope or order arms is both a sight and a sound. One, two, three – each as neat and sharp as a shot.

I got weekend leaves that I spent in London and it was easy to slip up in the evening after parade and come back again by a late train. So I saw a lot of Eileen.

But I had other problems. I was drawing seven and sixpence a pay day. The pay had gone up since I joined. In 1914 it was five shillings, but my mess bill was twelve shillings and sixpence. I must say I had never lived so well but then I had never lived with such rich men before or since. One of them had thirty thousand a year. We were messed by a contractor and had every known luxury – *pâté de foie gras*, caviar, oysters, game, fruit, all wonderfully cooked, and if I had not saved a few hundred pounds while I was at the front I would not have been able to come out. It was not even any use being teetotal because the drink bill was shared by the whole mess; whether you drank a lot or not at all made no difference. This is a bad system as it encourages drinking. However, I did not drink much – some beer with my lunch, wine with dinner and a glass of port to drink to the King. But the expenses must have bothered some of the other officers, too. Among them was a rifleman, a very good-looking young man, very smart at night in his rifleman's green undress uniform with a black patent leather despatch case and bandolier over his shoulder. He was an instructor of some kind seconded from his regiment. I imagine he got into difficulties and was caught cheating at cards. They played a lot, evidently for stakes he could not afford. There was no fuss or scandal, he merely disappeared, a ruined man. I saw later that he had resigned his commission and he would have had to resign from his clubs. I have little doubt that women were at the bottom of it. I was fortunately spared this because though I was in love I was still too young to get around much. I was also rather careful. The term gold-digger had not come into use yet but the gold-diggers were there, and I knew how they operated. Never having had money, I was always careful of it, for though my parents were not poverty-stricken, there had always been a lot of talk of money at home which made me realize that it was a scarce commodity and should not be thrown about.

While with the Household Battalion I saw a sight just at the Park entrance near our mess that I shall never forget: a herd of deer crossing the road in heavy mist. Being on the Thames and low-lying, we got a lot of mist. Windsor was famous for the Castle, the great park and the Barracks – Victoria Barracks, where a battalion of Foot Guards was always stationed, and Combermere, the Household Cavalry Barracks which we, though dismounted, used for our drill and other services. Our buttons had HB on them – *tout simple* – and so had the cap badge. Our stars of rank were flattened and elongated like those of the Household Cavalry. Everyone was very charming to me in the Battalion but I was out of my depth in age, in experience, except that I had been in action and most of the other officers had not, and above all financially.

Among the officers was an enormous captain from the Blues whom everyone called Tank. He was so big that when he had been in the ranks no issue boots were big enough for him and they had to be specially made. There was Lord Kilmory, who was always referred to by the non-commissioned officers as Major, Lord the Earl of Kilmory. There were Sparks of the West End antique-business family; Attenborough, connected with the great pawnbrokers; Haggie, an immensely wealthy man, and others; but with none of them was my contact more than superficial.

The mess was a private house at the Great Park gate near the elm avenue that led up to the Copper Horse, the equestrian statue of one of the Georges.

One of the things, of course, for which Windsor is famous other than the Castle is Eton College and we often saw the top-hatted boys in black jackets and striped trousers in the streets of the town.

My courtship of Eileen proceeded on established and respectable lines. Lunches. Dinners. Shows – seats in the stalls. I think we saw *Chu Chin Chow* three times. I bought her gardenias and little bunches of violets from flower women in the street. I wrote her letters since I could not telephone to the hospital. I kissed her. I petted her, though the word had not been invented then, in taxis. I pinched one of her black kid gloves and a little black voile handkerchief embroidered in the corners with roses and forget-me-nots. There is no doubt that I was madly in love with her. I had met her at a psychological moment when I had come almost directly out of battle.

On one special occasion I took her to dinner in one of the small private dining-rooms which then existed on the first floor of the Café Royale. They were designed for intimate meals *à deux* and even had a couch against one wall. The waiters who attended these tables were old men who had seen everything and were beyond surprise. I had ordered a special little dinner of turtle soup, salmon, pheasant, to be followed by crêpes suzette, with a bottle of burgundy to wash it down. But the whole affair was a failure. Before we had finished the soup my nose began to bleed and I spent the next hour pouring blood into a basin in the gentlemen's cloak room. I suppose this attack was due to my excitement, but it was a very embarrassing evening.

While I was in hospital at Reading my mother, realizing I needed a London base, had furnished a small apartment in Bolton Gardens for me. In Reading I found a bookshop where they had some pictures of horses and military prints. I bought several, including a set of coloured woodcuts – rather crude – of the generals and notables of the Napoleonic period to decorate the walls.

With some of the money I had saved while in France I bought my mother a blue arctic fox scarf which delighted me. It was the first thing I had ever given her with my own money. I have always liked giving presents rather than receiving them, partly I think because I have never wanted much. But in giving I have had some curious results. Once, many years later in New York, while buying some books for myself at a secondhand bookshop I saw a six-volume History of the Civil War which I sent to a friend who made a study of this period. I knew his library and knew he did not have it. He never forgave me, and told me if he wanted something he could afford to buy it for himself – an attitude that surprised me because it had never occurred to me that altruism could be suspect – or that some people, particularly in America, could think of any gift as a sprat to catch a mackerel.

Prostitutes were very thick on the ground in London. One night at about 11 p.m. I was accosted sixteen times between Piccadilly and Berkeley Street. I did not like being rude to the girls, some of whom were very pretty and well-dressed, so I devised a formula for dealing with them. I would say, 'It's no good, I'm afraid; I've just had a woman.' Then they gave up, knowing it was impossible to get blood out of a stone. I had one interesting encounter in the lift at the Earl's Court underground. I was alone with a tart who wanted me to go home with her. I declined the invitation and she kicked my shins, saying: 'You're too fucking particular!' She was right though I did not say so. Fortunately I was in uniform and wearing puttees.

At last I was passed off the square by Malcolm and was ready to go to France with the next draft when the news came through that the War Office had decided to disband the Household Battalion as it was proving difficult to get volunteers and the regiment refused to use the conscripts. This was a blow, particularly as I had made many friends – George Buchanan and Louis Alphonse Martin in particular, both lieutenants – whom I did not want to be parted from. There were, even now, very few of my friends left alive. Guy Handley, who had left the KOYLI and joined the Coldstream who were at the Victoria Barracks in Windsor only about a mile away from the Cavalry Barracks, was about the only one left, and it was he who suggested I come to them. He had been in the West African Frontier Force and was a fine soldier. I served under him in France till he was killed. Martin said he was going to the Coldstream too. He was a South African – a Boer who had fought against the British in '99.

The order from the Army Council disbanding our regiment was qualified by a notice that His Majesty the King would transfer any officer of the Household Battalion to any regiment he wished to go to without any loss of seniority. This made things much better. It was a splendid opportunity. Now was my chance to accomplish another of my life's ambitions. I could go to the Indian Cavalry. But I couldn't do it and at the same time stay in the London Command and be near Eileen, and the woman won. The woman always wins because a woman is a force of nature. It is no good saying what does he see in her or why does she like him. There are no such things as she and he. There are only vast forces before which these two – this boy and girl – are blown like torn paper in a storm.

So I made another plan. I'd go to the Coldstream with Guy and Martin. George Buchanan went to the Grenadiers, where he had a lot of friends. He was later blown up with them and had his neck broken, from which he recovered. One of the few who did. It happened through his being buried by one explosion up to the neck, and then the blast of the next shell lifted his head while his body was held stationary.

To join the Coldstream I had to be interviewed by the Colonel, who seemed quite pleased to accept me provided I had an income of £300 a year. He said I could not come out with less as a regular in peace time. I said: 'Yes, sir, I can manage that all right.'

Three hundred a year was nothing to me, nor was three thousand. I had not sixpence beyond my pay but I had a plan. I always seem to have had new plans. The Russian Revolution was now taking place and I thought when the war was over I would go to the Colonel and say, if I was still alive, that is (and if I was not there would be no problem), that my parents had been very well off but that all their money was invested in Russia and now they could not help me. This story was foolproof and might easily have been true. The regiment would then have found me some job, seconding me for instance to the West African Frontier Force or the King's African Rifles, or somewhere else, where I could save enough money to come back and serve in the regiment until it was spent. The alternative was a rich wife, but Eileen was not a rich girl, though if that fell through I could easily find one. This was a common practice in the army, and tailors and other shopkeepers would give young unmarried officers a great deal of credit, gambling on their either getting married to a girl with money, or on their inheriting money from their parents. They seldom lost anything by their patience. This was particularly true in the Brigade of Guards.

The Colonel accepted my assurance and I joined the Coldstream at Victoria Barracks next day. I had to get new uniforms and got a £60 allowance for them. I was sent to Anderson's, the regimental tailor. The Guards uniform is of a special cut, the trousers being a very pronounced plusfour type and the jacket having the buttons arranged in groups according to the regiment. The Grenadiers – the First Foot Guards – have their buttons ordinarily spaced, but we, the Second Foot Guards, have them arranged in pairs, the Scots Guards in threes, the Irish in fours, the Welsh in fives. The uniforms are made of heavy olive-green barathea with silk linings. The cap has a black woven silk border, a black patent leather peak with a gold edge, and our badge was a large six-pointed silver star on which a scarlet enamel cross of St George is centred (Order of the Garter). I also had to buy a new sword. The Brigade uses a much finer, more delicate weapon than the infantry of the line. It was all very grand. I was immensely proud of it. Again in a sense I had arrived at a point of destination which would one day become a point of departure. It was 1918. In July I would be twenty-one.

CHAPTER 19

THE MINSTREL BOY

THE move to the Coldstream was simply from Combermere to Victoria Barracks, just a taxi ride, since both were in Windsor. I now found myself on the square again under drill sergeants Lamb – a very tall thin man – and Ellis – a thickset man with the voice of a bull. Quick march, slow march, slope arms, order arms, present arms – all the old stuff which I had learnt with the House-hold Battalion with Foot Guard instructors, so I had no difficulty and soon passed out. I worked it out once that we did fourteen miles a day on the square. I doubt if it was really that but it was certainly ten or more.

I had a room in Barracks and drew a canvas mattress stuffed with straw (a donkey's breakfast) and bed boards to sleep on, like the men, and used this instead of my camp bed. I was training myself to be tough.

Things had advanced with Eileen and I saw her two or three times a week and at weekends. She went sick and was sent to hospital, where I visited her, taking her black hothouse grapes from Solomon's in Piccadilly, most of which I ate myself, to her amusement. She was also surprised at the way I ate them – skins, pips and all – because when I had been in hospital, I had got her to peel and de-pip each grape.

'Why did you do that?' she asked.

'To keep you with me longer,' I said.

I now bought myself an overcoat. The Guards did not wear khaki overcoats like the rest of the army. Ours were grey, almost the field grey of the German uniforms, double-breasted with gold buttons and a scarlet silk lining. I also got an undress blue uniform to wear at mess and in the evening if I went to London. It was dark blue with a high collar and a belt of the same material. The trousers – overalls – had a wide scarlet stripe, were rather tight-fitting and were worn over Wellington boots, being strapped under them at the instep. I was pretty pleased with all this and my gold-edged cap. I was also cultivating my moustache – a few miserable soft brown hairs that I fertilized with Vaseline, having been told it would make them grow. There was an army regulation to the effect that no officer should shave his upper lip. But I did shave mine to see if pruning would encourage the hairs or stiffen them.

Things were getting serious with Eileen. I asked her to marry me whenever I saw her and sent my servant to the post-office every Friday with a pre-paid 'Will-you-marry-me' telegram, to which I never got a real answer – just something cryptic like 'When will you be up next?'

Knowing I should soon go back to France, I went to see Dr Sinclair who had attended the family for years and persuaded him to give me enough morphia tablets to put myself out if I had to. He put them in a tiny glass tube and I carried them till the end of the war. They may have been quite harmless, just placebos, but this is something I never found out. My reason for wanting them was the horrible wounds I had seen on the Somme, and men dying out in no-man's-land who could not be rescued because of the machine-gun fire.

Every subaltern had to take his turn doing Castle guard. This was a pretty complicated piece of close order drill done in slow time. The guard marched through the Castle gate with the band playing, wheeled into line and went on changing direction half left a couple of times before halting in front of the guard they were relieving. The two officers, with swords drawn, saluted each other and the new guard marched on replacing the old guard. Before going on guard we practised the manœuvre on the barrack square, being directed by drill sergeant Lamb. The complication was that you had to count the steps you took before giving the order to change direction – a mistake and the guard would find itself marching into a wall. We could choose any music we liked for the band. My choice was 'Colonel Bogey'. A further complication was that if at any time during the operation a member of the Royal Family – even a royal baby – should appear on the lawn, we had to halt, present arms and continue from where we had left off when they went away.

I was terrified of finding myself in this position. Not only was there the guard to relieve, there was also the possibility that the officer in charge would be asked to dine with the Royal Family. This happened once or twice a month. The guard duties themselves were simple enough: mounting sentries at the gates of the Castle and various other places, and visiting them every few hours till the tour was over twenty-four hours later.

Then to my delight I saw my name on the ante-room noticeboard. I was to rejoin the BEF and should not have to do guard duty. I was given a week's embarkation leave which I spent seeing Eileen and my mother, who was staying at Bolton Gardens.

We had some trouble with the landlady of my small apartment when I took Eileen there. She would have no goings-on . . . not in her house . . . which was a respectable house.

Well, there were no real goings-on, but after we got married and went there in the afternoons sometimes for that purpose we had to show her our marriage lines.

There was a maid, Edith, who attended to my rooms and those in the rest of the house. Quite a pretty dark girl of twenty-five or so, who, I felt, would not be averse to a closer relationship, which made me nervous of her. I am quite sure she stole the gold wrist-watch I had been given but I never reported the loss to Mrs Thomson. I would not be instrumental in putting someone in prison for such a theft. But I am convinced it was Edith because someone else reported a loss of some kind and she went to prison anyway.

I was still on leave on April 26th when I received a telegram – 'Draft proceeds to France tomorrow 27th instant report here by 7 p.m. on that date acknowledge promptly. Cmdg.Res. Coldstream Windsor.' My reaction seems to have been to eat a lot of eggs. My diary reads: 'Breakfast Norfolk Hotel two eggs, lunch Stewart's Restaurant one egg, tea 8 Bolton Gardens two eggs, dinner 8 Bolton Gardens three eggs.' Between eating eggs I packed my gear, which was supposed to be limited to thirty-five pounds including blankets and bed-roll, in my Wolsey valise, but it was nearer 150 pounds by the time I had done. I had said goodbye to Eileen and my mother, returned to Windsor and left there again at 9.15 p.m. in charge of a draft of the sixty other ranks I was taking overseas – 56 Guardsmen, 3 corporals, 1 sergeant – all slightly drunk, a rabble accompanied by their wives and ladyfriends who, overcome by alcohol and affection, marched in the ranks with their men. Preceded by the fife and drum band only, we staggered to the station. We were met at Waterloo by Colonel Crighton – the regimental colonel – but he did not inspect the draft. No one could without having them propped up. But in spite of a long wait in London and another at Folkestone, I lost no one. Victoria Station presented the usual wartime spectacle: the endless drama of tired, unshaved, dirty men coming home for a week's leave, and clean, tidy men with shining buttons and badges going back to the war. Between them they completed the cycle of war-time life in which Blighty – home life – was hardly credible even while it was going on. The returning men in full packs, their rifles slung, their tin hats strapped to their packs, their overcoats shortened – roughly hacked off with their jack knives to knee length – their puttees still plastered with the mud of war, looked round them with astonishment. Women, girls, children, civilians. They lined up at the canteen for tea and sandwiches. Below the counter on the station concrete was a layer of French and Belgian soil that had fallen from their stamping feet. They wore their soft caps with an air. They smiled at each other like children. They had made it. They had got to the party after all. They looked with disgust at the Redcaps – the Military Police with their white pipe-clayed belts and spats. Bugger them. Fit men they looked. Safe at home with beer and clean beds. Beds with women in them while the rest were over there. That was just one side of the picture. The other was the returning traffic of men going back, saying goodbye to wives and sweethearts, to lovers of a night who had come to see them off, to mothers, to sisters. Crying women held children in their arms or led them by the hand. They were trying to be brave. I was trying to be brave and thanking God I had said my goodbyes before.

I brought my Guardsmen down the platform to the train. The NCOs and I numbered and entrained them. All correct and on parade. All sober though they had had to spend the night in London on their own. The rest would be easy. Just the train journey and the boat. We were convoyed over the Channel by two destroyers. On arriving at Boulogne I got the men some rations from the RTO and had an omelette (more eggs), French fried potatoes and coffee at the officers' club. On reaching Etaples we were met by guides and got into camp at 10 p.m., about twenty-five hours after leaving Windsor. No food, only cheese, bread and water in camp. My kit had not arrived or was lost, so I borrowed three blankets and slept on the floor of the hut.

The kits turned up next day and after a short rest we were sent up to the Guards Base Depot at Le Havre. The train we travelled in was in a bad state. No glass in the windows, and we passed a lot of damaged rolling-stock. Amiens had been badly hit since I was there last and the hotel I went to look for had completely disappeared. This was a new sensation. In those days we were not used to such things and I was shocked. Amiens was an open town full of women and children.

During the journey we lived on bully, biscuits and chocolate. But the base depot was splendidly run, beautifully neat and clean – a real Guards barracks. It was curious how one became almost homesick for this type of efficiency. It was a special kind of army housekeeping that belonged to our division and, I think, to us alone. There were little white wooden picket fences round everything. There were flower-beds with forget-me-nots, pansies and tulips, and grass lawns as neat as any at home. The baths were well organized, the water really hot and everything spotless. There were even beds of flowers cut out in the shape of the regimental crests – stars, grenades, leeks, thistles and shamrocks – done in arrangements of tulips, candytuft and wallflowers.

At this stage of the war they had stopped officer training at the base camps. Even the old Bull Ring at Etaples had ceased to exist. They just let us eat and sleep. On May 5th we left the base for the line. It was a five-mile march in full marching order to the railway station and we were led by the pipers of the Irish Guards in their saffron kilts. There is something very inspiring about this kind of music. It always brought to my mind the relief of Lucknow in the Indian Mutiny, when the beleaguered garrison heard the Highlanders marching towards them, as they played 'The Campbells are Coming'. That 'coming' theme is always very moving in war. We felt the same now that the Americans were on the way, and we heard them playing their *Over There – the Yanks are coming, hear them humming, over there, over there*. By now the British were very tired, the French were exhausted to the point of mutiny. There is no doubt that the Americans won the war, although it took me twenty years to see it. Just the fact that they were there was enough. At last we had someone behind us. A massive power, a steam-roller that nothing could stop. But they were only just beginning to come in. We saw a few odd officers and advance parties and mounted men with McLellan saddles that had cinches instead of girths. Thirty years later I changed my mind again and now think it might have been better if the Americans had not come in and the war had become a stalemate with a negotiated peace which would still have left Germany a great power.

We detrained at Rouen and were told we had all day to wait so we went to look at the Cathedral – it was heavily sandbagged. I climbed eight hundred and ten steps to the top of the tower to see the view and then had an excellent lunch of lobster mayonnaise, sweetbreads, strawberries and cream and a bottle of Graves that cost 130 francs. After lunch Kendal and Hasketh, the two officers with me, got off with a couple of girls and they asked me to go with them to translate. We went through a lot of tortuous streets until we came to the girls' lodgings, and there after I had negotiated a deal with them I left them at it and went to find a cousin of mine, Colonel Volly van der Byl, who was commanding a labour battalion of Cape Coloured troops. I had dinner with him and then went back to the station. I reached railhead next day, reported to Brigade and had tea with a staff officer who was writing a letter to a WAC officer about one of her girls who was pregnant by one of our men who, while he agreed the possibility of paternity, claimed only a partial liability but was still willing to marry her if he was given fourteen days' leave.

When I came out of the dugout I found an orderly in the RFC leading a saddled horse and as this seemed waste, I halted him and gave him a note for his CO saying I had borrowed the horse. I hoped he would not mind and I would send it back at once by mounted orderly when I reached our transport lines. It has always been a fixed principle of mine never to walk if I can ride. There were no repercussions.

I was back in the same area I had fought over in '16, though the Germans had taken back a lot of the ground we had won in those first battles. I was even able to visit peasants on whom I had been billeted two years before. I went to look for an old mill that I had liked. It had been built of very large chalk blocks, but had disappeared. I have never forgotten this mill and always meant one day to build a tower like it to live in. This was the Gaudiempre–St Amant–Humbercamp–Monchy area. The base was again Doullens. The best hotel there was *Les Quatre Sœurs Amantes*. As it was a near-brothel at the time, it seemed a very suitable name.

I was now with the 2nd Coldstream and posted to No. 4 Company. It was commanded by a short, stout man, a rancher from the Argentine, and a very fine soldier and horseman, who proved to me that short, fat men could ride well. He was much better on a horse than I was. In fact he was the equal of anyone except perhaps Knott, the Australian, who had been brought up on cattle stations and sheep runs. The battalion was commanded by Colonel Edwin Brassey, a very charming man, who had come from the Hussars. Major Ian Buller, the husband of the actress Lily Elsie whose picture had decorated my locker at school, was the second in command. He had transferred from the Lovat Scouts. I now drew a guardsman's uniform from the Quartermaster. The only difference between the officers and the other ranks was the woven shoulder stars. This at least prevented the officers being picked off by snipers as soon as an attack began, as had happened on the Somme when we wore riding breeches, field boots and Sam Browne belts. But it was a bit of a nuisance when we got mixed up with other units in an action. At one time, when on the flank of the division, I found myself with men from eighteen different regiments under my command, and they were difficult to handle until they saw the stars, quite rightly refusing to take orders from a young private, which is what I appeared to be.

The Germans were now preparing for an all-out effort before the Americans became effective, everyone was frantically digging new defence lines and putting up new wire. Otherwise things were quiet and we had no casualties except for three men who had boiled up some water out of a shell-hole to make tea. They had the idea it would be all right if they boiled it. It wasn't, and it killed them.

By now tanks were commonplace. The Germans had them. The French had a very fast one known as the Whippet. There was a story of some Whippets overrunning German infantry and emerging with their caterpillar tracks running with blood.

We now went into the line at Ayette, where there was a very good company headquarters in a chalk pit. It was here that I picked up a nice black and white pointer, wandering about behind the trenches, but I lost him again. He was an old dog and had been wounded, which made him very shell-shy, so that as soon as he heard a gun go off or a shell come over, he popped into the nearest dugout. We watched dog-fights and once I saw a German plane driven to the ground by five of ours.

The division was expecting to be attacked and was apparently not too happy about the quality of the troops on our flanks, and we were ordered to wire ourselves in so that if we were actually surrounded we could fight our way out to the rear without the danger of being outflanked. This had been done before, and was done again in the last war on the French coast, when one Guards Battalion fought till its strength was reduced to thirty-six men. Searchlights were being used on both sides to locate night bombing planes, and they made the night watches more interesting. We were shelled pretty often with mustard and tear gas. The gas shells landed like duds and then went off with a faint pop as they cracked, liberating the gas. We had a better pattern gas mask now that covered only the face, with a breathing tube that led to a container worn on the chest. There was a great deal of shelling of back areas and the shells passed over our heads in a continuous stream in both directions. Then the Germans started on us with trench mortars. For the last twenty yards one could see them coming and dodge them, with a bit of luck. I find from my diary that I was much upset because one of the officers wore khaki pyjamas, and decided that he must be mentally defective. I wonder why? I suppose I thought it was odd to want to wear khaki at night too.

My mother had given me a set of thick Jaeger wool pyjamas that I wore over the ordinary ones and they kept me beautifully warm in the sleeping-bag I had made by sewing blankets and an old eiderdown together. She was still worried about my weak chest and about my catching cold. But in spite of being wet a great part of the time I stayed well all through the war, apart from trench fever and scabies.

One officer's job both in and out of the line was to censor the men's letters. I tried not to read them and just looked for information that might give our position away or remarks about other units in the vicinity. There were spies about on both sides of the Channel ready to pick up any gossip they heard. Every *estaminet* had notices: *Taisez-vous. Méfiez-vous. Les oreilles ennemies vous écoutent.*

The men's letters were on the whole simple. A formula. They wanted to sleep with their wives or girls. They recalled – sometimes in detail – the last time they had done so. They wanted English beer, not these French slops. I would black out 'French'. They wanted a nice steak and kidney pie. How were the kids, the dog, the cat? They hoped this letter would find them as it leaves me – in the pink. How surprised the ladies would have been to find themselves in the position of the men who wrote the letters! Possibly up to their knees in mud. They worried about their women being faithful to them . . . The letters, most of them, were crude but very moving. Cries from the heart.

The incoming mail was a big event. The letters came up with the rations and Eileen wrote every day. There were rumours of our coming out of the line for a rest, to be fattened up for possible shock action. We were warned to expect an attack without artillery preparation. To do this, the Hun would have to mass at night, and lie in no-man's-land till he got the signal to attack. They were a long way from us. To prevent surprise the division sent out twelve officer's listening patrols each night. Each consisted of an officer, an NCO and a couple of Guardsmen. It was not too unpleasant to lie in no-man's-land with a telephone, some SOS rockets and a bag of bombs. Should anything suspicious be seen we were to telephone to Company HQ at once. Should the enemy attack suddenly we were to send up the rockets, fire a few rounds of rapid fire, throw our bombs and retire to our line. We lay in a circle facing in all directions and stayed quite still for five hours, coming in just before dawn.

Then we did a daylight raid with two officers, of whom I was one, and thirty-five men. We attacked the German line with the artillery giving us a box barrage so that the section we raided was cut off from both rear and flanks by a curtain of fire. We killed some Germans and brought back one prisoner for identification.

This was the purpose of the raid. We also captured a machine-gun and suffered no casualties ourselves.

We wore gas-masks for half an hour every day to keep us in practice. I found they made my mouth very sore as I dribbled into the mouthpiece. There were Chinese indentured labourers digging trenches behind us, strengthening the line still further. They wore blue smocks and had long pigtails.

Once when we went out to rest we were bombed at night. We lost a lot of transport animals and some officers' chargers. The mess cart received a direct hit and disappeared. After the raid we went out with flashlights to see what we could do. Some of the horses were screaming terribly and had to be shot.

What followed was routine trench warfare, shelling with HE, more gas, and a wonderful night march after a relief through Adinfer Wood, or rather the stumps that were left of it, by moonlight, the only sounds being the rattle of the men's equipment and the singing of the nightingales.

Martin now joined the battalion. Louis Alphonsus Martin, MC, DCM, MM, who had come with me from the Household Battalion to the Coldstream, and was the coolest man under fire I have ever served with. Nothing could frighten him. He was one of the dozen or so men I have loved. There can be love between men without any homosexual tinge, if not surpassing, at least equalling the love of women. They become, as it were, brothers without consanguinity. All love, apart from the actual sexual act, is really a matter of mutual trust, respect and affection – companionship. With a woman the added ingredient is sensuality.

Martin had fought against the British in the Boer War, had fought for them in South-West and East Africa, where he got his decorations, and then obtained a commission in the Household Battalion. He was a splendid fighting soldier with the Boer capacity for making a plan. Unfortunately, before we had been in France long, he went down with spleen trouble, the result of malaria contracted in East Africa. I missed him very much. Somehow when I was with him, and we were in the same Company, I was never frightened. Because, like everyone else, I was frightened a great deal of the time. But fear has its own compensations. One learns to control it. To attack it. To attack anything, even an emotion, is safer than standing still. One plays a

tremendous conjuring trick on oneself; by simulating courage it
comes. Moreover, in the Brigade of Guards one was aware of
serving with men who could not be equalled anywhere as soldiers,
except possibly by some German Guard regiments who had had
the same severe barrack-square training. This training at the
Depot first broke men, dissolving them in the acid of discipline,
and then rebuilt them mentally and physically into troops who
could not be defeated, as they have proved on the battlefields
of Europe and Africa.

I rode over to Loucheux with Martin the first time we came out
of the line after he joined us. There was a wonderful castle here,
like something out of a fairy tale, on the top of a hill with a moat
and a drawbridge. I met some Royal Flying Corps officers and
went joyriding with them a couple of times. It was interesting to
see our lines and those of the Germans below us. I became very
interested in the Air Force and talked to the Colonel about being
seconded to them. He said I would be stupid if I did so since I was
a regular soldier. There was no future in it. This was the cavalry
opinion and they considered themselves experts on the subject as
so many of their officers were pilots. There was as yet no regular
air arm. Officers were merely detached – seconded for temporary
service in the Royal Flying Corps. Cavalry officers were supposed
to be particularly good pilots, as they had 'hands'. 'Hands', in the
rider's sense, is a special feeling or relationship that exists between
the bit in the horse's mouth and the reins in the man's fingers.
Only a man with good hands can manage a difficult horse and
planes in those days were apparently as sensitive to good management as horses. The pilots early in the war fought duels in the air,
firing at each other with revolvers from the cockpit. Then the
French invented a method of firing a gun through the centre of
the propeller. This was the first great innovation. Then came
others, both in the air and on the ground, tracer bullets and
armour-piercing bullets for tanks, although the best method of
dealing with a tank was still held to be a Mills bomb under its
belly. The only problem was how to get it there and get away
alive.

I managed to get in quite a lot of riding when we were out of
the line and found it very interesting to coax a horse past a tank
if we met one rumbling and crashing along the road. One

certainly could not blame the horse for being nervous as many of them were not even used to motor-cars.

We received a great surprise in our part of the line one day when we were suddenly attacked by aircraft. It was the Richthofen Circus, as it was called. Baron Richthofen was a German air ace who operated with a picked squadron of planes all painted in brilliant colours – scarlet, yellow, blue and orange. Suddenly these monsters swooped down on us as if they were giant birds of prey, banked, and poured machine-gun fire into our trenches. This was, I think, almost the first time the infantry were strafed at close range from the air. It was a very frightening experience and took some standing up to. One had a great desire to run away. They were so big, so near, the roar of their engines so loud, their occupants – in goggles and flying helmets – so inhuman-looking, that for an instant or two one was bewildered. But that did not last long. We poured rifle and Lewis gun fire into them and they veered off. I do not think they were more than forty feet above us as they dived and banked. We did not bring any of them down but I do not think they liked our fire. They certainly did not come back for more. But our Lewis guns did bring down aeroplanes – one or two in the whole war – and the troops, by firing at them from the ground, disturbed them, kept them up, and made their reconnaissance more difficult.

I was now sent on another course – musketry – at Fort Mahon, a watering-place on the north coast, and again I got leave to go home. I was very lucky in having a home in France so near the line. I got a lift to Gobert's, the blacksmith's shop on the main road to Boulogne. As a boy I had bought my pigeons from him; he was a fancier. I passed the time of day with him and then walked to the Danfords', which was on the way home. They gave me a drink and Michael, their Irish terrier, was pleased to see me. Then I walked home – another four miles. My father was out – in the 1st Army School Mess, they said. So I sent an orderly in for him. The army had taken over our house as quarters for the senior officers. My father did not know who was asking for him but seemed very pleased to see me. Tears came into his eyes and for a moment he could not speak. There were times when he was very fond of me and others when he disliked me. I felt the same about him. I think we were too much alike. This emotionalism is a family characteristic. I cannot read aloud any passages from a book that I feel strongly about, and I can even bring tears into my own eyes when I write. My Uncle Montrose often had difficulties when he told stories about his adventures and the dogs and horses he had loved. One story in particular about a horse called Prince he had in Mexico caused him trouble, and it always ended with violent nose-blowing and eye-wiping.

After a weekend at home I hitch-hiked back to the course. Apart from practice in trenches with live ammunition being fired over our heads, which was not new to me but impressed some officers who had not been in action, and being subjected to a tank attack – they drove the tanks right over our trenches and that did impress me very much – there was nothing of much interest in the course. But I had a nice rest, plenty of sea bathing, had got home and seen Dad and had been gazetted a full lieutenant regular services.

I was on the way up and, although I did not know it, also on the way out.

Back to the line again and I spent my twenty-first birthday in the trenches. No one seemed to have remembered it though I did get a cake a week later. But no one remembered which birthday it was or that it had any special significance.

The Americans were now really pouring in and I was sent with five other officers and sixteen sergeants to go up the line with an American battalion on their first tour of duty. Major Ian Buller was in command of the party and he stayed at HQ with the American colonel. Each company commander had a senior subaltern to show him the ropes and each platoon officer had one of our long-service sergeants. It was a good plan and probably saved much confusion and many lives. We took them out on wiring parties and patrols in no-man's-land, showed them how to take over trenches from other units, the handling of stores, and gave them all the practical information which can only be learnt under actual active service conditions. I was very much impressed by the quality of their food and the excellence of their cook – a Negro. It was the first time I ever had creamed potatoes. The only trouble about him was that he could not cook if there was any shelling going on. In fact he was rather like the pointer than I had picked up – he went to pieces and wrung his hands. But fortunately we were not shelled much and seldom at meal times. I presume the German gunners also wanted to cook and eat in peace.

When our week with them was over I said goodbye and marched off with my NCOs. We went back independently, but after going about five miles I received a message that a platoon of Americans had been badly shelled and we went back to help them. Contrary to instructions, they had marched off in columns of fours, had been observed from a sausage balloon and had received a direct hit. There were about five dead and fifteen wounded. They were badly shaken up. We checked over the wounded, reorganized them and sent them on their way again, by sections, with an interval of thirty yards or so between them. In one stretcher they were carrying a man who was dead. They had forgotten to dress him. They had just picked him up and got to hell out of it. In the meantime he had bled to death and the stretcher was full to the top with blood. It was slopping round him like gravy. We said goodbye again and started off home once more – home being the 2nd Battalion trenches. On the way we saw a sausage balloon shot down in flames and passed the Scots Greys leading their horses along the road. I have no idea where they were going and they were the last cavalry I was to see in the war. Their grey horses were all pinkish brown. They had been washed down with permanganate of potash to make them less conspicuous.

I have written all this from the notes in my diary. But how strange it is to look at! All the names of places that were so important then and are now nothing, times that were vital – zero hours – days and nights of terror, what are they now? There are naturally no reports of battles as I never took the diary into action. We were not even supposed to keep one. But I liked writing it. I liked writing and, before I met Eileen, I wrote to my mother every day. Later I wrote to Eileen, who gave my mother the news.

But no one can describe war. Soldiers know it and so do many civilians, now more than ever seemed possible in those days. We did not think of killing women, children and old men then. Only boys and men in their prime. The pick of England, of France and Germany. It would have been the pick of America, too, had the war lasted long enough. I have known a Frenchwoman who had

lost nine of her men in war. Her grandfather in 1870, her husband
and brothers in World War I, and her sons in World War II. It is
easy for those who do not realize this to talk about the decadence
of France, but France has been bled white. England also lost a
whole generation of men who would have been leaders, the so-
called officer material.

For descriptions of war there are the war books. *All Quiet on
the Western Front, Company K*, and of the last war, *The Twenty
Thousand Thieves* take some beating. There are many other books
such as *Peter Jackson, Cigar Merchant, The Army Behind Barbed Wire*.
I had a collection of them once.

What I have done is not to write a war book or even to describe
the war, but to try to paint a picture of certain events, to show
their impact on the character of an individual. I happen to be that
man, that boy, and there my importance ends.

I sometimes wonder what Goya would have made of our war.
Is it not strange how soldiers adopt a war as if it was a child? But
what would Goya have done with bodies hanging like laundry,
like broken dolls, on the wire, with crows perched on the twisted
iron stakes? With the Highlanders killed in attack, lying on their
bellies with their skirts up like indecent girls, except that they were
men, bold men, who had died with their parts naked like their
ancestors at Flodden and Killiecrankie?

There is nothing fine about war. Only fear and sometimes a
terrible exultation, and such beauty that it can tear your heart out.
Patches of flowers – cornflowers and poppies – in a battlefield, the
singing of the larks, of nightingales in a wood that is no longer a
wood, the call of mating partridges in no-man's-land. A hatch of
swallowtail butterflies. I watched that once. While we were being
shelled, a dozen of them crawled out of their chrysalises and
sunned themselves into growth. I watched their wings unfold and
dry. Then I saw them fly away into the summer sunshine. What
was the rest of it? Routine, lice, baths, rations, the mail, fear of
being hit with your pants down in the latrine, patrols, fatigues,
carrying parties, courses to which both officers and NCOs were
sent as much for rest as for instruction. All this and much more –
friendships with men who are not only dead but forgotten, the
queer feeling that one knew the whole world when one was at
home. It was impossible to go into a restaurant or theatre without

meeting a friend. We were all friends then – a man one had served with, with whom one had been on a course, or travelled with in a train or a ship, or had met at a casualty clearing station, or in hospital. The uniforms were all familiar; we knew every badge in the army, we knew every medal. We were briefly but urgently, for those few years, one great family whose bond was the war, the King's uniform and the commission we held. Knowing this, it is not hard to see how Hitler welded his Germans into a weapon with which he threatened and nearly conquered the world. For men are lonely, they want to belong. We are still tribal in our hearts. As a species we are very new.

The men we met were part of us – part of the war. The *We*. Fighting soldiers. All soldiers were this in a sense, as differentiated from civilians. But only just. The ASC and RAMC, the padres and Army Pay Corps were a kind of social no-man's-land. Neither one thing nor the other, neither fish, fowl, nor good red herring, but still supportable. The staff were hated more than civilians. Redtabs were red flags to the infantry bull. Civilians were despised and regarded rather like children who did not know the facts of life. They were *Them*, as opposed to *Us*. The Germans were *Them*, too, but we were nearer to them than to civilians in many ways.

At home I had looked at boys in their teens, wondering how long they had to live. In every school in England a new list of names was read out every Sunday. The fallen who, failing to answer their last roll-call, would now have their names engraved on a thousand rolls of honour. The dead were *Us*, too.

It was strange the way the world was always divided into Us and Them. At school it was your own school, at home your own family, village or town. Without an Us there could be no I. A man could not exist isolated and remain a man. He must love someone, be attached to something, and if there is love then there must be its opposite – hate – or something near it.

I thought of Eileen; of girls, flappers, young women. Raphael Kirchner painted pictures of them. I carried one that reminded me of Eileen. Bruce Bairnsfather painted cartoons of us – 'Old Bill' and his mates. These two were the representative artists of our time.

The girls would continue to live. That was odd, too. That many of the teenage boys would die and the girls live on for years and years. It did not seem just somehow. But after all, what was justice? How did you define it?

Those of different age and sex were almost a different race. Men of my age and even twenty years older were soldiers. The babies would never be soldiers, or so we thought then, nor would the old men or children. Girls, mothers, grandmothers, were like the inhabitants of different countries with the years that separated them for boundaries.

I thought that never before had men been exposed at once to such pressures and such boredom. Never had young men had so much time to think, or even for haphazard undirected reading. Never had they been, in their prime, so separated from women, and never had they needed the solace of their company more. Not just their bodies but their femininity. Their softness, the sound of their voices. Living without the company of women was like living in a house without flowers, books or pictures. A house without a soul. I thought of the difference at home, of finding my mother there or not there. If she was out the place was empty.

Graham Wallace, writing of the pre-war period, described it as 'the proud tower built up through the great ages of European civilization was an edifice of grandeur and passion, of riches and beauty and dark cellars. Its inhabitants lived, as compared to a later time, with more magnificence, more extravagance and elegance; more careless ease, more gaiety, more pleasure in each other's company and conversation, more injustice and hypocrisy, more misery and want, more sentiment including false sentiment, less sufferance of mediocrity, more dignity in work, more delight in nature, more zest . . .'

This was the time into which I had been born and in whose death-throes I now participated.

CHAPTER 20

THE DOUBTFUL HERO

DURING this period of which I write and the days that followed my birthday, I was busy. We all were. The Hun was pulling out. We attacked positions held by no one, or by a skeleton force, a few snipers, and a machine-gun section or two. We had trouble with the water. Some of the wells were said to be poisoned. I am inclined to think they were because we were not allowed to drink from them. And now, as far as I am concerned, comes the *grande finale*, where everything ended with a bang – the attack at St Leger, by the 2nd Battalion of the Coldstream.

This was one of the high days of my life. We were holding a line of chalky trenches from which the Irish Guards had attacked the German positions a week before. They had taken them and then been driven back, having been unable to hold on owing to the casualties they had sustained. Some of their wounded were still crawling in. They were in a poor state from starvation and exposure. Our line ran more or less along a railway embankment with a wood on our right and the village of Croiseuilles on the left, behind the German line.

We made a few patrols, brought in more Irish wounded, and then received orders that we were to attack. I was not very optimistic about this because, unless the German position had changed a lot, there was no reason to suppose that we should succeed where the Irish had failed. There is nothing to choose between any of the Guards regiments. We were to have artillery support but no preparation, as it was meant to be a surprise and at dawn next day, having been moved during the night a mile or so to the right so that our flank was in the wood, we attacked, only to find that there were German machine-gunners concealed among the trees in our rear; they popped up once we were over the top and had to be dealt with before we could go on. Then we had to cross two sunken roads with machine-guns enfilading them – shooting down the roads as we crossed them. They could hardly miss. We jumped down the banks, ran across the road and scrambled up the opposite side. The banks were twenty feet high and we lost a lot of men.

The Germans had dugouts in the sides of the road which were impervious to our artillery which had plastered it. Jumping down the embankment, slipping and sliding, running across the road and up the bank the other side was an extraordinary and terrifying experience. For the German machine-guns it was like shooting fish in a barrel.

Getting to their first line we attacked with bombs and bayonets and drove the Germans back, killing a number of them and taking prisoners. They were cavalry, with white bands round their porkpie forage caps instead of the usual red. They were coming out with their hands up when the German barrage came down on us. It was a beautiful job. The whole world was a sea of flame, earth, debris, high explosive and steel. I was thrown into the air by what seemed to be a direct hit and landed on my belly. My runner was killed on one side of me, my orderly on the other. Our men had gone on by the time the dust had settled. I could see them against the skyline as I had the first time I was hit on the Somme in '16.

The orders were to leave all wounded where they fell. No one was to be helped till the attack had been pushed home. So I lay there in the long grass feeling very much alone. I was in the German wire. I could hear their machine-gun bullets hitting it – tsing . . . tsing. It was a very bright blue summer's day and every lark in the world was singing. All this I took in in a matter of seconds, for there is a great perception at the moment of death and I was sure I was dying. I had no feeling in my legs and I was afraid to put my hand back to see if I still had them.

This is when I decided that the parsons talked a lot of damn nonsense about death. There was nothing to it. Easy as rolling off a log. I thought this in those actual words. Then I looked at my watch and saw I had lived five minutes. I was in no actual pain and my mind was very clear. Had my legs been off, with both femoral arteries cut, I should not have lived five minutes. I then came to another philosophical conclusion: I decided that the two biggest things in a man's life were love and war. War I had had. Love I must get if I ever got out of this.

I now saw a lightly wounded Guardsman limping back. He was hit in the leg. I shouted to him and he dragged me into a shell-hole. He got the field dressing out of the bottom of my tunic where it was stitched into the lining. He told me his name was White. He did up the wound in my back and said: 'Well, that's done, sir.' I said: 'I'm still bleeding, I can feel it.' Blood feels funny when it runs out of you. First hot, like the water out of a tap, and then cold, clammy. He found another wound in the groin. This was a bad one. I could see the femoral artery like a bit of gas piping. Another hundred-thousandth of an inch and it would have been cut. Then White crawled out and got a field dressing from my runner's body. He put it on but I was still bleeding. There were four wounds and he had to go out twice more to get dressings from the dead, and all the time he was under direct machine-gun fire. Then we saw some Germans coming towards us. They still had their rifles but they looked a bit dazed and about ready to give up. However, as they were coming our way, to be on the safe side I got White to pull me up on to the edge of the shell-hole and prop me up so that my arms, head and chest were out and no one could see I was badly hit. I had my pistol in my hand. White hid in the bottom of the hole till they were quite near. Then he jumped out. The Germans dropped their rifles, said *Kamerad* and raised their hands when they saw him. I covered them with my pistol and told White to take the bolts out of their rifles and throw them away. I said: 'You've got to make them carry me.'

One of them had a groundsheet with him, one of those brown canvas ones with aluminium eyelets in it. They got that under me and carried me shoulder high, each one taking a corner, and White coming behind them with his rifle and fixed bayonet. One of them had protested about carrying me. He said:

'*Offizier! Offizier!*'

I said: 'Offizier, too!' pointing to the stars on my shoulder straps.

White said: 'You bloody well pick him up or I'll stick you.' He made a jab with his bayonet.

Everything went well till we got near the trench that had been our jumping-off point. As we were crossing the railway embankment a shell burst near us and they dropped me right on to the line. If White had not fired a round over their heads they would have bolted, but he got them back and herded them into the trench which was now occupied by some artillery observers and telephonists. I reported the position, which was confirmed before long as more of our wounded came back. The story they told was simple. It had been a repetition of the Irish attack. We had gained our objective.

The Germans were coming in with their hands up and then, suddenly realizing how few of us were left they started fighting again. Out of the seven hundred and fifty of us who had attacked at dawn there were now, at eight o'clock, less than two hundred effectives left.

This time I had really had it and I knew it. This was no Blighty one. The twin gods of war, Mr Luck and Mr Death, had met head on. But again my luck held. I was young, only twenty-one, I did not drink, I was fitter than I had ever been in my life. It was full summer – August – and for a month we had been following the Hun rearguards, often marching eighteen miles a day in fighting order, carrying ammunition, rifles, bombs, water-bottles and the rest. Sweating and light rations had made me as hard as nails and if anyone was fit to take bad wounds I was. One could ask no more than this. I was hit but alive, which was more than many of my friends and comrades were. Having been so near to death I was glad to be alive – just alive. Once again I had survived in a world where survival had become the exception.

The gunner told White to get me back to the gun emplacements. The Germans picked me up again. The gunner said: 'They'll fix you up there at the first-aid post.'

At the first-aid post I lost my Germans. They were sent back with a Corporal to Brigade HQ. They were the first prisoners to be brought in and would be questioned by the Intelligence Section. I lost Guardsman White, too. He had gone to get his wound dressed at the CCS. I lay on my artillery stretcher behind the gun emplacement, staring up at the blue sky and listening to the larks sing between the scream of the eighteen-pounder salvoes. I was in no pain. I was alive. I wondered if I would live through this experience. I thought again how easy death was, how I had conquered the fear of it when I thought I was bleeding to death. Fear only came seeping back now, when I found that I was not dying. I worried about the wound in my groin. Suppose I was no good . . . Two men picked up my stretcher and took me to the casualty clearing station about a mile back. There were already hundreds of men lying there in rows in the open. Such heavy casualties had not been expected and the RAMC were short of both doctors and orderlies.

I was given an anti-tetanus injection. A label to the effect that it had been done was tied on to my tunic. Later we were given cups of tea. Only those with arm or leg wounds that needed amputation were taken into the big Red Cross marquee. The rest of us lay there in the summer sunshine. My mind remained pretty clear. I remember the larks singing again. Those bloody larks. I thought how bloody silly it had been to expect us to do what the Irish Guards had failed to do. I remember being carried into various ambulances. Sometimes someone gave me water or tea in a tin cup or lit a cigarette and put it between my lips, but between rides we spent a lot of time just lying in big sheds, hundreds of us on our stretchers, just waiting, waiting for ambulances, for the hospital train, for the boat. It was a strange experience. We lay silent, dirty, bloody, verminous and stinking in a weird brotherhood of patience. Each of us lying like a dog that has been run over in a ditch, waiting for someone to come and pick him up.

I was still in no pain. Then we heard that a hospital train had come for us and we were moved in Ford ambulances that held four stretchers. All the way to the siding the man above me dripped blood on to me. There must have been a hole in his stretcher. The train stank of gangrene. We had begun to go rotten. I still only had the dressings Guardsman White had put on. They weren't changed till I was on the hospital ship. I heard the doctor say to the sister: 'This boy will die.' It occurred to me that 'this boy' was me. They had given me a shot of morphia but I could still hear and understand what was going on. I even heard the doctor's name – it was Linden Bell. Then he said: 'I wish I was going to look after him; it's an interesting case.' So I was interesting, too. Then he said: 'If his mother breastfed him he might pull through. A breastfed baby has a seventy per cent better chance of survival.' So if I lived I would owe it to Elsa's milk – an interesting thought.

I never, as some wounded young men did, cried for my mother or even thought of her – only of Eileen. Not that our wounded of any kind cried much or complained. It was what was in my mind, unstated. I wanted my girl. My woman. It was not that I did not love my mother but that she was at this point irrelevant. This was the brutal world of nature which, despite sonnets to daffodils and sunsets, is one of life, death and reproduction. Though, God knows, by then I had no desire to reproduce my kind or breed cannon-fodder for the next war. I had little confidence in the politicians. They had already betrayed us enough.

It had taken three days to get on the boat and have my wounds dressed. I was still in uniform and it was only on the ship that they changed me into pyjamas. I was in no great pain. As a rule you aren't to begin with. The force with which the projectile strikes the body seems to paralyse the nerves for a while. But only for a while. I asked the doctor who dressed me how I was hit and he told me, so that I now had an idea of my wounds. There was the one in the groin that I had seen, one in the back almost on the spine paralysing me from the waist downward so that I could only pass water through a catheter, and both my buttocks were blown half off. The trouble, as I was to find out later, was that whichever way I lay I was lying on a wound. Even on a water bed I could get no rest.

From the ship we were put into another hospital train and then out again on stretchers on the platform of a London station – Victoria, I think – where people came to look at us. They stared at our labels as if we were parcels about to be consigned somewhere, and that is precisely what we were, only we were animated parcels with some choice about our destination.

When I was asked which hospital I wanted to be sent to I hesitated a moment and thought of the Russian Hospital that Martin had said was so good when he was hit, but decided against it. It was, from what he said, a rather society sort of place with plenty of pretty débutantes visiting and holding the officers' hands. I decided that if I was going to live I had better go to some place that was more professional, so I said: 'Sister Agnes's, please.'

'The Edward the Seventh Hospital,' somebody said. So I was labelled and carried into another ambulance. Here again I was fortunate. The Brigade of Guards got preferential treatment and were asked where they wanted to go before the officers of line regiments.

I arrived at 9 Grosvenor Gardens at 3 a.m. on September 1st. I had been hit at dawn on August 27th. Sister Agnes came into the hall as I was carried in. She followed the bearers into the ward and supervised my transfer from the stretcher to the bed. She was a very small woman, less than five feet in height, in spite of the dyed yellow hair that she wore done high on her head. She had been very beautiful, and was said to have been one of King Edward's greatest friends. She was dressed in a nurse's uniform but with no cap. Round her neck on a gold chain she wore a large red cross made of rubies and diamonds. She stood very erect and her waist was the smallest I have ever seen. I doubt if it was eighteen inches.

She was a very remarkable woman, a great personality, and I and many other officers owe our lives to her. Her hospital was the proof of what good nursing can do. It was not a large place – there were, I think, about twenty beds – but the patients were nearly all very badly hurt. In the whole war only two men died there. She supervised everything. She attended every operation. She obtained the best specialists and surgeons in London. She got game and fruit from the King's estates and those of her friends. And above all she was fully staffed by well trained nurses. I had a private ward to begin with and a special nurse – Nurse Jones – who took care of me for six weeks and then had a breakdown. She even got up at night though she was on day duty to see if I was all right. She had been a maternity nurse and no baby could have been more gently treated. I had been very roughly handled at one time or another, with sticking bandages ripped off with the pus and scabs still adhering to the gauze. Nurses have to be hardened to survive the sights they see, particularly in war, but some of them were quite without sympathy. And so were some doctors. One of them, later, when I was convalescent in Hove, cost the British Government some thousands of pounds by disabling me when he pulled a jagged bit of shell casing out of my left buttock and damaged my sciatic nerve in the process. That buttock still had a sinus that would not heal and one day, as he was probing it to see what he could feel, he came upon this fragment.

I still do not know why it had not shown up in the X-ray, or why I was not X-rayed when he found it, and operated on properly. Instead, he took a long pair of forceps, grasped the fragment and dragged it out. This was the most painful thing I have ever suffered. I tore the pillow to pieces with my teeth as he did it and the feathers flew all over the ward. The piece, including its needle-sharp points, was nearly as big as my thumbnail.

I remained at Sister Agnes's hospital at 9 Grosvenor Gardens till September 26th; by that time, after five operations, I was considered out of danger and moved to an annexe at 19 Belgrave Square, and after a few weeks there I was sent to the Brighton Hospital. My recovery was remarkably fast considering that there were no such things as penicillin, sulpha drugs or plasma.

I have other memories of that time. I was so weak at first that I spent much time in tears. When anyone came to see me I cried. Eileen came, my mother, my aunt and other friends. But Eileen and Mother came every day. Being a nurse, Eileen got permission to come at any time since she could not choose her own time off to make it coincide with the hospital's visiting hours. There is no doubt that Eileen's visits kept me alive. It was she who gave me the will to live. Without her I should have died. I just lay there waiting for her daily visit.

Thirty years later, after we had been divorced, re-married to other people, and become friends again, she wrote and told me that all I did when she came to the hospital was to hold her hand and cry. But it was when I saw the white enamel trolley coming with the dressings that I really cried. Twice a day, it took over an hour to dress me. For each wound I had to be pulled about, raised and moved, and every movement was agony. But slowly I got better and stronger, and it was not too bad when I was well enough to read with a book-rest. Miss Fanny, Sister Agnes's sister, brought us books. She came round every morning with them and wrote letters for those who were unable to hold a pen. I made friends in the hospital; when I moved to a two-bed ward, Sydney Greville, who was the Controller of the Prince of Wales's household at the time, was in the next bed. I saw a lot of him until he died some two years later. He had nice apartments in St James's Palace where I used to visit him.

There was one incident that I used in *How Young They Died*.

Soon after I arrived in hospital and was alone with Eileen, I took her hand and put it on my genitals. I wanted to see if I was still operative in that direction. I imagine this must be a very common fear with all soldiers hit in that region.

As soon as I was fit to move again, and every hospital bed was needed, I was sent to a convalescent home at Hove. Eileen was already staying with relatives in Brighton. She met my train and I remember what she was wearing – a navy blue coat and skirt, a long knitted silk scarf of Brigade colours – dark red and dark blue. A black velvet beret she had made herself with a hat pin whose head was a large, round, carved mother-of-pearl Mah-Jong counter that I had had made up for her.

I was in uniform and carrying my circular red air-cushion. It looked like a doughnut. My buttock wounds, though healed, were still too tender to sit on without it. I was, however, able to sit on a saddle. I had tried this in a saddler's shop almost the first time I got out of hospital and on to the street.

Eileen was a beautiful girl, almost spectacular, with her walk and carriage. She was always stared at when we went into a restaurant, which flattered me.

At this point it is extremely hard to see how my mind worked. I had been very badly hit and had no reason to go back to the war. I had every excuse to stay out of it. No one could accuse me of cowardice or of trying to evade my duty. I hated the war. I was terrified of it, but with this there must have been some extraordinary pull, some fascination, that forced me back into it. Perhaps because I was so afraid? Was this a factor? I have always done what I have been afraid of doing. Then too I wanted to be in at the end. And the end was near now – it was October. And as a soldier there was more to be learnt. I also wanted to get back to the men I knew. To the regiment which had a strange kind of abstract reality for me, as if it was a place, a fixed point. Back to the sound of the guns, to the distant drumming of the greatest percussion instruments in the world, even to the smell of the dead. Perhaps the war had made such an impression on me that it seemed the only reality, and only soldiers appeared to me as people. It is impossible to follow a mind that had been disturbed like mine. In its confusion it could only follow the desires that were hidden in its core. To get married and to get back to the army. Soldiering was the one life I knew. As I see it now, these two desires were so basically simple that no thought was required to deal with them. I wanted to make love, that is to say, to breed – in principle – though I didn't want children; and I wanted to kill, or even be killed, for anyone who exposes himself to risks faces this possibility. It is the gamble, the titillation, that animates in a lesser way the ski-jumper, the fox-hunter, the big game-hunter. I was not ready for problems. I wanted things that were easily resolved, like lying down with a woman, and going to war with my comrades. I was too tired to think. I wanted an end, acts that were complete in themselves. Above all else I was still tired, hypnotized by the exhaustion of experience. These two ideas must have been the most fixed in my brain before it failed me.

For these things I needed no brain. Instinct would deal with the woman and a combination of atavism and training attend to the fighting. I had been very nearly reduced to an animal. Smart, sharp, quick to move in a difficult situation, but no longer a free man. The conditioning had been complete.

So when I came up before the board I forced them to pass me fit for active service. This was absurd. They knew it and I knew it, but I told them I wanted to be in at the end, to see the finish, that I was a regular, and they agreed, no doubt imagining me very brave – a real tiger – which was a lie. I did not want to go back at all, ever, but here again was this mysterious force that has always directed my life, that has driven me, that has never let me do what I wanted to do, and has acted so often in what has seemed at the time to be against my interests and against all common sense. By a curious coincidence the senior officer on the medical board was Major Linden Bell who had attended me on the hospital ship and said: 'This boy will die.' I reminded him of it and we both laughed.

CHAPTER 21

AFTERMATH

A COUPLE of weeks before my medical board, while we were walking on the Downs, we found a little rabbit-clipped lawn sheltered by gorse. Lying there listening to the guns in France and the singing larks – there always seemed to be larks – I told Eileen I had made up my mind to go back to the regiment if I could talk the medical board into passing me fit, but that I wanted to get married first. I had now returned to the ideas of love and war I had had when I was wounded, and I wanted the love bit before I continued with the other.

She agreed. We now spent all our time together, walking and going for bus rides. We had meals at the Metropole and the Ship. There were big aviaries of love-birds at the Metropole which seemed symbolic to me.

Then, one day, sitting on the stony beach at Brighton looking out to sea, to 'over there' and watching the rounded, water-worn pebbles being rolled in by the waves and rolling back again, I talked to Eileen about sex. I had been reading it up. There was little beyond Dr Marie Stopes's much discussed *Married Love* just out which I had bought. I had talked about it to the doctor in hospital. But there is a tragi-comic aspect to this conversation between a couple of virgins. I said: 'We can get married and we'll be all right as long as we don't have children.'

Eileen said: 'I don't want children much.'

I went on: 'There are only two principles of contraception: one is to stop the sperm reaching its destination and the other is to kill it before it gets there.'

This must have been some time in mid-October.

The next thing to do was to get permission to get married from the Regimental Colonel. I applied for an appointment to see him and told him I wished to get married. He asked a lot of questions about Eileen's background. Who was her father? What

did he do, and so on. In those days an officer, particularly in the
Brigade, had to marry within a certain class. His wife had to be a
lady. No actress was a lady. No secretary. I told him her father
had no profession. He had been going to be a doctor but had
come into money and retired before he had begun to work. Her
mother had been presented at Court. At last, satisfied with his
enquiries, he gave his permission.

I breathed a sigh of relief, saluted and went out. Soon it would
be all square and above board. I do not know what we should
have done if he had refused.

This going into the background of regular officers' wives is not
as snobbish as it might seem. A regiment is a kind of family
and it is essential that as far as possible occasions for friction
should be eliminated. This selective process exists today in democratic America when the girls young executives marry in big
corporations are looked over by the management.

Married subalterns are not popular in the army but I had
clinched the matter by saying my wife was an heiress and suggest-
ing that I could not afford to miss this opportunity. I proposed to
talk my way out of this later. Eventually her father did give her a
small allowance that almost clothed her.

As soon as the interview was over I returned to Brighton and
told Eileen of its success. I then went to a jeweller and looked at
wedding-rings. I chose one and said I would take it if he would
send his assistant with me to the registry office to make the
necessary arrangements as I had no idea of the procedure. I think
he was amused at the idea, and on October 30th, both of us as
nervous as kittens, we went through with what could hardly be
described as a ceremony with two witnesses picked from the
waiting-room.

We spent our honeymoon at the White Hart at Lewes, a very
fine old hotel with some of the best food I have ever eaten. The
best English cooking is as good as any in the world but you
seldom get it. It was so good and the hotel so expensive that, to
get value, I overate and gave myself a bilious attack and was ill
for three days.

We attended the Assizes and saw a young woman tried for the
murder of her mother. It appeared that she 'did not care for her
and wanted her clothes'. This was the motive. The court was most

impressive, with the judge in his red robes and all the barristers in wigs. At the end of an hour the jury gave their verdict of guilty. They were all staying at the White Hart with us, though we hardly saw them. The judge put on his black cap and condemned her to death. It was very impressive but perhaps not proper honeymoon entertainment. Still, it would have been stupid not to witness the majesty of the British Law – for it has majesty and dignity – in operation. The drama took place in the courthouse almost opposite the hotel.

We went for walks on the Downs. We visited the castle and bought a few souvenirs at an antique shop in the High Street – three brass cannon made by French prisoners in the Napoleonic Wars, four beechwood eggcups. These were interesting because they were too small to take the eggs laid by twentieth-century hens.

The honeymoon, despite fires in the bedroom, the good food and the comfort of the hotel, was not a success. I don't suppose they often are unless the couple have slept together before they get married. This was, however, the rock on which the ship of our romance was to founder some eighteen years later. Sex is certainly not everything in marriage, but sexual incompatibility may well in the end erode it. We got on splendidly as friends and companions but, as the French say, there is always one who kisses and one who extends the cheek. I have no doubt this would have been enough for many men, but I was too French in my outlook for it to last forever. I was a specimen of the classic *homme moyen sensuel*. I have a demonstrative nature. I have to touch the things I love. Women, cats, dogs, horses, objects of art, even trees and flowers. To me the hands are an extension of the eyes. It is not only blind men who feel this. The hands are the penultimate instruments of love, which is why many women are so interested in them. My mother often spoke of a man having beautiful hands. They have the same relation to the eyes as sound does to the printed word. We read something aloud because we know how it will sound. This is the charm of poetry, which is in fact a kind of music. I like to be touched by those with whom I have an intimate relationship – women and animals. This I assume is due to living in France where people are relatively uninhibited. Eileen, with her English upbringing, was unaccustomed to these contacts which meant so much to me. Had we been able to talk about things, had there been psychiatrists available, we might have worked things out. Only thirty years later when we became friends again by letter – hands across 6,000 miles of sea – did we solve the root cause of this trouble. She had been criminally attacked as a girl of twelve by her father's kennelman and never told anyone. That was the cause of the neuroses. I have seen photographs of her as quite a small girl, and even then she radiated an aura of something that any man must have found sexually appealing.

Then on November 11th came the Armistice. This seemed a good moment to inform our respective parents of what we had done. So we went up to London and told them. What could they do but make the best of it? Again, the *fait accompli*.

We went to see Eileen's father who, as an amateur carpenter, was doing war work in London making crutches. He was not particularly pleased at the news but promised Eileen £100 a year dress allowance. In those days £100 went a long way. A nice evening dress cost £10. A silk blouse six shillings. I remember going with her to buy one at Selfridge's because I had torn the one she had on and she could no longer wear it.

My mother was not pleased either, but what was done was done – and the only thing to do was to make the best of a bad job. As I pointed out, if I was old enough to go to war I was old enough to get married – an unanswerable argument that must have been used many times before and since. My Aunt Cass (Mrs J. Cundy) warned me to be careful about having children, as if I had not thought of it, and my Aunt Pim (Miss Euphemia Park of 8 Bolton Gardens) gave me £20 war loan certificates. Mrs Horsman, Eileen's mother, was upset at a registry office wedding and wanted one in a church. A white wedding with orange-blossom trimmings for her only daughter, thus fulfilling a mother's dream. I agreed but said I would have no part in the proceedings bar turning up at the church. Meanwhile we wanted to keep it quiet.

A secret marriage is romantic in all its aspects, with the difficulties, secret assignations and the excitement that goes with them, and a pleasant sense of sin. But it remains an irregular union and so we decided to formalize it by the usual public procedure. So on April 24, 1919, we were married at Christ Church, Lancaster

Gate, and had a reception afterwards at the Coburg Court Hotel. The most distinguished-looking man there was old John Leech, Oswald Norman's coachman, who looked like the Duke of Wellington. Eileen cut the cake with my sword and all the correct actions were performed. Toasts were drunk, bits of wedding-cake were packed up to be sent to people who could not come.

I recently received a letter from Eileen in which she said: 'How good-looking you were. Slightly drunk as you and Norman got lost in the tube and drank the Communion wine.'

Her letter brought it back to me. We went past the station and had to backtrack, but still got to the church early. For some reason we were shown into the vestry. As there was nothing to do, we poked about and found the wine in a cupboard and drank it.

(Norman Gwatkin, now General Sir Norman, was my best man. He was later Commandant at Sandhurst and was one of the finest-looking men in the British Army. He had passed out of Sandhurst just too late for the war.)

We got the usual wedding-presents: a silver tray, silver tea service, silver candlesticks, silver salt- and pepper-shakers, six silver toastracks, a silver cigarette box, two pairs of cut-glass decanters, flat flower bowls, flower vases, a few pictures, some china ornaments and dishes, a silver-topped Malacca walking-stick, a few cheques. One of my old-lady friends gave me a small first-aid set full of useful medicines in a japanned tin box. She had asked me what I wanted. I thought this would be useful if I went on foreign service.

I had several old-lady friends – seventy and over. I used to call on them and they would give me tea or dinner sometimes. One of them had the most peculiar furniture I have ever seen. Her husband had been a great hunter and the legs and backs of all the chairs and the legs of the tables were made of antlers – the horns of caribou, elk, wapiti and moose.

Eileen's going-away dress was an almost sky-blue Harris tweed suit made by 'Bill' in Bond Street at a cost of eighteen guineas, which was then considered an outrageous price.

Eileen looked very beautiful in a white satin dress made by Madame Buckmaster, which was supposed to convert into a dinner dress afterwards – of course it didn't. They never do. A wedding-dress remains a wedding-dress. Even if you dye it black, women always recognize its origin. It remains stained with invisible confetti spots. She had a very fine veil, an orange-blossom wreath, a bouquet and all the required trimmings. There is a great resemblance between brides and their cakes – white, decorated and admired. There were two bridesmaids in pink to whom I grudgingly gave presents – two small gold brooches shaped like wishbones.

Many years later in Africa, Eileen's veil came in very handy to keep the flies off the food on the dining-room table.

We had our second honeymoon at the annexe of the Barnett Cottage Home at Herne Bay, which was a charitable institution originally started by my aunt. The annexe was a small house that was used by the family when they wanted a few days' change in the bracing air of the East Coast. Herne Bay was at that time in the news, famous for the brides-in-the-bath murders. I remember going to see the bath. It was a white enamel tub standing on the verandah of the murder house. Mr Smith married ladies for their money and then killed them by the very simple, and perhaps humanitarian, method of drowning them like kittens, lifting up their legs so that their heads were submerged. He then reported this terrible accident to the police. His dear wife, to whom he had only been married a week or a month, had fainted in her bath and drowned. He naturally married under a false name each time but the third time someone recognized the similarity of the accidents, the police investigated, and finally ran him to ground just before our visit.

The other thing of interest on our Herne Bay honeymoon was the friendship that we struck up with some pedigree Anglo-Nubian goats. Most attractive animals with long floppy ears and Roman profiles – the whole face from forehead to lips being an arc.

On returning to the regiment at Windsor we took rooms in Park Street, opposite the royal stables, and settled down. We bought bicycles and had lovely rides and picnics in the country. I was looking forward to a bicycle tour of England one day. Before there were many cars, the bicycle was a wonderful means of getting about. But Eileen was not an ardent cyclist. I was too young to know then that few pretty women care for bicycles. But we had some pleasant and amusing times.

Among our wedding-presents had been a flat flower bowl and one day, to enliven the floral arrangement, I added four large crested newts that I had captured. This is the finest European newt – shiny black, with a splendidly serrated frill along the spine and a bright orange belly ornamented with small black spots disposed in an irregular manner. In brief, they were splendid amphibians who appeared to be very happy in the black bowl till my brother Ronald and his wife came to lunch. They seemed to disturb the newts in some way and they kept climbing on to the edge of the bowl and launching themselves at our guests, who did not care for reptilia.

We also had a little owl that I rode down in the Great Park. He got up in front of me and I galloped after him till he squatted down in the grass, hoping I had not seen him. But I had and I jumped down and stuffed him into my pocket. He lived in a canary cage when he was not flying about the apartment and ate the mice that the cooks caught in the barracks for me. But he was a slow eater and would sometimes sit for an hour with the back legs and tail of a mouse hanging out of his beak – all birds and reptiles swallow things head first – which disconcerted some people. I can see, looking back now, that Eileen from the very start had a great deal to put up with.

At this time, although I had been passed fit for service, I was unable to march far and so was made demobilization officer. I was given quite a fat book listing all professions and jobs. I had no idea there were so many. Men were released as there became room for them in industry or the firms they had worked for applied for them.

Lord Marsham, who wore a patch over one eye – he had lost it in the '14 retreat – often lent me his pony, a little black cob that I used to ride in the Great Park.

The pioneers were removing the Guards Division insignia from our limbers – it was an eye painted on a metal shield – and I asked them to save one for me, which they did. It was pierced by a bullet hole which made it even more interesting.

While we were in Windsor Eileen bought a Spirella corset. They were the latest thing and much more supple than the old kind. It fastened by being zipped up the side. This was the latest thing too – zippers. But as the fastening ran from under the arm to the hip it was almost impossible for a woman to put it on alone. One day when helping her I caught half an inch of her skin in the zipper. By the time I pulled the zipper back to release her and did her up again, we were both in hysterics. I was trying to smother my laughter because it was not serious and she was half crying, half laughing, and angry too. After that episode I was more careful as a ladies' maid.

I have always found expensive corsets and girdles with suspenders holding up silk stockings extremely attractive. This is probably due to the slight compression of the garment which streamlines a girl's body into seal-like svelteness, obviously a form of fetishism, like long hair and high heels – all no doubt rather decadent. Silk stockings were much more attractive to look at and touch than nylon. They shone slightly on the leg and were almost slippery – silky, in fact – to the touch. Some girls wore garters round their thighs to support the stockings. These were usually covered with ruched satin ribbon and sometimes decorated with the regimental badge of a husband or lover.

The theatrical stars of those and somewhat later days were George Robey (eyebrows), Harry Lauder, Harry Tate, Marie Lloyd, Little Tich, Dan Leno and Vesta Tilley, Gaby Deslys, Yvonne Printemps, with Josephine Baker and Mistinguette in Paris. There were beautiful actresses like Gladys Cooper, Lily Elsie, Doris Kean and Jessie Mathews appearing on the legitimate stage. The old war songs were still sung and there was wonderful entertainment to be had at such music halls as the Empire, the Alhambra and the Palladium. Singers, dancers, ballet, acrobats, conjurors, trick cyclists, animal acts, jugglers. When we could we went to shows of all kinds and saw world-famous variety artists who had learnt their business from father to son and mother to daughter for generations. All this has disappeared. It had gaiety and glamour. Even the musical-comedy chorus-girl has gone. Shows today are seldom gay or light.

I was always envious of men who could vamp any tune they had ever heard and soon had any group they were with singing the choruses. This was a gift I should like to have had but I have never been able to carry more than a single phrase of any tune in my head. Every mess in France had a Decca gramophone and day after day we played the same old records, but I never mastered one completely. Nor could I even remember the lyrics. I still like pop music, as it is called, and light opera, but have never been able to appreciate really serious music. In some ways I think I am very lucky in this as I have heard my musical friends go nearly mad when music which I quite enjoy is played. Obviously one hears more bad music than good and it is satisfactory to be able to enjoy it. I like anything which has a rhythm, a beat, a melody.

When I had demobilized the whole second battalion I put in for a new medical board. Having persuaded one board that I was fit, I now had to persuade another that there had been a slight mistake. I told them the truth – that I had wanted to get back to see the end, and they reversed the decision putting me on half pay. (I remained on half pay for five years and was then finally retired in 1927 on a pension of £12 per month as twenty-five per cent disabled.) By this time the battalion had moved to the Chelsea Barracks and we had taken rooms in Oakley Street.

One other thing occurred before I had the board. I had to refuse an appointment to the Egyptian Army that Sir Sydney Greville had nearly pushed through. I had talked to him about it in hospital as one of my ambitions, and he had pulled the necessary strings. The catch was I had to guarantee that I was not even engaged, much less married. This was a policy dating from Lord Kitchener's reorganization of the Egyptian forces. It would have been a very attractive job. To start as a Bimbashi – a rank corresponding to that of a major in the British Army – with the command of a detachment of cavalry mounted on entire Arabs, or, and this interested me even more, service in the desert with the Camel Corps who used racing camels. Here I would have been out of touch with everyone for weeks at a time, with some big game hunting and active service – skirmishes with slave traders, smugglers and frontier bandits. But all that was out now. No more soldiering.

We spent some time at Bridport in Dorset. The one thing I remember there was a man who bred game fowl, for which I have always had a passion. In their run, which was very large, he had the leg of a horse he got from the knacker's hanging on a wire.

The birds pecked at it all the time and ate the maggots which fell to the ground when it became fly-blown.

We next went to Condette to visit my people. The army was still occupying the big house and I went to call on the General, wearing uniform, and he asked if there was anything he could do for me.

I said: 'Yes, sir. I should like permission to ride some of the HQ horses.'

He said: 'Take any you like, my boy.' And so for the next couple of months I had a splendid time. The horses I liked best were a grey thoroughbred called Wee Joe – he was quite a big horse, over sixteen hands; a little brown mare called Kitty, a very fine jumper but difficult to ride because she liked to come up to the jump, stop and hop over like a buck; and Dancing Master, a big bay Kentucky pacer. He could do twelve miles an hour at a flying trot. Nobody liked him because he was very powerful and had a tendency to bolt, but he gave no trouble if you gave him his head. If you pulled, he pulled and off he'd go. There was a quiet mare, Christabel; I taught Eileen to ride on her.

This was a very happy interlude. We rode and made love under beautiful conditions in lovely country. The beach was so wild and empty that we could bathe naked and I often stripped and rode horses barebacked into the sea. This beach was an immense stretch of hard sand. At low tide there was a mile of it between the dunes and the sea, and it stretched for miles along the coast. So big was the area that a review of three British cavalry divisions was held there during the war.

Among the HQ officers was an Australian, Beck, a slim man with glasses, who rode as well as Knott in the 9th Yorkshire Light Infantry.

It was full summer – we rode, bathed, and went on picnics with the other officers and their wives. We went blackberrying in the forest. I went back to London a couple of times to see if I could get a job but had no luck. So I decided to accept my parents' offer of a cottage and stay in the village that I had always liked so much.

The village street at Condette had probably changed very little in a hundred years. The cottages were built on three sides of a square, the fourth side being the street, and consisted of three or

four rooms flanked on both sides by stables and outbuildings.
The women did all the garden work including digging. The men
bicycled to factories ten miles away. The vegetables the women
grew they took to market in their tented carts whose design had
not changed since before the Revolution. It seems probable that
since Roman times there had been cottages along the road, which
had a stream running along one side. Pigs were killed in the road,
their bowels and bladders washed in the streets. Women cleaned
their dishes in the stream. Children paddled and piddled in it.
Horses and cows drank from it. Ducks swam in it. It was an
artery, a string along which the cottages were threaded like
beads about the throat of the castle that had once protected them
from Viking raids.

The rest of the village was a little way off. Here was the church,
the cemetery, the *mairie*, the school, the *grande place* where fairs
and fêtes were held.

There were chickens everywhere, on every road. Pigeons on
the red-tiled roof tops. Watchdogs chained to their kennels.
There were country sounds – cock crow, hen cackle, pigeon coo,
dog barks, horses' hooves, iron-shod wheels of carts, the song of
a wren. In the summer heat a yellowhammer singing 'A little bit
of bread and no cheese . . . no cheese . . .' Cuckoos. A caged
canary on a cottage wall. These were the sounds of my youth –
rural, bucolic, still unchanged and untouched by war. This was
where I was going to live now, in the village of Condette in the
Pas de Calais. The next phase of my life was a reconstruction job
of trying to put Humpty Dumpty together again.

I am amazed that I have remembered in such detail things that
happened from fifty to seventy years ago. People, places, events,
fears and hopes that must all have made a deep impression on me.
Impressions were perhaps more vivid then because the world was
less crowded. Man, though gregarious, has a need for privacy
which is becoming harder and harder to obtain as the increasing
population presses on the existing space. Such memories are
of value only because they paint a picture of a vanished world.
Romantic, insanitary, relatively unmechanized. At once hypo-
critical and idealistic. A world which still had its roots in the
culture of Greece and Rome and was therefore explicable and

human even where it lacked humanity. There were precedents for everything. Everything had happened before. This is the era we have left behind us.

But on the surface there was nothing much new. There were more cars, and aeroplanes, as we called them, were obviously going to be put to civilian peacetime use. There were the million British dead, but dead men are never new. There was only the space they left and the women deprived of their love. There were the wounded, many of them outwardly recovered, but not those whose faces had been damaged, because plastic surgery was still in its infancy. It needed more wars, more automobile accidents, more sexual competition among women, to bring it to its present perfection. There were the limbless – hooked-armed, peg-legged – with war medals on their shabby vests and a minuscule pension in their pockets. A lot of medals were soon to find their way into the pawnshops. MM's, DSOs, DCMs, MCs, DSCs, even Victoria Crosses. Collectors' items now reposing in velvet-lined show-cases. There were wounded men still dressed in bright blue hospital suits, with scarlet neckerchiefs; topped off with their badged caps. Tigers, deer, sphinxes, knotted ropes, harps, French horns, stars, horses – the grand symbols of regiments that had for three hundred years fought on every continent.

Brass bands of crippled soldiers in the streets of London played for coppers. That was about the lot. The demobbed men back at their jobs. The women voting. The wounded wondering if this was what they had fought for. The dead being dug up by the War Graves Commission and replanted in neat garden rows, labelled. Name, rank, number, regiment. A final sorting-out.

There were still horses everywhere, in vans and under the saddle. The cavalry regiments were not yet disbanded. The generals would not give up something so pretty, and most of them were cavalrymen, as we had found to our cost. There were prostitutes on every West End corner – some of them very pretty – wrapped in luxurious furs.

But there were no pesticides, no jet planes, no antibiotics, no detergents, no plastics, no atomic bombs. Children seldom murdered each other, their parents or teachers. Most people had not yet heard of Freud The use of narcotics was restricted to a small number of adults. Most middle-class girls were virgins.

Christmas came again, another post-war Christmas. Men had been killed on Christmas Day in '14, '15, '16 and '17. Kids four years old did not know why their parents wept. Why should they? The plum puddings had silver shillings and sixpences in them. There were presents under the candlelit trees. 'Auld Lang Syne' and toasts to absent friends assumed a new and permanent significance. Never be back, those bastards wouldn't. Not a man Jack of 'em.

But we who were left were something special. Fighting soldiers of all ranks, we had been going to stand together and make a new England. A new world, perhaps. It remained 'perhaps'. It ended with yearly regimental dinners for the thinning ranks of the survivors – officers only, of course – who told of more and more improbable exploits to anyone polite enough to listen. Black tie, miniature medal affairs, speeches and drinks. And pipers playing if it was a Scottish unit.

There were still emperors, kings, shahs and rajahs sitting on their thrones. But termites were working under the gilt. One cannot see termites. They work in the dark. There were still great empires: The British, French, Dutch, Belgian, Portuguese and Spanish. Civilized society was still stratified. A layer cake of wealth and breeding in which every individual had a recognized place. A mould that could only be broken by a combination of luck or very special talents. It was possible in those days to place people socially by the way they dressed or spoke. How curious this sounds today, with titled singers and athletes, and peers taking in lodgers.

The world was still on the gold standard though we no longer saw a sovereign or a louis. That we should ever come off it was inconceivable, because gold was much more than a metal. Gold represented a fixed value. Now there are none. No values, neither financial, moral, spiritual nor emotional. Or perhaps there are, but if so, they are new, explicable only to the present generation of golden-beds and golden handshakes.

This was the world into which, after a final medical board, I had been retired. If I could have got a good job I would have taken it, but it soon became apparent that I was completely unequipped for civil life, having gone straight from school into the army. No one, as thousands have since found out, is less fitted for business than an ex-officer who has learnt only to obey orders and to give them. The lies, bickering, give and take, chance your arm and blow your own trumpet of the civilian world is utterly alien to him.

This is why we decided to remain in France. My half pay – of about £20 a month as far as I remember – went a long way with a very favourable exchange. And so began the next phase of my life. Childhood. Boyhood. The Army. All were in the past.

I had returned to Condette where I had always been so happy. It was a return to the earth – the soil – because I began to lead the life of a peasant. Digging the ground, raising vegetables, milking my goat, breeding rabbits and poultry to eat. Above all, now that I had it, I realized that this was what I had needed. Silence, isolation. Living on a kind of emotional island with the girl I loved. Now that I could let go, I broke down, avoided strangers, cried easily, had terrible nightmares, in one of which I almost strangled Eileen, thinking she was a German.

Eileen seemed to accept this way of life. She was a country girl born in Norfolk and had later lived with her parents in Berkhampstead, which was then quite rural. She too, I think, was tired after the war years, the hospital work and endless hectic rush of social life that was inevitable for any attractive girl.

What we had was a kind of idyll. We lived in our private bubble out of time, in space that was bounded by the hedges of our garden.

After later wars I should probably have been put into a psychiatric hospital, which might well have been the end of me. In this French cottage I found what I wanted: silence, peace, the earth, the company of animals, and a woman to make love to. The catharsis of sex with love. Something very different from shacking up with a broad. It was a lot more than a biological function – a matter of glands. That I should write this shows how square I am. Such ideas date a man.

In those distant days we did not know anything about battle fatigue. Shell-shock had to reduce a man to gibbering idiocy before it was considered an adequate excuse for avoiding action. A man who did not go forward in battle was court-martialled for

cowardice and shot – *pour encourager les autres*. And it did. Going
forward, you had a good chance of survival. If you ran away, you
had none. In that war we stayed with our units till we were
wounded, killed or the war ended. I once sat as the junior member
of a General Court Martial, but thank God the case did not in-
volve the possibility of a death sentence. That would have been
terrible as, being the junior member, I had to vote first so as not
to be influenced by my superiors, two field officers and a general
as far as I remember. The accused was represented by an officer
who had been a barrister, known, I think, as 'the soldier's friend'.
We wore our best uniforms and swords borrowed from divisional
headquarters.

I have tried to give a picture of my early life – the story of a
middle-class, middle-income group boy precipitated into the
greatest war the world will ever see. Hundreds of millions may
be killed in some atomic holocaust, but it will not be war in
the classic sense. Men will require a different kind of courage
and qualities which we may not have possessed.

These memoirs have been written as an addition to the existing
literature of personal experience between 1897 and 1922. With
this behind me I shall write of the period that followed the war.
Fifty years in which more strange and terrible events took place
than have ever been recorded before. Another great war. Revolutions. The horror of the German concentration camps which
destroyed one's concept of a civilized nation. The obliteration
of two Japanese cities by atomic bombs. The Russians' sputnik.
Americans landing on the moon. The unbelievable and often
irresponsible advances of science. The breakup of empires. The
fall of kings. The rise of the United Nations. Jet aircraft. The
contraceptive pill. These things, and many others, have been
the gigantic backdrop against which I have lived since the First
World War and must, within a few years, die

For the moment I was alone but for my wife. My parents
seemed irrelevant. My friends were dead – killed in the war or the
'flu epidemic of '18, the tiny balance left dispersed by the circumstances of peace. The brotherhood of arms is a fragile structure
that can only exist in the shadow of death and danger. Most of the
men I now knew were three or four years younger than I or
twenty years older. I had reached a point where I was prepared to

claim friendship with any of them merely because they were there